Journey of Souls

◄◄-►►

Case Studies of Life between Lives

Michael Newton, Ph.D.

LLEWELLYN PUBLICATIONS
Woodbury, Minnesota

FIFTH REVISED EDITION, Twenty-seventh Printing, 2009

FOURTH EDITION, First printing, 1995
THIRD EDITION, First printing, 1995
SECOND EDITION, Second printing, 1994
FIRST EDITION, First printing, 1994

Cover Art and Design: Anne Marie Garrison
Book Design and Layout: Susan Van Sant

Library of Congress Cataloging-in-Publication Data (first edition)
    Newton, Michael, 1931-
    Journey of souls: case studies of life between lives / Michael Newton.
        p.   cm.
    ISBN 13: 978-1-56718-485-3
    ISBN 10: 1-56718-485-5 (pbk.)
    1. Spiritualism.   2. Death—Miscellanea.   3. Reincarnation—case studies.   I. Title.
    BF 1275.D2N48   1994
    133.9'01'3—dc20   94-15730
                                                                    CIP

Llewellyn Publications
A Division of Llewellyn Worldwide, Ltd.
2143 Wooddale Drive, Dept. 978-1-56718-485-3
Woodbury, MN 55125-2989
www.llewellyn.com
Llewellyn is a registered trademark of Llewellyn Worldwide, Ltd.

Printed in the United States of America

See Through the Eyes of the Immortal Soul

Why are you here on Earth? Where will you go after death? What will happen to you when you get there? Many books have been written about past lives, but there has been little about the ongoing existence of our souls as we await rebirth—until this startling and provocative book.

When Dr. Michael Newton, a certified Master Hypnotherapist, began regressing his clients back in time to access their memories of former lives, he stumbled onto a discovery of enormous proportions: that it is possible to "see" into the spirit world through the mind's eye of subjects who are in a hypnotized or superconscious state; and that clients in this altered state were able to tell him what their soul was doing between lives on Earth.

What you are about to read will shake your preconceptions about death. Over many years, the author has taken hundreds of people into the spirit world. The 29 cases recounted here encompass the reports of the very religious, the spiritually noncommitted, and those in-between—all of whom displayed a remarkable consistency in the way they answered questions about the spirit world.

Dr. Newton learned that the healing process of finding one's place in the spirit world was far more meaningful for his clients than describing their former lives on Earth. *Journey of Souls* represents many years of his research and insights to help you understand the purpose behind your life choices, and how and why your soul—and the souls of those you love—lives eternally.

"This remarkable, fast-moving book uncovers some of the mysteries of life in the spirit world."

—*NAPRA Trade Journal*

"*Journey of Souls* is the first truly new metaphysical information to come out in years. The book is essential reading for anyone wanting to know what awaits them on the other side."

—Dick Sutphen

"Here is a briliant and perceptive approach to our next thrust in trying to understand the nature of existence."

—*The Association for Past-Life Research & Therapies Newsletter*
Winafred B. Lucas, Ph.D. and Carole Clark, M.S.W.-

Readers Respond to Journey of Souls

Journey of Souls is a masterpiece which will be long remembered after other books in this field are forgotten. Congratulations.

—Frank
Boston, MA

Your book has made me aware of my inner self and given me a sense of purpose in life. It was spiritual without religious dogma. How can I thank you?

—Vicki
Amsterdam, Netherlands

After I purchased *Journey of Souls* I carried it with me wherever I went because I could not put it down. Your book touched me as no other has.

—Viola
Toronto, Canada

I believe your spiritually gifted book has no comparison with any existing literature on the Spirit World, its laws and processes.

—Joti
Istanbul, Turkey

You have given the world a great gift with your book *Journey of Souls* which rings with such truth that it is overwhelming.

—Madole
Kona, Hawaii

I must tell you that *Journey of Souls* is the most serious and interesting book I know describing the period of life between incarnations. No other book has such detail. Its power comes from your critical manner in questioning your patients.

Zeljko
Tubingen, Germany

Journey of Souls is a classic that should be in every library. I wonder if you have any idea of the hearts it has touched?

—J.C.
Dublin, Ireland

To Peggy, beloved wife and soulmate.

Besides the enormous contributions of my wife, special acknowledgements to Norah Mayper, John Fahey, and those associates who gave me time out of their lives for editing, advice, and encouragement. And to all my subjects, whose fortitude made this research possible by allowing me to travel the pathways of their minds alongside them.

About the Author

Michael Duff Newton holds a doctorate in Counseling Psychology, is a certified Master Hypnotherapist and a member of the American Counseling Association. He has been on the faculty of higher educational institutions as a teacher while active in private practice in Los Angeles. Dr. Newton developed his own age regression techniques in order to effectively take hypnosis subjects beyond their past life memories to a more meaningful soul experience between lives. The author is considered to be a pioneer in uncovering the mysteries about our life in the spirit world, first reported in this best-selling book. *Journey of Souls* has been translated into ten languages. Dr. Newton has an international reputation as a spiritual regressionist, appearing on numerous radio and TV talk shows and as a lecturer at New Age expositions. In 1998, he received the annual award for the "Most Unique Contribution" in bridging mind, body and spirit from the National Association of Transpersonal Hypnotherapists. He was honored for his years of clinical soul memory research and discoveries into the cosmology of the afterlife. The author is a historian, amateur astronomer and world traveler. He and his wife, Peggy, now make their home in the Sierra Nevada Mountains of northern California.

Other Books By Author

Destiny of Souls (Llewellyn, 2001)
Life Between Lives (Llewellyn, 2004)
Memories of the Afterlife (Llewellyn, 2009)

To Write to the Author

If you wish to contact the author, please write to the author in care of Llewellyn Worldwide, and we will forward your request. Both the author and the publisher appreciate hearing from you and learning of your enjoyment of this book and how it has helped you. Llewellyn Worldwide cannot guarantee that every letter written to the author can be answered, but all will be forwarded. Please write to:

Dr. Michael Newton
c/o Llewellyn Worldwide
2143 Wooddale Drive, Dept. 978-1-56718-485-3
Woodbury, MN 55125-2989, U.S.A.

Please enclose a self-addressed, stamped envelope or $1.00 to cover costs.
If outside the U.S.A., enclose international postal reply coupon.

❦ CONTENTS ❧

You would know the hidden realm
where all souls dwell.
The journey's way lies
through death's misty fell.
Within this timeless passage
a guiding light does dance,
Lost from conscious memory,
but visible in trance.

M.N.

Introduction

ARE you afraid of death? Do you wonder what is going to happen to you after you die? Is it possible you have a spirit which came from somewhere else and will return there after your body dies, or is this just wishful thinking because you are afraid?

It is a paradox that humans, alone of all creatures of the Earth, must repress the fear of death in order to lead normal lives. Yet our biological instinct never lets us forget this ultimate danger to our being. As we grow older, the specter of death rises in our consciousness. Even religious people fear death is the end of personhood. Our greatest dread of death brings thoughts about the nothingness of death which will end all associations with family and friends. Dying makes all our earthly goals seem futile.

If death were the end of everything about us, then life indeed would be meaningless. However, some power within us enables humans to conceive of a hereafter and to sense a connection to a higher power and even an eternal soul. If we do actually have a soul, then where does it go after death? Is there really some sort of heaven full of intelligent spirits outside our physical universe? What does it look like? What do we do when we get there? Is there a supreme being in charge of this paradise? These questions are as old as humankind itself and still remain a mystery to most of us.

The true answers to the mystery of life after death remain locked behind a spiritual door for most people. This is because we have built-in amnesia about our soul identity which, on a conscious level, aids in the merging of the soul and human brain. In the last few years the general public has heard about people who temporarily died and then came back to life to tell about seeing a long tunnel, bright lights, and even brief encounters with friendly spirits. But none of these accounts written in the many books on reincarnation has ever given us anything more than a glimpse of all there is to know about life after death.

This book is an intimate journal about the spirit world. It provides a series of actual case histories which reveal in explicit detail what happens to us when life on Earth is over. You will be taken beyond the spiritual tunnel and enter the spirit world itself to learn what transpires for souls before they finally return to Earth in another life.

I am a skeptic by nature, although it will not seem so from the contents of this book. As a counselor and hypnotherapist, I specialize in behavior modification for the treatment of psychological disorders. A large part of my work involves short-term cognitive restructuring with clients by helping them connect thoughts and emotions to promote healthy behavior. Together we elicit the meaning, function, and consequences of their beliefs because I take the premise that no mental problem is imaginary.

In the early days of my practice, I resisted past life requests from people because of my orientation toward traditional therapy. While I used hypnosis and age-regression techniques to determine the origins of disturbing memories and childhood trauma, I felt any attempt to reach a former life was unorthodox and non-clinical. My interest in reincarnation and metaphysics was only intellectual curiosity until I worked with a young man on pain management.

This client complained of a lifetime of chronic pain on his right side. One of the tools of hypnotherapy to manage pain is directing the subject to make the pain worse so he or she can also learn to lessen the aching and thus acquire control. In one of our sessions involving pain intensification, this man used the imagery of being stabbed to recreate his torment. Searching for the origins of this image, I eventually uncovered his former life as a World War I soldier who was killed by a bayonet in France, and we were able to eliminate the pain altogether.

With encouragement from my clients, I began to experiment with moving some of them further back in time before their last birth on Earth. Initially I was concerned that a subject's integration of current needs, beliefs, and fears would create fantasies of recollection. However, it didn't take long before I realized our deep-seated memories offer a set of past experiences which are too real and connected to be ignored. I came to appreciate just how therapeutically important the link is between the bodies and events of our former lives and who we are today.

Then I stumbled on to a discovery of enormous proportions. I found it was possible to see into the spirit world through the mind's eye of a hypnotized subject who could report back to me of life *between* lives on Earth.

The case that opened the door to the spirit world for me was a middle-aged woman who was an especially receptive hypnosis subject. She had been talking to me about her feelings of loneliness and isolation in that delicate stage when a subject has finished recalling their most recent past life. This unusual individual slipped into the highest state of altered consciousness almost by herself. Without realizing I had initiated an overly short command for this action, I suggested she go to the source of her loss of companionship. At the same moment I inadvertently used one of the trigger words to spiritual recall. I also asked if she had a specific *group* of friends whom she missed.

Suddenly, my client started to cry. When I directed her to tell me what was wrong, she blurted out, "I miss some friends in my group and that's why I get so lonely on Earth." I was confused and questioned her further about where this group of friends was actually located. "Here, in my permanent home," she answered simply, "and I'm looking at all of them right now!"

After finishing with this client and reviewing her tape recordings, I recognized that finding the spirit world involved an extension of past life regression. There are many books about past lives, but none I could find which told about our life as souls, or how to properly access the spiritual recollections of people. I decided to do the research myself and with practice I acquired greater skill in entering the spirit world through my subjects. I also learned that finding their place in the spirit world was far more meaningful to people than recounting their former lives on Earth.

How is it possible to reach the soul through hypnosis? Visualize the mind as having three concentric circles, each smaller than the last and within the other, separated only by layers of connected mind-consciousness. The first outer layer is represented by the conscious mind which is our critical, analytic reasoning source. The second layer is the subconscious, where we initially go in hypnosis to tap into the storage area for all the memories that ever happened to us in this life and former lives. The third, the innermost core, is what we are now calling the superconscious mind. This level exposes the highest center of Self where we are an expression of a higher power.

The superconscious houses our real identity, augmented by the subconscious which contains the memories of the many alter-egos assumed by us in our former human bodies. The superconscious may not be a level at all, but the soul itself. The superconscious mind represents our highest center of wisdom and perspective, and all my information about life after death comes from this source of intelligent energy.

How valid is the use of hypnosis for uncovering truth? People in hypnosis are neither dreaming nor hallucinating. We don't dream in chronological sequences nor hallucinate in a directed trance state. When subjects are placed in trance, their brain waves slow from the Beta wake state and continue to change vibration down past the meditative Alpha stage into various levels within the Theta range. Theta is hypnosis—not sleep. When we sleep we go to the final Delta state where messages from the brain are dropped into the subconscious and vented through our dreams. In Theta, however, the conscious mind is not unconscious, so we are able to receive as well as send messages with all memory channels open.

Once in hypnosis, people report the pictures they see and dialogue they hear in their unconscious minds as literal observations. In response to questions, subjects cannot lie, but they may misinterpret something seen in their unconscious mind, just as we do in the conscious state. In hypnosis, people have trouble relating to anything they don't believe is the truth.

Some critics of hypnosis believe a subject in trance will fabricate memories and bias their responses in order to adopt any theoretical framework suggested by the hypnotist. I find this generalization to be a false premise. In my work, I treat each case as if I were hearing the information for the first time. If a subject were somehow able to overcome hypnosis procedure and construct a deliberate fantasy about the spirit world, or free-associate from pre-set ideas about their afterlife, these responses would soon become inconsistent with my other case reports. I learned the value of careful cross-examination early in my work and I found no evidence of anyone faking their spiritual experiences to please me. In fact, subjects in hypnosis are not hesitant in correcting my misinterpretations of their statements.

As my case files grew, I discovered by trial and error to phrase questions about the spirit world in a proper sequence. Subjects in a superconscious state are not particularly motivated to volunteer information about the whole plan of soul life in the spirit world. One must have the right set of keys for specific doors. Eventually, I was able to perfect a reliable method of memory access to different parts of the spirit world by knowing which door to open at the right time during a session.

As I gained confidence with each session, more people sensed I was comfortable with the hereafter and felt it was all right to speak to me about it. The clients in my cases represent some men and women who were very religious, while others had no particular spiritual beliefs at all. Most fall somewhere in between, with a mixed bag of personal philosophies about life. The astounding thing I found as I progressed with my research was that once subjects were regressed back into their soul state they all displayed a remarkable consistency in responding to questions about the spirit world. People even use the same words and graphic descriptions in colloquial language when discussing their lives as souls.

However, this homogeneity of experience by so many clients did not stop me from continually trying to verify statements between my subjects and corroborate specific functional activities of souls. There were some differences in narrative reporting between cases, but this was due more to the level of soul development than to variances in how each subject basically saw the spirit world.

The research was painfully slow, but as the body of my cases grew I finally had a working model of the eternal world where our souls live. I found thoughts about the spirit world involve universal truths among the souls of people living on Earth. It was these perceptions by so many different types of people which convinced me their statements were believable. I am not a religious person, but I found the place where we go after death to be one of order and direction, and I have come to appreciate that there is a grand design to life and afterlife.

When I considered how to best present my findings, I determined the case study method would provide the most descriptive way in which the reader could evaluate client recall about the afterlife. Each case I have selected represents a direct dialogue between myself and a subject. The case testimonies are taken from tape recordings from my sessions. This book is not intended to be about my subjects' past lives, but rather a documentation of their experiences in the spirit world relating to those lives.

For readers who may have trouble conceptualizing our souls as non-material objects, the case histories listed in the early chapters explain how souls appear and the way in which they function. Each case history is abbreviated to some extent because of space constraints and to give the reader an orderly arrangement of soul activity. The chapters are designed to show the normal progression of souls into and out of the spirit world, incorporated with other spiritual information.

The travels of souls from the time of death to their next incarnation has come to me from over thirty years of life between lives hypnotherapy. The travels of souls from the time of death to their next incarnation has engaged my study since the 1970s, growing with each decade. However, most of the LBL cases in this book were collected within the past ten years. It surprised me at first, that I had people who remembered parts of their soul life more clearly after distant lifetimes than recent ones. Yet, for some reason, no one subject was able to recall the entire chronology of soul activities I have presented in this book. My clients remember certain aspects of their spiritual life quite vividly, while other experiences are hazy to them. As a result, even with these twenty-nine cases, I found I could not give the reader the full range of information I have gathered about the spirit world. Thus, my chapters contain details from more cases than just the twenty-nine listed.

The reader may consider my questioning in certain cases to be rather demanding. In hypnosis, it is necessary to keep the subject on track. When working in the spiritual realm, the demands on a facilitator are higher than with past life recall. In trance, the average subject tends to let his or her soul-mind wander while watching interesting scenes unfold. My clients often want me to stop talking so they can detach from reporting what they see and just enjoy their past experiences as souls. I try to be gentle and not overly structured, but my sessions are usually single ones which run three hours in length and there is a lot to cover. People may come long distances to see me and not be able to return.

I find it very rewarding to watch the look of wonder on a client's face when his or her session ends. For those of us who have had the opportunity to actually see our immortality, a new depth of self-understanding and empowerment emerges. Before awakening my subjects, I often implant appropriate post-suggestion memories. Having a conscious knowledge of their soul life in the spirit world and a history of physical existences on planets gives these people a stronger sense of direction and energy for life.

Finally, I should say that what you are about to read may come as a shock to your preconceptions about death. The material presented here may go against your philosophical and religious beliefs. There will be those readers who will find support for their existing opinions. For others, the information offered in these cases will all appear to be subjective tales resembling a science fiction story. Whatever your persuasion, I hope you will reflect upon the implications for humanity if what my subjects have to say about life after death is accurate.

1

Death and Departure

⊶ Case 1 ⊷

S. (Subject): Oh, my *god!* I'm not really dead—am I? I mean, my body is dead—I can see it below me—but I'm floating ... I can look down and see my body lying flat in the hospital bed. Everyone around me *thinks* I'm dead, but I'm not. I want to shout, *hey, I'm not really dead!* This is so incredible ... the nurses are pulling a sheet over my head ... people I know are crying. I'm supposed to be dead, but I'm still *alive!* It's strange, because my body is absolutely dead while I'm moving around it from above. *I'm alive!*

THESE are the words spoken by a man in deep hypnosis, reliving a death experience. His words come in short, excited bursts and are full of awe, as he sees and feels what it is like to be a spirit newly separated from a physical body. This man is my client and I have just assisted him in recreating a past life death scene while he lies back in a comfortable recliner chair. A little earlier, following my instructions during his trance induction, this subject was age-regressed in a return to childhood memories. His subconscious perceptions gradually coalesced as we worked together to reach his mother's womb.

I then prepared him for a jump back into the mists of time by the visual use of protective shielding. When we completed this important step of mental conditioning, I moved my subject through an imaginary time tunnel to his last life on Earth. It was a short life because he had died suddenly from the influenza epidemic of 1918.

As the initial shock of seeing himself die and feeling his soul floating out of his body begins to wear off a little, my client adjusts more readily to the visual images in his mind. Since a small part of the conscious, critical portion of his mind is still functioning, he realizes he is recreating a former experience. It takes a bit longer than usual since this subject is a younger soul and not so used to the cycles of birth, death, and rebirth as are many of my other clients.

Yet, within a few moments he settles in and begins to respond with greater confidence to my questions. I quickly raise this subject's subconscious hypnotic level into the superconscious state. Now he is ready to talk to me about the spirit world, and I ask what is happening to him.

S: Well … I'm rising up higher … still floating … looking back at my body. It's like watching a movie, only I'm in it! The doctor is comforting my wife and daughter. My wife is sobbing (subject wiggles with discomfort in his chair). I'm trying to reach into her mind … to tell her everything is all right with me. She is so overcome by grief I'm not getting through. I want her to know my suffering is gone … I'm free of my body … I don't need it any more … that I will wait for her. I want her to know that … but she is … not listening to me. Oh, I'm moving away now …

And so, guided by a series of commands, my client starts the process of moving further into the spirit world. It is a road many others have traveled in the security of my office. Typically, as memories in the superconscious state expand, subjects in hypnosis become more connected to the spiritual passageway. As the session moves forward, the subject's mental pictures are more easily translated into words. Short descriptive phrases lead to detailed explanations of what it is like to enter the spirit world.

We have a great deal of documentation, including observations from medical personnel, which describes the out-of-body near-death experiences of people severely injured in accidents. These people were considered clinically dead before medical efforts brought them back from the other side. Souls are quite capable of leaving and returning to their host bodies, particularly in life-threatening situations when the body is dying. People tell of hovering over their bodies, especially in hospitals, watching doctors perform life-saving procedures on them. In time these memories fade after they return to life.

In the early stages of hypnosis regression into past lives, the descriptions of subjects mentally going through their past deaths do not contradict the reported statements of people who have actually died in this life for a few minutes. The difference between these two groups of people is that subjects in hypnosis are not remembering their experiences of temporary death. People in a deep trance state are capable of describing what life is like after permanent physical death.

What are the similarities of afterlife recollection between people reporting on their out-of-body experiences as a result of a temporary physical trauma and a subject in hypnosis recalling death in a past life? Both find themselves floating around their bodies in a strange way, trying to touch solid objects which dematerialize in front of them. Both kinds of reporters say they are frustrated in their attempts to talk to living people who don't respond. Both state they feel a pulling sensation away from the place where they died and experience relaxation and curiosity rather than fear.

All these people report a euphoric sense of freedom and brightness around them. Some of my subjects see brilliant whiteness totally surrounding them at the moment of death, while others observe the brightness is farther away from an area of darker space through which they are being pulled. This is often referred to as the tunnel effect, and has become well known with the public.

My second case will take us further into the death experience than Case 1. The subject here is a man in his sixties describing to me the events of his death as a young woman called Sally, who was killed by Kiowa Indians in an attack on a wagon train in 1866. Although this case and the last one relate death experiences after their most immediate past lives, a particular death date in history has no special relevance because it is recent. I find no significant differences between ancient and modern times in terms of graphic spirit world recall, or the quality of lessons learned.

I should also say the average subject in trance has an uncanny ability to zero in on the dates and geographic locations of many past lives. This is true even in earlier periods of human civilization, when national borders and place names were different than exist today. Former names, dates, and locations may not always be easily recalled in every past life, but descriptions about returning to the spirit world and life in that world are consistently vivid.

The scene in Case 2 opens on the American southern plains right after an arrow has struck Sally in the neck at close range. I am always careful with death scenes involving violent trauma in past lives because the subconscious mind often still retains these experiences. The subject in this case came to me because of a lifetime of throat discomfort. Release therapy and deprogramming is usually required in these cases. In all past life recall, I use the time around death for quiet review and place the subject in observer status to soften pain and emotion.

← Case 2 →

Dr. N: Are you in great pain from the arrow?

S: Yes … the point has torn my throat … I'm dying (subject begins to whisper while holding his hands at the throat). I'm choking … blood pouring down … Will (husband) is holding me … the pain … terrible … I'm getting out now … it's over, anyway.

Note: Souls often leave their human hosts moments before actual death when their bodies are in great pain. Who can blame them? Nevertheless, they do stay close by the dying body. After calming techniques, I raise this subject from the subconscious to the superconscious level for the transition to spiritual memories.

Dr. N: All right, Sally, you have accepted being killed by these Indians. Will you please describe to me the exact sensation you feel at the time of death?

S: Like … a force … of some kind … pushing me up out of my body.

Dr. N: Pushing you? Out where?

S: I'm ejected out the top of my head.

Dr. N: And what was pushed out?

S: Well—me!

Dr. N: Describe what "me" means. What does the thing that is you look like going out of the head of your body?

S: (pause) Like a … pinpoint of light … radiating …

Dr. N: How do you radiate light?

S: From … my energy. I look sort of transparent white … my soul …

Dr. N: And does this energy light stay the same after leaving your body?

S: (pause) I seem to grow a little ... as I move around.

Dr. N: If your light expands, then what do you look like now?

S: A ... wispy ... string ... hanging ...

Dr. N: And what does the process of moving out of your body actually feel like to you?

S: Well, it's as if I shed my skin ... peeling a banana. I just lose my body in one swoosh!

Dr. N: Is the feeling unpleasant?

S: Oh no! It's wonderful to feel so free with no more pain, but ... I am ... disoriented ... I didn't expect to die ... (sadness is creeping into my client's voice and I want him to stay focused on his soul for a minute more, rather than what is taking place on the ground with his body)

Dr. N: I understand, Sally. You are feeling a little displacement at the moment as a soul. This is normal in your situation for what you have just gone through. Listen and respond to my questions. You said you were floating. Are you able to move around freely right after death?

S: It's strange ... it's as if I'm suspended in air that isn't air ... there are no limits ... no gravity ... I'm weightless.

Dr. N: You mean it's sort of like being in a vacuum for you?

S: Yes ... nothing around me is a solid mass. There are no obstacles to bump into ... I'm drifting ...

Dr. N: Can you control your movements—where you are going?

S: Yes ... I can do some of that ... but there is ... a pulling ... into a bright whiteness ... it's so *bright!*

Dr. N: Is the intensity of whiteness the same everywhere?

S: Brighter ... away from me ... it's a little darker white ... gray ... in the direction of my body ... (starts to cry) oh, my poor body ... I'm not ready to leave yet. (subject pulls back in his chair as if he is resisting something)

Dr. N: It's all right, Sally, I'm with you. I want you to relax and tell me if the force that took you out of your head at the moment of death is still pulling you away, and if you can stop it.

S: (pause) When I was free of my body the pulling lessened. Now, I feel a nudge ... drawing me away from my body ... I don't want to go yet ... but, something wants me to go soon ...

Dr. N: I understand, Sally, but I suspect you are learning you have some element of control. How would you describe this thing that is pulling you?

S: A ... kind of magnetic ... force ... but ... I want to stay a little longer ...

Dr. N: Can your soul resist this pulling sensation for as long as you want?

S: (there is a long pause while the subject appears to be carrying on an internal debate with himself in his former life as Sally) Yes, I can, if I really want to stay. (subject starts to cry) Oh, it's awful what those savages did to my body. There is blood all over my pretty blue dress ... my husband Will is trying to hold me and still fight with our friends against the Kiowa.

Note: I reinforce the imagery of a protective shield around this subject, which is so important as a foundation to calming procedures. Sally's soul is still hovering over her body after I move the scene forward in time to when the Indians are driven off by the wagon train rifles.

Dr. N: Sally, what is your husband doing right after the attack?

S: Oh, good ... he isn't hurt ... but ... (with sadness) he is holding my body ... crying over me ... there is nothing he can do for me, but he doesn't seem to realize that yet. I'm cold, but his hands are around my face ... kissing me.

Dr. N: And what are you doing at this moment?

S: I'm over Will's head. I'm trying to console him. I want him to feel my love is not really gone ... I want him to know he has not lost me forever and that I will see him again.

Dr. N: Are your messages getting through?

S: There is so much grief, but he ... feels my essence ... I know it. Our friends are around him ... and they separate us finally ... they want to reform the wagons and get started again.

Dr. N: And what is going on now with your soul?

S: I'm still resisting the pulling sensation ... I want to stay.

Dr. N: Why is that?

S: Well, I know I'm dead ... but I'm not ready to leave Will yet and ... I want to watch them bury me.

Dr. N: Do you see or feel any other spiritual entity around you at this moment?

S: (pause) They are near ... soon I will see them ... I feel their love as I want Will to feel mine ... they are waiting until I'm ready.

Dr. N: As time passes, are you able to comfort Will?

S: I'm trying to reach inside his mind.

Dr. N: And are you successful?

S: (pause) I ... think a little ... he feels me ... he realizes ... love...

Dr. N: All right, Sally, now we are going to move forward in relative time again. Do you see your wagon train friends placing your body in some kind of grave?

S: (voice is more confident) Yes, they have buried me. It's time for me to go ... they are coming for me now ... I'm moving ... into a brighter light ...

Contrary to what some people believe, souls often have little interest in what happens to their bodies once they are physically dead. This is not callousness over personal situations and the people they leave behind on Earth, but an acknowledgement of these souls to the finality of mortal death. They have a desire to hurry on their way to the beauty of the spirit world.

However, many other souls want to hover around the place where they died for a few Earth days, usually until after their funerals. Time is apparently accelerated for souls and days on Earth may be only minutes to them. There are a variety of motivations for the lingering soul. For instance, someone who has been murdered or killed unexpectedly in an accident often does not want to leave right away. I find these souls are frequently bewildered or angry. The hovering soul syndrome is particularly true of deaths with young people.

To abruptly detach from a human form, even after a long illness, is still a jolt to the average soul and this too may make the soul reluctant to depart at the moment of death. There is also something symbolic about the normal three- to five-day funeral arrangement periods for souls. Souls really have no morbid curiosity to see themselves buried because emotions in the spirit world are not the same as we experience here on Earth. Yet, I find soul entities appreciate the respect given to the memory of their physical life by surviving relatives and friends.

As we saw in the last case, there is one basic reason for many spirits not wanting to immediately leave the place of their physical death. This comes from a desire to mentally reach out to comfort loved ones before progressing further into the spirit world. Those who have just died are not devastated about their death, because they *know* those left on Earth will see them again in the spirit world and probably later in other lives as well. On the other hand, mourners at a funeral generally feel they have lost a loved one forever.

During hypnosis, my subjects do recall frustration at being unable to effectively use their energy to mentally touch a human being who is unreceptive due to shock and grief. Emotional trauma of the living may overwhelm their inner minds to such an extent that their mental capabilities to communicate with souls are inhibited. When a newly departed soul does find a way to give solace to the living—however briefly—they usually are satisfied and want to then move on quickly away from Earth's astral plane.

I had a typical example of spiritual consolation in my own life. My mother died suddenly from a heart attack. During her burial service, my sister and I were so filled with sadness our minds were numb at the ceremony. A few hours later we returned to my mother's empty house with our spouses and decided to take a needed rest. My sister and I must have reached the receptive Alpha state at about the same time. Appearing in two separate rooms, my mother came through our subconscious minds as a dream-like brush of whiteness above our heads. Reaching out, she smiled, indicating her acceptance of death and current well-being. Then she floated away. Lasting only seconds, this act was a meaningful form of closure, causing both of us to release into a sound sleep of the Delta state.

We are capable of feeling the comforting presence of the souls of lost loved ones, especially during or right after funerals. For spiritual communication to come through the shock of mourning it is necessary to try to relax and clear your mind, at least for short periods. At these moments our receptivity to a paranormal experience is more open to receive positive communications of love, forgiveness, hope, encouragement, and the reassurance your loved one is in a good place.

When a widow with young children says to me, "A part of my husband comes to me during the difficult times," I believe her. My clients tell me as souls they are able to help those on Earth connect their inner minds to the spirit world itself. As it has been wisely said, people are not really gone as long as they are remembered by those left on Earth. In the chapters ahead, we will see how specific memory is a reflection of our own soul, while collective memories are the atoms of pure energy for all souls. Death does not break our continuity with the immortal soul of those we love simply because they have lost the physical personhood of a mortal body. Despite their many activities, these departed souls are still able to reach us if called upon.

Occasionally, a disturbed spirit does not want to leave the Earth after physical death. This is due to some unresolved problem which has had a severe impact on its consciousness. In these abnormal cases, help is available from higher, caring entities who can assist in the adjustment process from the other side. We also have the means to aid disturbed spirits in letting go on Earth, as well. I will have more to say about troubled souls in Chapter Four, but the enigma of ghosts portrayed in books and movies has been greatly overblown.

How should we best prepare for our own death? Our lives may be short or long, healthy or sick, but there comes that time when we all must meet death in a way suited for us. If we have had a long illness leading to death, there is time to adequately prepare the mind once initial shock, denial, and depression have passed. The mind takes a short cut through this sort of progression when we face death suddenly. As the end of our physical life draws near, each of us has the capacity to fuse with our higher consciousness. Dying is the easiest period in our lives for spiritual awareness, when we can sense our soul is connected to the eternity of time.

Although there are dying people who find acceptance to be more difficult than resignation, caregivers working around the dying say most everyone acquires a peaceful detachment near the end. I believe dying people are given access to a supreme knowledge of eternal consciousness and this frequently shows in their faces. Many of these people realize something universal is out there waiting and it will be good.

Dying people are undergoing a metamorphosis of separation by their souls from an adopted body. People associate death as losing our life force, when actually the opposite is true. We forfeit our body in death, but our eternal life energy unites with the force of a divine oversoul. Death is not darkness, but light.

My clients say after recalling former death experiences they are so filled with rediscovered freedom from their earthbound bodies that they are anxious to get started on their spiritual journey to a place of peace and familiarity. In the cases which follow, we will learn what life is like for them in afterlife.

2

Gateway to the Spirit World

FOR thousands of years the people of Mesopotamia believed the gates into and out of heaven lay at opposite ends of the great curve of the Milky Way, called the River of Souls. After death, souls had to wait for the rising doorway of Sagittarius and the autumn equinox, when day and night are equal. Reincarnation back to Earth could only take place during the spring equinox through the Gemini exit in their night sky.

My subjects tell me that soul migration is actually much easier. The tunnel effect they experience when leaving Earth is the portal into the spirit world. Although souls leave their bodies swiftly, it seems to me entry into the spirit world is a carefully measured process. Later, when we return to Earth in another life, the route back is described as being more rapid.

The location of the tunnel in relation to the Earth has some variations between the accounts of my subjects. Some newly dead people see it opening up next to them right over their bodies, while others say they move high above the Earth before they enter the tunnel. In all cases, however, the time lapse in reaching this passageway is negligible once the soul leaves Earth. Here are the observations of another individual in this spiritual location.

↤ Case 3 ↦

Dr. N: You are now leaving your body. See yourself moving further and further away from the place where you died, away from the plane of Earth. Report back to me what you are experiencing.

S: At first ... it was very bright ... close to the Earth ... now it's a little darker because I have gone into a tunnel.

Dr. N: Describe this tunnel for me.

S: It's a ... hollow, dim vent ... and there is a small circle of light at the other end.

Dr. N: Okay, what happens to you next?

S: I feel a tugging ... a gentle pulling ... I think I'm supposed to drift through this tunnel ... and I do. It is more gray than dark now, because the bright circle is expanding in front of me. It's as if ... (client stops)

Dr. N: Go on.

S: I'm being summoned forward ...

Dr. N: Let the circle of light expand in front of you at the end of the tunnel and continue to explain what is happening to you.

S: The circle of light grows very wide and ... I'm out of the tunnel. There is a ... cloudy brightness ... a light fog. I'm filtering through it.

Dr. N: As you leave the tunnel, what else stands out in your mind besides the lack of absolute visual clarity?

S: (subject lowers voice) It's so ... still ... it is such a quiet place to be in ... I am in the place of spirits ...

Dr. N: Do you have any other impressions at this moment as a soul?

S: *Thought!* I feel the ... power of thought all around me. I ...

Dr. N: Just relax completely and let your impressions come through easily as you continue to report back to me exactly what is happening to you. Please go on.

S: Well, it's hard to put into words. I feel ... thoughts of love ... companionship ... empathy ... and it's all combined with ... anticipation ... as if others are ... waiting for me.

Dr. N: Do you have a sense of security, or are you a little scared?

S: I'm not scared. When I was in the tunnel, I was more ... disoriented. Yes, I feel secure ... I'm aware of thoughts reaching out to me

... of caring ... nurturing. It is strange, but there is also the under-standing around me of just who I am and why I am here now.

Dr. N: Do you see any evidence of this around you?

S: (in a hushed tone) No, I sense it—a harmony of thought every-where.

Dr. N: You mentioned cloud-like substances around you right after leaving the tunnel. Are you in a sky over Earth?

S: (pause) No—not that—but I seem to be floating through cloud stuff which is different from Earth.

Dr. N: Can you see the Earth at all? Is it below you?

S: Maybe it is, but I haven't seen it since I went in the tunnel.

Dr. N: Do you sense you are still connected to Earth through an-other dimension, perhaps?

S: That's a possibility—yes. In my mind Earth seems close ... and I still feel connected to Earth ... but I know I'm in another space.

Dr. N: What else can you tell me about your present location?

S: It's still a little ... murky ... but I'm moving out of this.

This particular subject, having been taken through the death experi-ence and the tunnel, continues to make tranquil mental adjustments to her bodiless state while pulling further into the spirit world. After some initial uncertainty, her first reported impressions reflect an inviting sense of well-being. This is a common feeling among my subjects.

Once through the tunnel, our souls have passed the initial gateway of their journey into the spirit world. Most now fully realize they are not really dead, but have simply left the encumbrance of an Earth body which has died. With this awareness comes acceptance in varying degrees depending upon the soul. Some subjects look at these surroundings with continued amazement while others are more matter-of-fact in reporting to me what they see. Much depends upon their respective maturity and recent life experiences. The most common type of reaction I hear is a relieved sigh followed by something on the order of, "Oh, wonderful, I'm home in this beautiful place again."

There are those highly developed souls who move so fast out of their bodies that much of what I am describing here is a blur as they home into their spiritual destinations. These are the pros and, in my opinion, they are a distinct minority on Earth. The average soul does not move that rapidly and some are very hesitant. If we exclude the rare cases of highly disturbed spirits who fight to stay connected with their dead bodies, I find it is the younger souls with fewer past lives who remain attached to Earth's environment right after death.

Most of my subjects report that as they emerge from the mouth of the tunnel, things are still unclear for awhile. I think this is due to the density of the nearest astral plane surrounding Earth, called the *kamaloka* by Theosophists. The next case describes this area from the perspective of a more analytical client. The soul of this individual demonstrates considerable observational insight into form, colors, and vibrational levels. Normally, such graphic physical descriptions by my subjects occur deeper into the spirit world after they get used to their surroundings.

⤛ Case 4 ⤜

Dr. N: As you move further away from the tunnel, describe what you see around you in as much detail as possible.

S: Things are … layered.

Dr. N: Layered in what way?

S: Umm, sort of like … a cake.

Dr. N: Using a cake as a model, explain what you mean?

S: I mean some cakes have small tops and are wide at the bottom. It's not like that when I get through the tunnel. I see layers … levels of light … they appear to me to be … translucent … indented …

Dr. N: Do you see the spirit world here as made up of a solid structure?

S: That's what I'm trying to explain. It's not solid, although you might think so at first. It's layered—the levels of light are all woven together in … stratified threads. I don't want to make it sound like things are not symmetrical—they are. But I see variations in thickness and color refraction in the layers. They also shift back and forth. I always notice this as I travel away from Earth.

Dr. N: Why do you think this is so?

S: I don't know. I didn't design it.

Dr. N: From your description, I picture the spirit world as a huge tier with layers of shaded sections from top to bottom.

S: Yes, and the sections are rounded—they curve away from me as I float through them.

Dr. N: From your position of observation, can you tell me about the different colors of the layers?

S: I didn't say the layers had any major color tones. They are all variations of white. It is lighter … brighter where I'm going, than where I have been. Around me now is a hazy whiteness which was much brighter than the tunnel.

Dr. N: As you float through these spiritual layers, is your soul moving up or down?

S: Neither. I am moving across.

Dr. N: Well, then, do you see the spirit world at this moment in linear dimensions of lines and angles as you move across?

S: (pause) For me it is … mostly sweeping, non-material energy which is broken into layers by light and dark color variations. I think something is … pulling me into my proper level of travel and trying to relax me, too …

Dr. N: In what way?

S: I'm hearing sounds.

Dr. N: What sounds?

S: An … echo … of music … musical tingling … wind chimes … vibrating with my movements … so relaxing.

Dr. N: Other people have defined these sounds as vibrational in nature, similar to riding on the resonance from the twang of a tuning fork. Do you agree or disagree with this description?

S: (nods in assent) Yes, that's what this is … and I have a memory of scent and taste, too.

Dr. N: Does this mean our physical senses stay with us after death?

S: Yes, the memory of them … the waves of musical notes here are so beautiful … bells … strings … such tranquility.

Many spirit world travelers report back to me about the relaxing sensations of musical vibrations. Noise sensations start quite early after death. Some subjects tell me they hear humming or buzzing sounds right after leaving their physical bodies. This is similar to the noise one hears standing near telephone wires and may vary in volume before souls pull away from what I believe to be the Earth's astral plane. People have said they hear these same sounds when under general anesthesia. These flat, ringing sounds become more musical when we leave the tunnel. This music has been appropriately called energy of the universe because it revitalizes the soul.

With subjects who speak about spiritual layering, I mention the possibility that they could be seeing astral planes. In metaphysical writing, we read a lot about planes above the Earth. Beginning with ancient Indian scriptures called the Vedas, followed by later Eastern texts, astral planes have historically represented a series of rising dimensions above the physical or tangible world, which blend into the spiritual. These invisible regions have been experienced by people over thousands of years through meditative, out-of-body observations of the mind. Astral planes also have been described as being less dense as one moves farther away from the heavy influences of Earth.

The next case represents a soul who is still troubled after passing through the spiritual tunnel. This is a man who, at age thirty-six, died of a heart attack on a Chicago street in 1902. He left behind a large family of young children and a wife who was deeply loved. They were very poor.

↞ Case 5 ↠

Dr. N: Can you see clearly yet as you travel beyond the tunnel?

S: I'm still passing through these … foamy clouds around me.

Dr. N: I want you to move all the way through this and tell me what you see now.

S: (pause) Oh … I'm out of it … my God, this place is *big!* It's so bright and clean—it even smells good. I am looking at a beautiful ice palace.

Dr. N: Tell me more.

S: (with amazement) It's enormous … it looks like bright, sparkling crystal … colored stones shining all around me.

Dr. N: When you say crystalline, I think of a clear color.

S: Well, there are mostly grays and white … but as I float along I do see other colors … mosaics … all glittery.

Dr. N: Look into the distance from within this ice palace—do you see any boundaries anywhere?

S: No, this space is infinite … so majestic … and peaceful.

Dr. N: What are you feeling right now?

S: I … can't fully enjoy it … I don't want to go further … Maggie … (subject's widow)

Dr. N: I can see you are still disturbed about the Chicago life, but does this inhibit your progress into the spirit world?

S: (subject jerks upright in my office chair) *Good!* I see my guide coming towards me—she knows what I need.

Dr. N: Tell me what transpires between you and your guide.

S: I say to her I can't go on … that I need to know Maggie and the children are going to be okay.

Dr. N: And how does your guide respond?

S: She is comforting me—but I'm too loaded down.

Dr. N: What do you say to her?

S: (shouting) I tell her, "Why did you allow this to happen? How could you do this to me? You made me go through such pain and hardship with Maggie and now you cut off our life together."

Dr. N: What does your guide do?

S: She is trying to soothe me. Telling me I did a good job and that I will see my life ran its intended course.

Dr. N: Do you accept what she says?

S: (pause) In my mind … information comes to me … of the future on Earth … that the family is getting on without me … accepting that I am gone ... they are going to make it ... and we will all see each other again.

Dr. N: And how does this make you feel?

S: I feel ... peace ... (with a sigh) ... I am ready to go on now.

Before touching on the significance of Case 5 meeting his guide here, I want to mention this man's interpretation of the spirit world appearing as an ice palace. Further into the spirit world, my subjects will talk about seeing buildings and being in furnished rooms. The state of hypnosis by itself does not create these images. Logically, people should not be recalling such physical structures in a non-material world unless we consider these scenes of Earth's natural environment are intended to aid in the soul's transition and adjustment from a physical death. These sights have individual meaning for every soul communicating with me, all of whom are affected by their Earth experiences.

When the soul sees images in the spirit world which relate to places they have lived or visited on Earth, there is a reason. An unforgotten home, school, garden, mountain, or seashore are seen by souls because a benevolent spiritual force allows for terrestrial mirages to comfort us by their familiarity. Our planetary memories never die—they whisper forever into the soul-mind on the winds of mythical dreams just as images of the spirit world do so within the human mind.

I enjoy hearing from subjects about their first images of the spirit world. People may see fields of wildflowers, castle towers rising in the distance, or rainbows under an open sky when returning to this place of adoration after an absence. These first ethereal Earth scenes of the spirit world don't seem to change a great deal over a span of lives for the returning soul, although there is variety between client descriptions. I find that once a subject in trance continues further into the spirit world to describe the functional aspects of spiritual life, their comments become more uniform.

The case I have just reviewed could be described as a fairly unsettled spirit bonded closely to his soulmate, Maggie, who was left behind. There is no question that some souls do carry the negative baggage of a difficult past life longer than others, despite the calming influences of the spirit world. People tend to think all souls become omniscient at death. This is not completely true because adjustment periods vary. The time of soul adjustment depends upon the circumstances of death, attachments of each soul to the memories of the life just ended, and level of advancement.

I frequently hear anger during age-regression when a young life ends suddenly. Souls reentering the spirit world under these conditions are often bewildered and confused over leaving people they love without much warning. They are unprepared for death and some feel sad and deprived right after leaving their bodies.

If a soul has been traumatized by unfinished business, usually the first entity it sees right after death is its guide. These highly developed spiritual teachers are prepared to take the initial brunt of a soul's frustration following an untimely death. Case 5 will eventually make a healthy adjustment to the spirit world by allowing his guide to assist him during the balance of his incoming trip.

However, I have found our guides do not encourage the complete working out of thought disorders at the spiritual gateway. There are more appropriate times and places for detailed reviews about karmic learning lessons involving life and death, which I will describe later. The guide in Case 5 offered a brief visualization of accelerated Earth time as a means of soothing this man about the future of his wife and children so he could continue on his journey with more acceptance.

Regardless of their state of mind right after death, my subjects are full of exclamations about rediscovered marvels of the spirit world. Usually, this feeling is combined with euphoria that all their worldly cares have been left behind, especially physical pain. Above all else, the spirit world represents a place of supreme quiescence to the traveling soul. Although it may at first appear we are alone immediately following death, we are not isolated or unaided. Unseen intelligent energy forces guide each of us through the gate.

New arrivals in the spirit world have little time to float around wondering where they are or what is going to happen to them next. Our guides and a number of soulmates and friends wait for us close to the gateway to provide recognition, affection, and the assurance we are all right. Actually, we feel their presence from the moment of death because much of our initial readjustment depends upon the influence of these kindly entities toward our returning soul.

3

Homecoming

SINCE encountering friendly spirits who meet us after death is so important, how do we recognize them? I find a general consensus of opinion among subjects in hypnosis about how souls look to each other in the spirit world. A soul may appear as a mass of energy, but apparently it is also possible for non-organic soul energy to display human characteristics. Souls often use their capacity to project former life forms when communicating with each other. Projecting a human life form is only one of an incalculable number of appearances which can be assumed by souls from their basic energy substance. Later on, in Chapter Six, I will discuss another feature of soul identity—the possession of a particular color aura.

Most of my subjects report the first person they see in the spirit world is their personal guide. However, after any life we can be met by a soulmate. Guides and soulmates are not the same. If a former relative or close friend appears to the incoming soul, their regular guide might be absent from the scene. I find that usually guides are somewhere in close proximity, monitoring the incomer's arrival in their own way. The soul in my next case has just come through the spiritual gateway and is met by an advanced entity who obviously has had close connections with the subject over a prolonged series of past lives. Although this soulmate entity is not my client's primary guide, he is there to welcome and provide loving encouragement for her.

⊶ Case 6 ⊶

Dr. N: What do you see around you?

S: It's as if … I'm drifting along on … pure white sand … which is shifting around me … and I'm under a giant beach umbrella—with brightly colored panels—all vaporized, but banded together, too …

Dr. N: Is anyone here to meet you?

S: (pause) I … thought I was alone … but … (a long hesitation) in the distance … uh … light … moving fast towards me … oh, my gosh!

Dr. N: What is it?

S: (excitedly) Uncle Charlie! (loudly) Uncle Charlie, I'm over *here!*

Dr. N: Why does this particular person come to meet you first?

S: (in a preoccupied far-off voice) Uncle Charlie, I've missed you so much.

Dr. N: (I repeat my question)

S: Because, of all my relatives, I loved him more than anybody. He died when I was a child and I never got over it. (on a Nebraska farm in this subject's most immediate past life)

Dr. N: How do you know it's Uncle Charlie? Does he have features you recognize?

S: (subject is squirming with excitement in her chair) Sure, sure—just as I remember him—jolly, kind, lovable—he is next to me. (chuckles)

Dr. N: What is so funny?

S: Uncle Charlie is just as fat as he used to be.

Dr. N: And what does he do next?

S: He is smiling and holding out his hand to me …

Dr. N: Does this mean he has a body of some sort with hands?

S: (laughs) Well, yes and no. I'm floating around and so is he. It's … in my mind … he is showing all of himself to me … and what I am most aware of … is his hand stretched out to me.

Dr. N: Why is he holding out his hand to you in a materialized way?

S: (pause) To … comfort me … to lead me … further into the light.

Dr. N: And what do you do?

S: I'm going with him and we are thinking about the good times we spent together playing in the hay on the farm.

Dr. N: And he is letting you see all this in your mind so you will know who he is?

S: Yes ... as I knew him in my last life ... so I won't be afraid. He knows I am still a little shocked over my death. (subject had died suddenly in an automobile accident)

Dr. N: Then, right after death, no matter how many deaths we may have experienced in other lives, it is possible to be a little fearful until we get used to the spirit world again?

S: It's not really fear—that's wrong—more like I'm apprehensive, maybe. It varies for me each time. The car crash caught me unprepared. I'm still a little mixed up.

Dr. N: All right, let's go forward a bit more. What is Uncle Charlie doing now?

S: He is taking me to the ... place I should go ...

Dr. N: On the count of three, let's go there. *One—two—three!* Tell me what is happening.

S: (long pause) There ... are ... other people around ... and they look ... friendly ... as I approach ... they seem to want me to join them ...

Dr. N: Continue to move towards them. Do you get the impression they might be waiting for you?

S: (recognition) Yes! In fact, I realize I have been with them before ... (pause) *No, don't go!*

Dr. N: What's happening now?

S: (very upset) Uncle Charlie is leaving me. Why is he going away?

Dr. N: (I stop the dialogue to use standard calming techniques in these circumstances, and then we continue.) Look deeply with your inner mind. You must realize why Uncle Charlie is leaving you at this point?

S: (more relaxed, but with regret) Yes ... he stays in a ... different place than I do ... he just came to meet me ... to bring me here.

Dr. N: I think I understand. Uncle Charlie's job was to be the first person to meet you after your death and see you were okay. I'd like to know if you feel better now, and more at home.

S: Yes, I do. That's why Uncle Charlie has left me with the others.

A curious phenomenon about the spirit world is that important people in our lives are always able to greet us, even though they may already be living another life in a new body. This will be explained in Chapter Six. In Chapter Ten, I will examine the ability of souls to divide their essence so they can be in more than one body at a time on Earth.

Usually at this juncture in a soul's passage, the carry-on luggage of Earth's physical and mental burdens are diminishing for two reasons. First, the evidence of a carefully directed order and harmony in the spirit world has brought back the remembrance of what we left behind before we chose life in physical form. Secondly, there is the overwhelming impact of seeing people we thought we would never meet again after they died on Earth. Here is another example.

⊷ Case 7 ⊶

Dr. N: Now that you have had the chance to adjust to your surroundings in the spirit world, tell me what effect this place has on you.

S: It's so ... warm and comforting. I'm relieved to be away from Earth. I just want to stay here always. There is no tension, or worries, only a sense of well-being. I'm just floating ... how beautiful ...

Dr. N: As you continue to float along, what is your next major impression as you pass the spiritual gateway?

S: (pause) Familiarity.

Dr. N: What is familiar?

S: (after some hesitation) Uh mm ... people ... friends ... are here, I think.

Dr. N: Do you see these people as familiar people on Earth?

S: I ... have a sensation of their presence ... people I knew ...

Dr. N: All right, keep moving along. What do you see next?

S: Lights ... soft ... kind of cloudy-like.

Dr. N: As you are moving, does this light continue to look the same?

S: No, they are growing ... blobs of energy ... and I know they are people!

Dr. N: Are you moving toward them, or are they coming toward you?

S: We are drifting toward each other, but I am going slower than they are because ... I'm uncertain what to do ...

Dr. N: Just relax and continue floating while reporting back to me everything you see.

S: (pause) Now I'm seeing half-formed human shapes—from the waist up only. Their outlines are transparent, too ... I can see through them.

Dr. N: Do you see any sort of features to these shapes?

S: (anxiously) *Eyes!*

Dr. N: You see just eyes?

S: ... There is only a trace of a mouth—it's nothing. (alarmed) The eyes are all around me now ... coming closer ...

Dr. N: Does each entity have two eyes?

S: That's right.

Dr. N: Do these eyes have the appearance of human eyes with an iris and pupil?

S: No ... different ... they are ... larger ... black orbs ... radiating light ... towards me ... thought ... (then with a relieved sigh) oh!

Dr. N: Go on.

S: I'm starting to recognize them—they are sending images into my mind—thoughts about themselves and ... the shapes are changing ... into people!

Dr. N: People with physical human features?

S: Yes. Oh ... *look!* It's *him!*

Dr. N: What do you see?

S: (begins to laugh and cry at the same time) I think it's … *yes*—it's Larry—he is in front of everybody else—he is the first one I really see … *Larry, Larry!*

Dr. N: (after giving my subject a chance to recover a little) The soul entity of Larry is in front of an assortment of people you know?

S: Yes, now I know the ones I want most to see are in front … some of my other friends are in the back.

Dr. N: Can you see them all clearly?

S: No, the ones in back are … hazy … far off … but, I have the sensation of their presence. Larry is in front … coming up to me … *Larry!*

Dr. N: Larry is the husband from your last life you told me about earlier?

S: (subject rushes on) Yes—we had such a wonderful life together—Gunther was so strong—everyone was against our marriage in his family—Jean deserted from the navy to save me from the bad life I was living in Marseilles—always wanting me …

This subject is so excited her past lives are tumbling one on top of the other. Larry, Gunther, and Jean were all former husbands, but the same soulmate. I was glad we had a chance to review earlier who these people were in sessions before this interval of recall in the spirit world. Besides Larry, her recent American husband, Jean was a French sailor in the nineteenth century and Gunther was the son of German aristocrats living in the eighteenth century.

Dr. N: What are the two of you doing right now?

S: Embracing.

Dr. N: If a third party were to look at the two of you embracing at this moment, what would they see?

S: (no answer)

Dr. N: (the subject is so engrossed in the scene with her soulmate there are tears streaming down her face. I wait a moment and then try again.) What would you and Larry look like to someone watching you in the spirit world right now?

S: They would see … two masses of bright light whirling around each other, I guess … (subject begins to settle down and I help wipe the tears off her face with a tissue)

Dr. N: And what does this signify?

S: We are hugging … expressing love … connecting … it makes us happy …

Dr. N: After you meet your soulmate, what happens next?

S: (subject tightly grips the recliner arms) Oh—they are all here—I only sensed them before. Now more are coming closer to me.

Dr. N: And this happens after your husband comes near you?

S: Yes … *Mother!* She is coming over to me … I've missed her so much … oh, Mom … (subject begins to cry again)

Dr. N: All right …

S: Oh, please don't ask me any questions now—I want to enjoy this … (subject appears to be in silent conversation with her mother of the last life)

Dr. N: (I wait for a minute) Now, I know you are enjoying this meeting, but I need you to help me know what is going on.

S: (in a faraway voice) We … we are just holding each other … it's so good to be with her again …

Dr. N: How do you manage to hold each other with no bodies?

S: (with a sigh of exasperation at me) We envelop each other in light, of course.

Dr. N: Tell me what that is like for spirits?

S: Like being wrapped in a bright-light blanket of love.

Dr. N: I see, then ….

S: (subject interrupts with a high pitched laugh of recognition) *Tim!* … it's my brother—he died so young (a drowning accident at age fourteen in her last life). It's so wonderful to see him here. (subject waves her arm) And there is my best girl friend Wilma—from next door—we are laughing together over boys like we did while sitting up in her attic.

Dr. N: (after subject mentions her aunt and a couple of other friends) What do you think determines the sequence of how all these people come here to greet you?

S: (pause) Why, how much we all mean to each other—what else?

Dr. N: And with some, you have lived many lives, while with others perhaps only one or two?

S: Yes … I have been with my husband the most.

Dr. N: Do you see your guide around anywhere?

S: He is here. I see him floating off to the side. He knows some of my friends, too …

Dr. N: Why do you call your guide a "him?"

S: We all show what we want of ourselves. He always relates to me with a masculine nature. It's right and very natural.

Dr. N: And does he watch over you in all your lives?

S: Sure, and after death too … here, and he is always my protector.

Our reception committee is planned in advance for us as we enter the spirit world. This case demonstrates how uplifting familiar faces can be to the incoming younger soul. I find there are a different number of entities waiting in greeting parties after each life. Although the meeting format varies, depending on a soul's special needs, I have learned there is nothing haphazard about our spiritual associates knowing exactly when we are due and where to meet us upon our arrival in the spirit world.

Frequently, an entity who is significant to us will be waiting a little in front of the others who want to be on hand as we come through the gateway. The size of welcoming parties not only changes for everyone after each life, but is drastically reduced to almost nothing for more advanced souls where spiritual comfort becomes less necessary. Case 9, at the end of this chapter, is an example of this type of spiritual passage.

Cases 6 and 7 both represent one of the three ways newly arrived souls are received back into the spirit world. These two souls were met shortly after death by a principal entity, followed by others of decreasing influence. Case 7 recognized people more quickly than Case 6. When we meet such spirits in a gathering right after our death, we find they have been spouses, parents, grandparents, siblings, uncles, aunts, cousins, and dear friends in our past lives. I have witnessed some gut-wrenching emotional scenes with my clients at this stage of their passage.

The emotional meetings which take place between souls at this interval in a spiritual passage are only a prelude to our eventual placement within a specific group of entities at our own maturity level. These meetings provide another emotional high for a subject in superconscious recall. Spiritual organizational arrangements, involving how groups form and are cross-matched with other entities, will be described in subsequent chapters.

For the present, it is important we understand welcoming entities may not be part of our own particular learning group in the spirit world. This is because all the people who are close to us in our lives are not on the same developmental level. Simply because they choose to meet us right after death out of love and kindness does not mean they will all be part of our spiritual learning group when we arrive at the final destination of this journey.

For instance, in Case 6, Uncle Charlie was clearly a more advanced soul than my subject and may even have been serving in the capacity of a spiritual guide. It was evident to me that one of the primary tasks of Uncle Charlie's soul was to help Case 6 as a child in the life just ended, and his responsibility continued right after my subject's death. With Case 7, the important first contact was Larry, a true soulmate on the same level as this subject. Notice also in Case 7, that my subject's spiritual guide was not conspicuous among her former relatives and friends. However, as the scene unfolded, there were indications of a spiritual guide orchestrating the whole meeting process while remaining in the background. I see this in many cases.

The second manner in which we are met right after death involves a quiet, meaningful encounter with one's spiritual guide where no one else is revealed in the immediate vicinity, as in Case 5. Case 8 further illustrates this sort of meeting. What type of after-death meeting we do experience appears to involve the particular style of our spiritual guide along with requisites of our individual character. I find the duration of this first meeting with our guides does vary after each life depending upon the circumstances of that life.

Case 8 shows the very close relationships people have with their spiritual guides. Many guides have strange sounding names, while others are rather conventional. I find it interesting that the old-fashioned religious term of having a "guardian angel" is now used metaphysically to denote an empathetic spirit. To be honest, this is a term I once denigrated as being foolishly loaded with wishful thinking and representing an out-dated mythology at odds with the modern world. I don't have that belief anymore about guardian angels.

I am repeatedly told that the soul itself is androgynous, and yet, in the same breath, clients declare sex is not an unimportant factor. I have learned all souls can and do assume male and female mental impressions toward other entities as a form of identity preference. Cases 6 and 7 show the importance of the newly arrived soul in seeing familiar "faces" identified by gender. This is also true of the next case. Another reason why I selected Case 8 is to indicate how and why souls choose to visually appear in human form to others in the spirit world.

⊷ Case 8 ⊶

Dr. N: You have just started to actually leave the Earth's astral plane now, and are moving further and further into the spirit world. I want you to tell me what you feel.

S: The silence … so peaceful …

Dr. N: Is anyone coming to meet you?

S: Yes, it's my friend Rachel. She is always here for me when I die.

Dr. N: Is Rachel a soulmate who has been with you in other lives, or is she someone who always remains here?

S: (with some indignation) She doesn't *always* stay here. No, she is with me a lot—in my mind—when I need her. She is my own guardian (said with possessive pride).

Note: The attributes of guides as differentiated from soulmates and other supportive entities will be examined in Chapter Eight.

Dr. N: Why do you call this entity a "she"? Aren't spirits supposed to be sexless?

S: That's right—in a literal way, because we are capable of both attributes. Rachel wants to show herself to me as a woman for the visual knowing and it is a mental thing as well with her.

Dr. N: Are you locked into male or female attributes during your spiritual existence?

S: No. As souls there are periods in our existence when we are more inclined toward one gender than another. Eventually, this natural preference evens out.

Dr. N: Would you describe how Rachel's soul actually looks to you at this moment?

S: (quietly) A youngish woman … as I remember her best … small, with delicate features … a determined expression on her face … so much knowledge and love.

Dr. N: Then you have known Rachel on Earth?

S: (responding with nostalgia) Once, long ago, she was close to me in life … now she is my guardian.

Dr. N: And what do you feel when you look at her?

S: A calmness … tranquility … love …

Dr. N: Do you and Rachel actually look at each other with eyes in a human way?

S: (hesitates) Sort of … but different. You see the mind behind what we take to be eyes, because that is what we relate to on Earth. Of course, we can do the same thing as humans on Earth, too …

Dr. N: What can you do on Earth with your eyes that can also be done in the spirit world?

S: When you look into a certain person's eyes on the ground—even people you have just met—and see a light you have known before … well, that tells you something about them. As a human you don't know why—but your soul remembers.

Note: I have heard about the light of spiritual identity being reflected in the human eyes of a soulmate expressed in a variety of ways from many clients. As for myself, I have knowingly experienced this instant recognition only once in my life at the moment I first saw my own wife. The effect is startling, and a bit eerie as well.

Dr. N: Are you saying that sometimes on Earth when two people look at each other, they may feel they have known one another before?

S: Yes, it's deja vu.

Dr. N: Let's go back to Rachel in the spirit world. If your guardian did not project an image of herself in human form to you, would you have known her anyway?

S: Well, naturally we can always identify each other by the mind. But, it's nicer this way. I know it sounds crazy, but it's a ... social thing ... seeing a familiar face puts you at ease.

Dr. N: Seeing human features of people you knew in past lives is a good thing then, particularly in the readjustment period right after leaving Earth?

S: Yeah, otherwise you feel a little lost at first ... lonesome ... and maybe confused, too ... seeing people as they were helps me get used to things here faster when I first come back, and seeing Rachel is always a big boost.

Dr. N: Does Rachel present herself to you in human form right after each death on Earth as a way of getting you readjusted to the spirit world?

S: (eagerly) Oh, yes—she does! And she gives me security. I feel better when I see others I have known before too ...

Dr. N: And do you speak to these people?

S: No one speaks, we communicate by the mind.

Dr. N: Telepathically?

S: Yes.

Dr. N: Is it possible for souls to have private conversations which cannot be telepathically picked up by others?

S: (pause) ... for intimacy—yes.

Dr. N: How is this done?

S: By touch—it's called touching communication.

Note: When two spirits come so close to each other they are conjoined, my subjects say they can send private thoughts by touch which passes between them as "electrical sound impulses." In most instances, subjects in hypnosis do not wish to talk to me about these personal confidences.

Dr. N: Could you clarify for me how human features can be projected by you as a soul?

S: From ... my mass of energy ... I just think of the features I want ... but I can't tell you what gives me the ability to do this.

Dr. N: Well, then, can you tell me why you and the other souls project certain features at different times?

S: (long pause) It depends on where you are in your movements around here … when you see another … and your state of mind then.

Dr. N: That's what I want to get at. Tell me more about recognition.

S: You see, recognition depends on a person's … feelings when you meet them here. They will show you what *they* want you to see of themselves and what they think *you* want to see. It also depends on the circumstances of your meeting with them.

Dr. N: Can you be more specific? What different circumstances can cause energy forms to materialize in a certain way toward other spirits?

S: It is the difference between your being on their turf or your turf. They may choose to show you one set of features in one place, while in another you might see something else.

Note: Spiritual "territory" will be explained as we proceed further into the spirit world.

Dr. N: Are you telling me that a soul may show you one face at the gateway to the spirit world and another image later in a different situation?

S: That's right.

Dr. N: Why?

S: Like I was telling you, a lot of how we present ourselves to each other depends on what we are feeling right then … what relationship we have with a certain person and where we are.

Dr. N: Please tell me if I understand all this correctly. The identity souls project to each other depends on timing and location in the spirit world as well as mood, and maybe psychological states of mind when they meet?

S: Sure, and it works both ways … it's interconnecting.

Dr. N: Then, how can we know the true character of a soul's consciousness with all these changes in each other's image?

S: (laughs) The image you project never hides who you really are from the rest of us. Anyway, it's not the same kind of emotion we know on Earth. Here it is more ... abstract. Why we project certain features and thoughts ... is based on a ... confirmation of ideas.

Dr. N: Ideas? Do you mean your sentiments at the time?

S: Yes ... sort of ... because these human features were part of our physical lives in other places when we discovered things ... and developed ideas ... it is all a ... continuum for us to use here.

Dr. N: Well, if in each of our past lives we have a different face, which one do we assume between lives?

S: We mix it up. You assume those features which the person you see will most recognize as you, depending on what you want to communicate.

Dr. N: What about communication without projecting features?

S: Sure, we do that—it's normal—but I mentally associate with people more quickly with features.

Dr. N: Do you favor projecting a certain set of facial features?

S: Hmm ... I like the face with the mustache ... having a rock-hard jaw ...

Dr. N: You mean when you were Jeff Tanner, the cowpuncher from Texas in the life we discussed earlier?

S: (laughs) That's it—and I have had faces like Jeff's in other lives, too.

Dr. N: But, why Jeff? Was it just because he was you in your last life?

S: No, I felt good as Jeff. It was a happy, uncomplicated life. Damn, I looked great! My face resembled those billboard smoking ads you used to see along the highway. (chuckling) I enjoy showing off my handle-bar mustache as Jeff.

Dr. N: But that was only one life. People not associated with you in that life may not recognize you here.

S: Oh, they would get it was me soon enough. I could change to something else, but I like myself as Jeff the best right now.

Dr. N: So, this goes back to what you were saying about all of us really only having one identity, regardless of the number of facial features we might project as souls?

S: Yeah, you see everyone as they truly are. Some only want their best side to show because of what you might think of them—they don't fully appreciate that it is what you are striving for which is important, not how you appear. We get a lot of laughs about how spirits think they *should* look, even taking faces they never had on Earth, and that's okay.

Dr. N: Are we talking about the more immature souls, then?

S: Yes, usually. They can get stuck ... we don't judge ... in the end they are going to be all right.

Dr. N: I think of the spirit world as a place of supreme all-knowing intelligent consciousness and you make it appear that souls have moods and vanity as though they were back on Earth?

S: (burst of laughter) People are people no matter how they look on their physical worlds.

Dr. N: Oh, do you see souls who have gone to planets other than Earth?

S: (pause) Once in a while ...

Dr. N: What features do souls from other planets besides Earth show you?

S: (evasively) I ... kind of stick with my own people, but we can assume any features we want for communication ...

Note: Gaining information from the subjects I have had who are able to recall leading physical past lives in non-human form on other worlds is always challenging. Recollection of these experiences are usually limited to older, more advanced souls, as we will see later.

Dr. N: Is this ability to transmit features to each other as souls a gift the creator provided for us based upon spiritual need?

S: How should I know—I'm not God!

The concept of souls having fallibility comes as a surprise to some people. The statements of Case 8 and all my other clients indicate most of us are still far from perfect beings in the spirit world. The essential purpose of reincarnation is self-improvement. The psychological ramifications of our development, both in and out of the spirit world, is the foundation of my work.

We have seen the importance of meeting other entities while entering the spirit world. Besides uniting with our guides and other familiar beings, I have mentioned a third form of reentry after death. This is the rather disconcerting manner in which a soul is met by no one.

Although it is an uncommon occurrence for most of my clients, I still feel a little sorry for those subjects who describe how they are pulled by unseen forces all alone to their final destinations, where contact is finally made with others. This would be akin to landing in a foreign country where you have been before, but without any baggage handlers or a tourist information desk to assist you with directions. I suppose what bothers me the most about this type of entry is the apparent lack of any soul acclimation.

My own conceptions of what it must be like to be alone at the spiritual gateway and beyond is not shared by those souls who utilize the option of going solo. Actually, people in this category are experienced travelers. As older, mature souls, they seem to require no initial support system. They know right where they are going after death. I suspect the process is accelerated for them as well, because they manage to more rapidly wind up where they belong than those who stop to meet others.

Case 9 is a client who has had a great number of lives, spanning thousands of years. About eight lives before his current one, people finally stopped meeting him at the spiritual gate.

⊷ Case 9 ⊶

Dr. N: What happens to you at the moment of death?

S: I feel a great sense of release and I move out fast.

Dr. N: How would you characterize your departure from Earth into the spirit world?

S: I shoot up like a column of light and I'm on my way.

Dr. N: Has it always been this fast for you?

S: No, only after my last series of lives.

Dr. N: Why?

S: I know the way, I don't need to see anybody—I'm in a hurry.

Dr. N: And it doesn't bother you that you are not met by anyone?

S: (laughs) There was a time when it was good, but I don't require that sort of thing anymore.

Dr. N: Whose decision was it to allow you to enter the spirit world without assistance?

S: (pause and then with a shrug) It was ... a mutual decision ... between my teacher and me ... when I knew I could handle things by myself.

Dr. N: And you don't feel rather lost or lonely right now?

S: Are you kidding? I don't need my hand held anymore. I know where I'm going and I'm anxious to get there. I'm being pulled along by a magnet and I just enjoy the ride.

Dr. N: Explain to me how this pulling process works which will take you to your destination?

S: I am riding on a wave ... a beam of light.

Dr. N: Is this beam electromagnetic, or what?

S: Well ... it's similar to the bands of a radio with someone turning the dial and finding the right frequency for me.

Dr. N: Are you saying you are being guided by an invisible force without much voluntary control and that you can't speed things up as you did right after death?

S: Yes. I must go with the wave bands of light ... the waves have direction and I'm flowing with it. It's easy. They do it all for you.

Dr. N: Who does it for you?

S: The ones in control ... I don't really know.

Dr. N: Then you are not in control. You don't have the responsibility of finding your own destination.

S: (pause) My mind is in tune with the movement ... I flow with the resonance ...

Dr. N: Resonance? You hear sounds?

S: Yes, the wave beam ... vibrates ... I am locked into this, too.

Dr. N: Let's go back to your statement about the radio. Is your spiritual travel influenced by vibrational frequencies such as high, medium, and low resonance quality?

S: (laughing) That's not bad—yes, and I'm on a line, like a homing beacon of sound and light ... and it's part of my own tonal pattern—my frequency.

Dr. N: I'm not sure I understand how light and vibration combine to set up directional bands.

S: Think of a monster tuning fork inside a flashing strobe light.

Dr. N: Oh, then there is energy here?

S: We have energy—within an energy field. So, it isn't just the lines we travel on ... we generate energy *ourselves* ... we can use these forces depending on our experience.

Dr. N: Then your maturity level does give you some element of control in the rate and direction of travel.

S: Yes, but not right here. Later, when I am settled I can move around much more on my own. Now, I'm being pulled and I'm supposed to go with it.

Dr. N: Okay, stay with this and describe to me what happens next.

S: (short pause) I'm moving alone ... being homed into my proper space ... going where I belong.

In hypnosis, the analytical conscious mind works in conjunction with the unconscious mind to receive and answer messages directed to our deep-seated memories. The subject in Case 9 is an electrical engineer and thus he utilized some technical descriptions to express his spiritual sensations. This client's predisposition to explain his thoughts on soul travel in technical terms was encouraged, but not dictated, by my suggestions. All subjects bring their own segments of knowledge to bear on answering my questions about the spirit world. This case used physical laws familiar to him to describe motion, whereas another person might have said souls move in this tract within a vacuum.

Before continuing with the passage of souls into the spirit world, I want to discuss those entities who either have not made it this far after physical death, or will be diverted from the normal travel route.

4

The Displaced Soul

THERE are souls who have been so severely damaged they are detached from the mainstream of souls going back to a spiritual home base. Compared to all returning entities, the number of these abnormal souls is not large. However, what has happened to them on Earth is significant because of the serious effect they have on other incarnated souls.

There are two types of displaced souls: those who do not accept the fact their physical body is dead and fight returning to the spirit world for reasons of personal anguish, and those souls who have been subverted by, or had complicity with, criminal abnormalities in a human body. In the first instance, displacement is of the soul's own choosing, while in the second case, spiritual guides deliberately remove these souls from further association with other entities for an indeterminate period. In both situations, the guides of these souls are intimately concerned with rehabilitation, but because the circumstances are quite different between each type of displaced soul, I will treat them separately.

The first type we call ghosts. These spirits refuse to go home after physical death and often have unpleasant influences on those of us who would like to finish out our own human lives in peace. These displaced souls are sometimes falsely called "demonic spirits" because they are accused of invading the minds of people with harmful intent. The subject of negative spirits has produced serious investigations in the field of parapsychology. Unfortunately, this area of spirituality has also attracted a fringe element of the unscrupulous associated with the occult, who prey on the emotions of susceptible people.

The troubled spirit is an immature entity with unfinished business in a past life on Earth. They may have no relation to the living person who is disrupted by them. It is true that some people are convenient and receptive conduits for negative spirits who wish to express their querulous nature. This means that someone who is in a deep meditative state of consciousness might occasionally pick up annoying signal patterns from a discarnated being whose communications can range from the frivolous to provocative. These unsettled entities are not spiritual guides. Real guides are healers and don't intrude with acrimonious messages.

More often than not, these uncommon haunted spirits are tied to a particular geographic location. Researchers who have specialized in the phenomena of ghosts indicate those disturbed entities are caught in a no-man's land between the lower astral planes of Earth and the spirit world. From my own research, I don't believe these souls are lost in space, nor are they demonic. They choose to remain within the Earth plane after physical death for a time by their own volition due to a high level of discontent. In my opinion, they are damaged souls because they evidence confusion, despair, and even hostility to such an extent they want their guides to stay away from them. We do know a negative, displaced entity can be reached and handled by various means, such as exorcism, to get them to stop interfering with human beings. Possessing spirits can be persuaded to leave and eventually make a proper transition into the spirit world.

If we have a spirit world governed by order, with guides who care about us, how can maladaptive souls who exert negative energy upon incarnated beings be allowed to exist? One explanation is that we still have free will, even in death. Another is that since we endure so many upheavals in our physical universe, then spiritual irregularities and deviations from the normal exodus of souls ought to be anticipated as well. Also ghosts only represent a divided portion of a disturbed soul's energy while the rest has returned to the spirit world for reunification. Discarnate, unhappy spirits who trap themselves are possibly part of a grand design. When they are ready, these souls will be taken by the hand away from Earth's astral plane and guided to their proper place in the spirit world.

I turn now to the far more prevalent second type of disturbed soul. These are souls who have been involved with evil acts. We should first speculate if a soul can be considered culpable or guilt-free when it occupied the offending criminal brain? Is the soul mind or human ego responsible, or are they the same? Occasionally, a client will say to me, "I feel possessed by an inner force which tells me to do bad things." There are mentally ill people who feel driven by opposing forces of good and evil over which they believe they have no control.

After working for years with the superconscious minds of people under hypnosis, I have come to the conclusion that the five-sensory human can negatively act upon a soul's psyche. We express our eternal self through dominant biological needs and the pressures of environmental stimuli which are *temporary* to the incarnated soul. Although there is no hidden, sinister self within our human form, some souls are not fully assimilated. People not in harmony with their bodies feel detached from themselves in life.

This condition does not excuse souls from doing their utmost to prevent evil involvement on Earth. We see this in human conscience. It is important we distinguish between what is exerting a negative force on our mind and what is not. Hearing an inner voice which may suggest self-destruction to ourselves or someone else is not a demonic spiritual entity, an alien presence, nor a malevolent renegade guide. Negative forces emanate from ourself.

The destructive impulses of emotional disorders, if left untreated, inhibit soul development. Those of us who have experienced unresolved personal trauma in our lives carry the seeds of our own destruction. This anguish affects our soul in such a way that it seems we are not whole. For instance, excessive craving and addictive behavior, which is the outgrowth of personal pain, inhibits the expression of a healthy soul and may even hold a soul in bondage to its host body.

Does the extent of contemporary violence mean that we have more souls "going wrong" today than in the past? If nothing else, our over-population and mind-altering drug culture should support this conclusion. On the positive side, Earth's international level of consciousness toward human suffering appears to be rising.

I've been told that in every era of Earth's bloody history there has always been a significant number of souls unable to resist and successfully counter human cruelty. Certain souls, whose hosts have a genetic disposition to abnormal brain chemistry, are particularly at risk in a violent environment. We see how children can be so damaged by physical and emotional family abuse that, as adults, they commit premeditated acts of atrocity without feelings of remorse. Since souls are not created perfect, their nature can be contaminated during the development of such a life form.

If our transgressions are especially serious we call them evil. My subjects say to me no soul is inherently evil, although it may acquire this label in human life. Pathological evil in humans is characterized by feelings of personal impotence and weakness which is stimulated by helpless victims. Although souls who are involved with truly evil acts should generally be considered at a low level of development, soul immaturity does not automatically invite malevolent behavior from a damaged human personality. The evolution of souls involves a transition from imperfection to perfection based upon overcoming many difficult body assignments during their task-oriented lives. Souls may also have a predisposition for selecting environments where they consistently don't work well, or are subverted. Thus, souls may have their identity damaged by poor life choices. However, all souls are held accountable for their conduct in the bodies they occupy.

We will see in the next chapter how souls receive an initial review of their past life with guides before moving on to join their friends. But what happens to souls who have, through their bodies, caused extreme suffering to another? If a soul is not capable of ameliorating the most violent human urges in its host body, how is it held accountable in afterlife? This brings up the issue of being sent to heaven or hell for good and bad deeds because accountability has long been a part of our religious traditions.

On the wall of my office hangs an Egyptian painting, "The Judgment Scene," as represented in the Book of the Dead, which is a mythological ritual of death over 7,000 years old. The ancient Egyptians had an obsession with death and the world beyond the grave because, in their cosmic pantheon, death explained life. The picture shows a newly deceased man arriving in a place located between the land of the living and the kingdom of the dead. He stands by a set of scales about to be judged for his past deeds on Earth. The master of ceremonies is the god Anubis, who carefully weighs the man's heart on one pan of the scale against the ostrich feather of truth on the opposite side. The heart, not the head, represented the embodiment of a person's soul-conscience to the Egyptians. It is a tense moment. A crocodile-headed monster is crouched nearby with his mouth open, ready to devour the heart if the man's wrongs outweigh the good he did in life. Failure at the scales would end the existence of this soul.

I get quite a few comments from my clients about this picture. A metaphysically oriented person would insist no one is denied entrance into the kingdom of afterlife, regardless of how unfavorably balanced the scales might be toward past conduct. Is this belief true? Are all souls given the opportunity to transmute back into the spirit world the same way, irrespective of their association with the bodies they occupied?

To answer this question, I should begin by mentioning that a large segment of society believes all souls do not go to the same place. More moderate theology no longer stresses the idea of hellfire and brimstone for sinners. However, many religious sects indicate a spiritual coexistence of two mental states of good and evil. For the "bad" soul there are ancient philosophical pronouncements denoting a separation from the God-Essence as a means of punishment after death.

The Tibetan Book of the Dead, a source of religious belief thousands of years older than the Bible, describes the state of consciousness between lives (the Bardo) as a time when "the evil we have perpetrated projects us into spiritual separation." If the peoples of the East believed in a special spiritual location for evil doers, was this idea similar to the concept of purgatory in the Western world?

From its earliest beginnings, Christian doctrine defined purgatory as a transitory state of temporary banishment for sins of a minor nature against humanity. The Christian purgatory is supposed to be a place of atonement, isolation, and suffering. When all negative karma is removed, these souls are eventually allowed into heaven. On the other hand, souls committing major (deadly) sins are condemned to hell forever.

Does hell exist to permanently separate good souls from bad ones? All my case work with the spirits of my subjects has convinced me there is no residence of terrible suffering for souls, except on Earth. I am told all souls go to one spirit world after death where everyone is treated with patience and love.

However, I have learned that certain souls do undergo separation in the spirit world, and this happens at the time of their orientation with guides. They are not activated along the same travel routes as other souls. Those of my subjects who have been impeded by evil report that souls whose influence was too weak to turn aside a human impulse to harm others will go into seclusion upon reentering the spirit world. These souls don't appear to mix with other entities in the conventional manner for quite a while.

I have also noticed that those beginner souls who are habitually associated with intensely negative human conduct in their first series of lives must endure individual spiritual isolation. Ultimately, they are placed together in their own group to intensify learning under close supervision. This is not punishment, but rather a kind of purgatory for the restructuring of self-awareness with these souls.

Because wrongdoing takes so many forms on Earth, spiritual instruction and the type of isolation used is varied for each soul. The nature of these variations apparently is evaluated during orientation at the end of each life. Relative time of seclusion and reindoctrination is not consistent either. For instance, I have had reports about maladjusted spirits who have returned back to Earth directly after a period of seclusion in order to expunge themselves as soon as possible by a good incarnated performance. Here is an example, as told to me by a soul who was acquainted with one of these spirits.

◂◂ Case 10 ▸▸

Dr. N: Do souls bear responsibility for their involvement with flawed human beings who injure others in life?

S: Yes, those who have wronged others savagely in a life—I knew one of those souls.

Dr. N: What do you know about this entity? What happened after this soul returned to the spirit world following that life?

S: He … had hurt a girl … terribly … and did not rejoin our group. There was extensive private study for him because he did so poorly while in that body.

Dr. N: What was the extent of his punishment?

S: Punishment is … a wrong interpretation … it's regeneration. You have to recognize this is a matter for your teacher. The teachers are more strict with those who have been involved with cruelty.

Dr. N: What does "more strict" mean to you in the spirit world?

S: Well, my friend didn't go back with us … his friends … after this sad life where he hurt this girl.

Dr. N: Did he come through the same spiritual gateway as yourself when he died?

S: Yes, but he did not meet with anybody … he went directly to a place where he was alone with the teacher.

Dr. N: And then what happened to him?

S: After awhile … not long … he returned to Earth again as a woman … where people were cruel … physically abusive … it was a deliberate choice … my friend needed to experience that …

Dr. N: Do you think this soul blamed the human brain of his former host body for hurting the girl?

S: No, he took what he had done ... back into himself ... he blamed his own lack of skill to overcome the human failings. He asked to become an abused woman himself in the next life to gain understanding ... to appreciate the damage he had done to the girl.

Dr. N: If this friend of yours did not gain understanding and continued involving himself with humans who committed wrongful acts, could he be destroyed as a soul by someone in the spirit world?

S: (long pause) You can't destroy energy exactly ... but it can be reworked ... negativity which is unmanageable ... in many lives ... can be readjusted.

Dr. N: How?

S: (vaguely) ... Not by destruction ... remodeling ...

Case 10 did not respond further to this line of questioning, and other subjects who know something about these damaged souls are rather sparse with their information. Later, we will learn a bit more about the formation and restoration of intelligent energy.

Most errant souls are able to solve their own problems of contamination. The price we pay for our misdeeds and the rewards received for good conduct revolve around the laws of karma. Perpetrators of harm to others will do penance by setting themselves up as future victims in a karmic cycle of justice. The Bhagavad Gita, another early Eastern scripture which has stood the test of thousands of years, has a passage which says, "souls of evil influence must redeem their virtue."

No study of life after death would have any meaning without addressing how karma relates to causality and justice for all souls. Karma by itself does not denote good or bad deeds. Rather it is the *result* of one's positive and negative actions in life. The statement, "there are no accidents in our lives," does not mean karma by itself impels. What it does is propel us forward by teaching lessons. Our future destiny is influenced by a past from which we cannot escape, especially when we injure others.

The key to growth is understanding we are given the ability to make mid-course corrections in our life and having the courage to make necessary changes when what we are doing is not working for us. By conquering fear and taking risks, our karmic pattern adjusts to the effects of new choices. At the end of every life, rather than having a monster waiting to devour our souls, *we* serve as our most severe critic in front of teacher-guides. This is why karma is both just and merciful. With the help of our spiritual counselors and peers we decide on the proper mode of justice for our conduct.

Some people who believe in reincarnation also think if negative souls do not learn their lessons within a reasonable span of lives, they will be eliminated and replaced by more willing souls. My subjects deny this premise.

There is no set path of self-discovery designed for all souls. As one subject told me, "souls are assigned to Earth for the duration of the war." This means souls are given the time and opportunity to make changes for growth. Souls who continue to display negative attitudes through their human hosts must overcome these difficulties by continually making an effort to change. From what I have seen, no negative karma remains attached to a soul who is willing to work during their many lives on this planet.

It is an open question whether a soul should be held entirely at fault for humanity's irrational, unsocialized, and destructive acts. Souls must learn to cope in different ways with each new human being assigned to them. The permanent identity of a soul stamps the human mind with a distinctive character which is individual to that soul. However, I find there is a strange dual nature between the soul mind and human brain. I will discuss this concept further in later chapters, after the reader learns more about the existence of souls in the spirit world.

5

Orientation

AFTER those entities who meet us during our homecoming have dispersed, we are ready to be taken to a space of healing. This will be followed by another stop involving the soul's reorientation to a spiritual environment. In this place we are often examined by our guide.

I tend to call the cosmology of all spiritual locations as *places*, or *spaces*, simply for convenient identification because we are dealing with a non-physical universe. The similarity of descriptions among clients of what they do as souls at the next two combined stops is remarkable, although they do have different names for them. I hear such terms as: chambers, travel berths, and interspace stopover zones, but the most common is "the place of healing."

I think of the healing station as a field hospital, or MASH unit, for damaged souls coming off Earth's battlefields. I have selected a rather advanced male subject who has been through this revitalization process many times to describe the nature of this next stop.

⤜ Case 11 ⤞

Dr. N: After you leave the friends who greeted you following your death, where does your soul go next in the spirit world?

S: I am alone for a while ... moving through vast distances ...

Dr. N: Then what happens to you?

S: I am being guided by a force I can't see, into a more enclosed space—an opening into a place of pure energy.

Dr. N: What is this area like?

S: For me … it is the vessel of healing.

Dr. N: Give me as much detail as possible about what you experience here.

S: I'm propelled in and I see a bright warm beam. It reaches out to me as a stream of liquid energy. There is a … vapor-like … steam swirling around me at first … then gently touching my soul as if it were alive. Then it is absorbed into me as fire and I am bathed and cleansed from my hurts.

Dr. N: Is someone bathing you, or is this light beam enveloping you from out of nowhere?

S: I am alone, but it is directed. My essence is being bathed … restoring me after my exposure to Earth.

Dr. N: I have heard this place is similar to taking a refreshing shower after a hard day's work.

S: (laughs) After a lifetime of work. It's better and you don't get wet, either.

Dr. N: You also don't have a physical body anymore, so how can this energy shower heal a soul?

S: By reaching into … my being. I'm so tired from my last life and with the body I had.

Dr. N: Are you saying the ravages of the physical body and the human mind leaves an emotional mark on the soul after death?

S: God, yes! My very expression—who I am as a being—was affected by the brain and body I occupied.

Dr. N: Even though you are now separated from that body forever?

S: Each body leaves … an imprint … on you, at least for a while. There are some bodies I have had that I can never get away from altogether. Even though you are free of them you keep some of the outstanding memories of your bodies in certain lives.

Dr. N: Okay, now I want you to finish with your shower of healing and tell me what you feel.

S: I am suspended in the light … it permeates through my soul … washing out most of the negative viruses. It allows me to let go of the bonds of my last life … bringing about my transformation so I can become whole again.

Dr. N: Does the shower have the same effect upon everyone?

S: (pause) When I was younger and less experienced, I came here more damaged—the energy here seemed less effective because I didn't know how to use it to completely purge the negativity. I carried old wounds with me longer despite the healing energy.

Dr. N: I think I understand. So, what do you do now?

S: When I am restored, I leave here and go to a quiet place to talk to my guide.

This place I have come to call the shower of healing is only a prelude for the rehabilitation of returning souls. The orientation stage which immediately follows (especially with younger souls), involves a substantial counseling session with one's guide. The newly refreshed soul arrives at this station to undergo a debriefing of the life just ended. Orientation is also designed as an intake interview to provide further emotional release and readjustment back into the spirit world.

People in hypnosis who discuss the type of counseling which goes on during orientation say their guides are gentle but probing. Imagine your favorite elementary school teacher and you have the idea. Think of a firm but concerned entity who knows all about your learning habits, your strong and weak points, and your fears, who is always ready to work with you as long as you continue to try. When you don't, everything remains stationary in your development. Nothing can be hidden by students from their spiritual teachers. No subterfuge or deception exists in a telepathic world.

There are a multitude of differences in orientation scenes depending upon the souls' individual makeup and their state of mind after the life just ended. Souls report their orientation often takes place in a room. The furnishings of these settings and the intensity of this first conference can vary after each life. The case below gives a brief example of an orientation scene which attests to the desire of higher forces to bring comfort to the returning soul.

◄← Case 12 →►

S: At the center of this place I found my bedroom where I was so happy as a child. I see my rose-covered wallpaper and four-poster bed with the squeaky springs under a thick, pink quilt made for me by my grandmother. My grandmother and I used to have heart-to-heart chats whenever I was troubled and she is here, too—just sitting on the edge of my bed with my favorite stuffed animals around her—waiting for me. Her wrinkled face is full of love, as always. After a while I see she is actually my guide Amephus. I talk to Amephus about the sad and happy times of the life I have finished. I know I made mistakes, but she is so kind to me. We laugh and cry together while I reminisce. Then we discuss all the things I didn't do that I might have done with my life. But in the end it's okay. She knows I must rest in this beautiful world. I'm going to relax. I don't care if I ever go back to Earth again because my real home is here.

Apparently, the more advanced souls do not require any orientation at this stage. This does not mean the ten percent of my clients in this category just sail right by their guides with a wave upon their return from Earth. Everybody is held accountable for their past lives. Performance is judged upon how each individual interpreted and acted upon their life roles. Intake interviews for the advanced souls are conducted with master teachers later. The less experienced entities are usually given special attention by counselors because the abrupt transition from the physical to a spiritual form is more difficult for them.

The next case I have selected has a more in-depth therapeutic spiritual orientation. The exploration of attitudes and feelings with a view to reorienting future behavior is typical of guides. The client in Case 13 is a strong, imposing thirty-two-year-old woman of above-average height and weight. Dressed in jeans, boots, and a loose-fitting sweat shirt, Hester arrived at my office one day in a state of agitation.

Her presenting problems fell into three parts. She was dissatisfied with her life as a successful real estate broker as being too materialistic and unfulfilling. Hester also felt she lacked feminine sexuality. She mentioned having a closet full of beautiful clothes which were "hateful to wear." This client then told me how she had easily manipulated men all her life because, "There is a male aggression about me which also makes me feel incomplete as a woman." As a young girl, she avoided dolls and wearing dresses because she was more interested in competitive sports with boys.

Her masculine feelings had not changed with age, although she had found a man who became her husband because he accepted her dominance in their relationship. Hester said she enjoyed sex with him as long as she was in physical control and that he found this exciting. In addition, my client complained of headaches on the right side of her head above the ear which, after extensive medical examinations, doctors had attributed to stress.

During our session, I learned this subject had experienced a recent series of male lives, culminating with a short life as a prosecuting attorney called Ross Feldon in the state of Oklahoma during the 1880s. As Ross, my client had committed suicide at age thirty-three in a hotel room by shooting himself in the head. Ross was in despair over the direction his life had taken as a courtroom prosecutor.

As the dialogue progresses, the reader will notice displays of intense emotion. Regression therapists call this "heightened response" being in a state of revivification (meaning to give new life) as opposed to the alternative trance state where subjects are observer-participants.

◄◄ Case 13 ►►

Dr. N: Now that you have left the shower of healing, where are you going?

S: (apprehensively) To see my advisor.

Dr. N: And who is that?

S: (pause) … Dees … no … his name is Clodees.

Dr. N: Did you talk to Clodees when you entered the spirit world?

S: I wasn't ready yet. I just wanted to see my parents.

Dr. N: Why are you going to see Clodees now?

S: I … am going to have to make some kind of … accounting … of myself. We go through this after all my lives, but this time I'm really in the soup.

Dr. N: Why?

S: Because I killed myself.

Dr. N: When a person kills himself on Earth does this mean they will receive some sort of punishment as a spirit?

S: No, no, there is no such thing here as punishment—that's an Earth condition. Clodees will be disappointed that I bailed out early and didn't have the courage to face my difficulties. By choosing to die as I did means I have to come back later and deal with the same thing all over again in a different life. I just wasted a lot of time by checking out early.

Dr. N: So, no one will condemn you for committing suicide?

S: (reflects for a moment) Well, my friends won't give me any pats on the back either—I feel sadness at what I did.

Note: This is the usual spiritual attitude toward suicide, but I want to add that those who escape from chronic physical pain or almost total incapacity on Earth by killing themselves feel no remorse as souls. Their guides and friends also have a more accepting view toward this motivation for suicide.

Dr. N: All right, let's proceed into your conference with Clodees. First describe your surroundings as you enter this space to see your advisor.

S: I go into a room—with walls … (laughs) Oh, it's the Buckhorn!

Dr. N: What's that?

S: A great cattleman's bar in Oklahoma. I was happy as a patron there—friendly atmosphere—beautiful wood paneling—the stuffed leather chairs. (pause) I see Clodees is sitting at one of the tables waiting for me. Now we are going to talk.

Dr. N: How do you account for an Oklahoma bar in the spirit world?

S: It's one of the nice things they do for you to ease your mind, but that's where it ends. (then with a deep sigh) This talk is not going to be like a party at the bar.

Dr. N: You sound a little depressed at the prospect of an intimate conversation with your guide about your last life?

S: (defensively) Because I blew it! I have to see him to explain why things didn't work out. Life is so *hard!* I try to do it right … but …

Dr. N: Do what right?

S: (with anguish) I had an agreement with Clodees to work on setting goals and then following through. He had expectations for me as Ross. Damn! Now I have to face him with this …

Dr. N: You don't feel you met the contract you had with your advisor about lessons to be learned as Ross?

S: (impatiently) No, I was terrible. And, of course, I'll have to do it all over again. We never seem to get it perfect. (pause) You know, if it weren't for Earth's beauty—the birds—flowers—trees—I would never go back. It's too much trouble.

Dr. N: I can see you are upset, but don't you think …

S: (breaks in with agitation) You can't get away with a *thing* either. Everybody here knows you so well. There is nothing I can keep from Clodees.

Dr. N: I want you to take a deep breath and go further into the Buckhorn Bar and tell me what you do.

S: (subject gulps and squares her shoulders) I float in and sit down across from Clodees at a round table near the front of the bar.

Dr. N: Now that you are near Clodees, do you think he is as upset as you are over this past life?

S: No, I'm more upset with myself over what I did and didn't do and he knows that. Advisors can be displeased but they don't humiliate us, they are too superior for that.

The counseling input of a directive guide gives the healing process of our soul a boost during orientation, but that does not mean the defensive barriers to progress are completely removed. The painful emotional memories from our past do not die as easily as our bodies. Hester must see her negative past life script as Ross clearly, without distorted perceptions.

Recreating spiritual orientation scenes during hypnosis assists me as a therapist. I have found the techniques of psychodramatic role playing to be useful in exposing feelings and old beliefs related to current behavior. Case 13 had quite a long orientation which I have condensed. At this juncture of the case I shifted my questioning to involve the subject's guide.

As the proceedings unfold with Ross Feldon's life, I will take the role of a third party intermediary between Ross and Clodees. Within this counseling mode I also want to initiate a role transference where Hester-Ross will speak the thoughts of Clodees. The integration of a subject with their guide is a means of eliciting assistance from these higher entities and bringing problems into sharper focus. I sometimes sense even my own guide is directing me in these sessions.

I am cautious about summoning up guides without good cause. Facilitating communication directly with a client's guide always has an uncertain outcome. If my intrusion is clumsy or unnecessary, guides will block a subject's response by silence or use metaphoric language which is obscure.

I have had guides speak through a subject's vocal chords in raspy tones which are so discordant I can hardly understand the responses to questions. When subjects talk for their guides, rather than guides speaking for themselves through the subject, usually the cadence of speech is not as broken. In this case, Clodees comes through Hester-Ross easily and allows me some latitude in working with *his* client.

> **Dr. N:** Ross, we both need to understand what is happening psychologically to you right from the start of your orientation with Clodees. I want you to assist me. Are you willing to do this?
>
> **S:** Yes, I am.
>
> **Dr. N:** Good, and now you are going to be able to do something unusual. On the count of three, you will have the ability to assume the dual roles of Clodees and yourself. This ability will enable you to speak to me about your thoughts and those of your guide as well. It will seem that you will actually become your guide when I question you. Are you ready?
>
> **S:** (with hesitation) I ... think so.
>
> **Dr. N:** (rapidly) *One—two—three!* (I place my palm on the subject's forehead to stimulate the transference.) *Now, be Clodees speaking his thoughts through you.* You are sitting at a table across from the soul of Ross Feldon. What do you say to him? *Quickly!* (I want the subject to react without thinking critically about the difficulty of my command)
>
> **S:** (subject reacts slowly, speaking as his own guide) You know ... you could have done better...

Dr. N: *Quickly now*—be Ross Feldon again. Move to the other side of the table and answer Clodees.

S: I ... tried ... but I fell short of the goal ...

Dr. N: Switch places again. Become the voice of Clodees' thoughts and answer Ross. *Quickly!*

S: If you could change anything about your life, what would it be?

Dr. N: *Respond as Ross.*

S: Not to be ... corrupted ... by power and money.

Dr. N: *Answer as Clodees.*

S: Why did you let these things detract from your original commitment?

Dr. N: (I lower my voice) You are doing fine. Keep switching chairs back and forth at the table. Now answer your guide's question.

S: I wanted to belong ... to feel important in the community ... to rise above others and be admired ... for my strength.

Dr. N: Respond as Clodees.

S: Especially by women. I observed you tried to dominate them sexually as well, making conquests without attachments.

Dr. N: Speak as Ross.

S: Yes ... that's true ... (shakes head from side to side) I don't have to explain—you know everything anyway.

Dr. N: Respond as Clodees.

S: Oh, but you do. You must bring your self-awareness to bear on these matters.

Dr. N: Answer as Ross.

S: (defiantly) If I hadn't exerted power over these people they would have controlled me.

Dr. N: Respond as Clodees.

S: This lacks merit and was unworthy of you. What you became is not how you started. We chose your parents carefully.

Note: The Feldon family were farmers of modest means who displayed honesty, forbearance, and sacrificed much so Ross could study law.

Dr. N: Answer as Ross.

S: (in a rush) Yes—I know—they brought me up to be idealistic— to help the little guy, and I wanted this, too, but it didn't work for me. You saw what happened. I was in debt when I began as a lawyer … ineffective … of no consequence. I didn't want to be poor any- more, defending people who couldn't pay me. I hated the farm—the pigs and the cows. I liked being around substantial people and when I joined the establishment as a prosecutor, I had the idea of reform- ing the system and helping farm people. It was the system that was wrong.

Dr. N: Respond as Clodees.

S: Ah, you were corrupted by the system—explain this to me.

Dr. N: Answer as Ross.

S: (hotly) People had to pay fines they couldn't afford—others I sent to jail because of offenses they didn't mean to commit—others I had hung! (voice breaks) I became a legal killer.

Dr. N: Respond as Clodees.

S: Why did you feel responsible for prosecuting criminals who were guilty of hurting others?

Dr. N: Answer as Ross.

S: Few of those … most were … just ordinary people like my par- ents who got caught up in the system … needing money to survive … and there were those who were … sick in the head …

Dr. N: Respond as Clodees.

S: What about the victims of the people you prosecuted? Didn't you choose a life of law to help society and to make the farms and the towns safer with justice?

Dr. N: Answer as Ross.

S: (loudly) *Don't you see, it didn't work for me—I was turned into a murderer by a primitive society!*

Dr. N: Respond as Clodees.

S: And so you murdered yourself?

Dr. N: Answer as Ross.

S: I got off track … I couldn't go back to being a nobody … and I couldn't go forward.

Dr. N: Respond as Clodees.

S: Too easily you became a participant with those whose motivations were for personal gain and notoriety. This was not you. Why did you hide from yourself?

Dr. N: Answer as Ross.

S: (with anger) Why didn't you help me more—when I started as a public defender?

Dr. N: Respond as Clodees.

S: What benefit do you get from thinking I should pick you up at every turn?

Dr. N: (I ask Hester to respond as Ross, but when she remains silent after the last question, I step in) Ross, if I may interrupt—I believe Clodees is inquiring into the payoff for you from both the pain you feel now and strokes you get from blaming him over your last life.

S: (pause) Wanting sympathy … I guess.

Dr. N: Okay, respond as Clodees to this thought.

S: (very slowly) What more would you have me do? You didn't reach far enough inside yourself. I placed thoughts in your mind of temperance, moderation, responsibility, original goals, your parents' love—you ignored these thoughts and were stubborn to alternative action.

S: (Ross responds without my command) I know I missed the signs you set up … I wasted opportunities … I was afraid …

Dr. N: Respond as Clodees to your statement.

S: What do you value most about who you are?

Dr. N: Answer your guide.

S: That I had the desire to change things on Earth. I started with wanting to make a difference for the people of Earth.

Dr. N: Respond as Clodees.

S: You left that assignment early and now I see you missing opportunities again—being afraid to take risks—taking paths which damage you—trying to become someone who is not you and there is sadness again.

Recreating the orientation stage does produce abrupt transitions during my hypnosis sessions. While Case 13 is speaking as Clodees, notice how her responses take on a more lucid and decisive quality which is different from either my client Hester, or her former self as Ross. I am not always successful with my subjects translating their guides' comments so insightfully in former spiritual orientations. Nevertheless, past life memories often spill over into contemporary problems in whatever spiritual setting is selected.

Whether my subject or her guide actually directed the conversation in the Buckhorn Bar scene while I moved the time frame around does not matter to me. After all, Ross Feldon as a person is dead. But Hester is caught in the same quagmire, and I want to do what I can to break this destructive pattern of behavior. I spend a few minutes reviewing with this subject what her guide has indicated about lack of self-concept, alienation, and lost values. After asking Clodees for his continued assistance, I close the orientation scene and immediately take Hester to a later spiritual stage just before her rebirth today.

Dr. N: With all the knowledge of who you were as Ross, and having a greater understanding of your real spiritual identity after your stay in the spirit world, why did you choose your current body?

S: I chose to be a woman so people would not feel intimidated by me.

Dr. N: Really? Then why did you take the body of such a strong, forceful woman in the twentieth century?

S: They won't see a prosecuting attorney dressed in black in a courtroom—this time I am a surprise package!

Dr. N: A surprise package? What does that mean?

S: As a woman, I knew I would be less intimidating to men. I can catch them off guard and scare them to death.

Dr. N: What kind of men?

S: The big guys—the power structure in society—catch then when they are lulled into a false sense of security because I'm a woman.

Dr. N: Catch them and do what?

S: (drives her right fist into the left palm) Nail them—to save the little guy from the sharks who want to eat up all the small fish in this world.

Dr. N: (I move my subject into the present while she remains in the superconscious state) Let me understand your reason for choosing to be a woman in this life. You wanted to help the same sort of people who you were unable to help as a man in your previous life—is this correct?

S: (sadly) Yeah, but it's not the best way. It's not working out for me like I thought. I'm still too strong and macho. Energy is pouring out of me in the wrong direction.

Dr. N: What wrong direction?

S: (wistfully) I'm doing it again. Misusing people. I chose the body of a woman who is intimidating to men and I don't feel like a woman.

Dr. N: Give me an example?

S: Sexually and in business. I'm in the power game again ... pushing aside principles ... getting off track as before (as Ross). This time I manipulate real estate deals. I'm too interested in acquiring money. I want status.

Dr. N: And how does this hurt you, Hester?

S: The influence of money and position is a drug to me as it was in my last life. My being a woman now has done nothing to change my desire to control people. So ... stupid ...

Dr. N: Then do you think your motivations were wrong in choosing to be a female?

S: Yes, I do feel more natural living as a man. But I thought as a woman this time around I would be ... more subtle. I wanted this chance to try again in a different sex and Clodees let me take it. (client slumps down in her chair) What a blunder.

Dr. N: Don't you think you are being a little hard on yourself, Hester? I have the sense you also chose to be a woman because you wanted a woman's insight and intuition to give you a different perspective to tackle your lessons. You can have masculine energy, if you want to call it that, and still be feminine.

Before finishing this case, I should touch on the issue of homosexuality. Most of my subjects select the bodies of one gender over another 75 percent of the time. This pattern is true of all but the advanced souls, who maintain more of a balance in choosing to be men and women. A gender preference by a majority of earthbound souls does not mean they are unhappy the other 25 percent of the time as males or females.

Hester is not necessarily gay or bi-sexual because of her body choice. Homosexuals may or may not be comfortable with their anatomy as humans. When I do have a client who is gay, they often ask if their homosexuality is the result of choosing to be "the wrong sex" in this life. When their sessions are over this inquiry is usually answered.

Regardless of the circumstances which lead souls to make gender choices, this decision was made before arriving on Earth. Sometimes I find that gay people have chosen in advance of their current lives to experiment with a sex that was seldom used in former lives.

Being gay carries a sexual stigma in our society which presents a more difficult road in life. When this road is chosen by one of my clients, it can usually be traced to a karmic need to accelerate personal understanding of the complex differences in gender identity as related to certain events in their past. Case 13 chose to be a woman in this life to try and get over the stumbling blocks experienced as Ross Feldon.

Would Hester have benefited from knowing about her past as Ross from birth rather than having to wait over thirty years and undergo hypnosis? Having no conscious memory of our former existences is called amnesia. This human condition is perplexing to people attracted to reincarnation. Why should we have to grope around in life trying to figure out who we are and what we are supposed to do and wondering if some spiritual divinity really cares about us? I closed my session with this woman by asking about her amnesia.

Dr. N: Why do you think you had no conscious memory about your life as Ross Feldon?

S: When we choose a body and make a plan before coming back to Earth, there is an agreement with our advisors.

Dr. N: An agreement about what?

S: We agree … not to remember … other lives.

Dr. N: Why?

S: Learning from a blank slate is better than knowing in advance what could happen to you because of what you did before.

Dr. N: But wouldn't knowing about your past life mistakes be valuable in avoiding the same pitfalls in this life?

S: If people knew all about their past, many might pay too much attention to it rather than trying out new approaches to the same problem. The new life must be … taken seriously.

Dr. N: Are there any other reasons?

S: (pause) Without having old memories, our advisors say there is less preoccupation for … trying to … avenge the past … to get even for the wrongs done to you.

Dr. N: Well, it seems to me that so far this has been part of the motivation and conduct in your life as Hester.

S: (forcefully) That's why I came to you.

Dr. N: And do you still think a total blackout of our eternal spiritual life on Earth is essential to progress?

S: Normally, yes, but it's not a total blackout. We get flashes from dreams … during times of crisis … people have an inner knowing of what direction to take when it is necessary. And sometimes your friends can fudge a little …

Dr. N: By friends, you mean entities from the spirit world?

S: Uh-huh … they give you hints, by flashing ideas—I've done it.

Dr. N: Nevertheless, you had to come to me to unlock your conscious amnesia.

S: (pause) We have … the capacity to know when it is necessary. I was ready for change when I heard about you. Clodees allowed me to see the past with you because it was to my benefit.

Dr. N: Otherwise, your amnesia would have remained intact?

S: Yes, that would have meant I wasn't supposed to know certain things yet.

In my opinion, when clients are unable to go into hypnosis at any given time, or if they have only sketchy memories in trance, there is a reason for this blockage. This does not mean these people have no past memories, just that they are not ready to have them exposed.

My client knew something was hindering her growth and wanted it revealed. The superconscious identity of the soul houses our continuous memory, including goals. When the time in our lives is appropriate, we must harmonize human material needs with our soul's purpose for being here. I try to take a common sense approach in bringing past and present experiences into alignment.

Our eternal identity never leaves us alone in the bodies we choose, despite our current status. In reflection, meditation, or prayer, the memories of who we really are do filter down to us in selective thought each day. In small, intuitive ways—through the cloud of amnesia—we are given clues for the justification of our being.

After desensitizing the source of her headaches, I completed my session with Hester by reinforcing her choice to be a woman for reasons other than intimidating men. I gave her permission to lower her defenses a little and be less aggressive. We discussed options for restructuring occupational goals toward the helping professions and the possibilities of volunteer service work. She was finally able to see her life today as a great opportunity for learning rather than a failure of gender choice.

After a case is completed, I never cease to admire the brutal honesty of souls. When a soul has led a productive life beneficial to themselves and those around them, I notice they return to the spirit world with enthusiasm. However, when subjects like Case 13 report they wasted a past life, especially from early suicide, then they describe going back rather dejected.

When orientation is upsetting to a subject, I find an underlying reason is the abruptness with which a soul is once again in full possession of all past knowledge. After physical death, unencumbered by a human body, the soul has a sudden influx of perception. The stupid things we did in life hit us hard in orientation. I see more relaxation and greater clarity of thought as I move my subjects further into the spirit world.

Souls are created in a positive matrix of such love and wisdom that when a soul starts to come to a planet like Earth and join the physical beings who have evolved from a primitive state, the violence is a shock. Humans have the raw, negative emotions of anger and hate as an outgrowth of their fear and pain connected with survival going back to the Stone Age.

Both positive and negative emotions are mixed between soul and host for their mutual benefit. If a soul only knew love and peace, it would gain no insight and never truly appreciate the value of these positive feelings. The test of reincarnation for a soul coming to Earth is the conquering of fear in a human body. A soul grows by trying to overcome all negative emotions connected to fear through perseverance in many lifetimes, often returning to the spirit world bruised or hurt, as Case 13 indicated. Some of this negativity can be retained, even in the spirit world, and may reappear in another life with a new body. On the other hand, there is a trade-off. It's in joy and unabashed pleasure that the true nature of an individual soul is revealed on earth in the face of a happy human being.

Orientation conferences with our guides allow us to begin the long process of self-evaluation between lives. Soon we will have another conference, this time with more master beings in attendance. In the last chapter, I referred to the ancient Egyptian tradition of newly deceased souls being taken into a Hall of Judgement to account for their past life. In one form or another, the concept of a torturous courtroom trial awaiting us right after death has been part of the religious belief system of many cultures. Occasionally, a susceptible individual in a traumatic situation will say they had an out-of-body experience with nightmarish visions of being taken by frightening specters into an afterlife of darkness where they were sentenced in front of demonic judges. In these cases, I suspect a strong preconditioned belief system of hell.

In the quiet, relaxing state of hypnosis, with continuity on all mental levels, my subjects report that the initial orientation session with their guides prepares them to go before a panel of superior beings. However, the words courtroom and trial are not used to describe these proceedings. A number of my cases have called these wise beings, directors and even judges, but most refer to them as a Council of Masters or Elders. This board of review is generally composed of between three and seven members and since souls appear before them after arriving at their home base, I will go into this conference in more detail at the end of the next chapter.

All soul evaluation conferences, be they with our guides, peers, or a panel of masters have one thing in common. The feedback and past life analysis we receive in terms of judgement is based upon the original <u>intent</u> of our choices as much as the actions of a lifetime. Our motivations are questioned and criticized, but not condemned in such a way as to make us suffer. As I explained in Chapter Four, this does not mean souls are exonerated for their acts which harmed others simply because they are sorry. Karmic payment will come in a future life. I have been told that our spiritual masters constantly remind us that because the human brain does not have an innate moral sense of ethics, conscience is the soul's responsibility. Nevertheless, there is overwhelming forgiveness in the spirit world. This world is ageless and so too are our learning tasks. We will be given other chances in our struggle for growth.

When the initial conference with our guide is over, we leave the place of orientation and join a coordinated flow of activity involving the transit of enormous numbers of other souls into a kind of central receiving station.

6

Transition

ALL souls, regardless of experience, eventually arrive at a central port in the spirit world which I call the staging area. I have said there are variations in the speed of soul movement right after death, depending upon spiritual maturity. Once past the orientation station there seems to be no further travel detours for anyone entering this space of the spirit world. Apparently, large numbers of returning souls are conveyed in a spiritual form of mass transit.

Sometimes souls are escorted by their guides to this area. I find this practice is especially true for the younger souls. Others are directed through by an unseen force which pulls them into the staging area and then beyond to waiting entities. From what I am able to determine, accompaniment by other entities depends upon the volition of one's guide. In most cases haste is not an issue, but souls do not dawdle along on this leg of their journey. The feelings we have along this path depend on our state of mind after each life.

The assembly and transfer of souls really involves two phases. The staging area is not an encampment space. Spirits are brought in, collected, and then projected out to their proper final destinations. When I hear accounts of this particular junction, I visualize myself walking with large numbers of travelers through the central terminal of a metropolitan airport which has the capacity to fly all of us out in any direction. One of my clients described the staging area as resembling "the hub of a great wagon wheel, where we are transported from a center along the spokes to our designated places."

My subjects say this region appears to them as having a large number of unacquainted spirits moving in and out of the hub in an efficient manner with no congestion. Another person called this area "the Los Angeles free-way without gridlock." There may be other similar wheel hubs with free-way-type on and off ramps in the spirit world, but each client considers their own route to and from this center to be the only one.

The observations I hear about the nature of the spirit world when en-tering the staging area have definitely changed from those first impressions of layering and foggy stratification. It is as if the soul is now traveling through the loosely-wound arms of a mighty galactic cloud into a more unified celestial field. While their spirits hover in the open arena of the staging area preparing for further transport out to prescribed spaces, I en-joy listening to the excitement in the voices of my subjects. They are dazzled by an eternal world spread out before them and believe that somewhere within lies the nucleus of creation.

When they look at the fully opened canopy around them, subjects will state that the spirit world appears to be of varied luminescence. I hear nothing about the inky blackness we associate with deep space. The gath-erings of souls that clients see in the foreground in this amphitheater ap-pear as myriads of sharp star lights all going in different directions. Some move fast while others drift. The more distant energy concentrations have been pictured as "islands of misty veils." I am told the most outstanding characteristic of the spirit world is a continuous feeling of a powerful mental force directing everything in uncanny harmony. People say this is a place of pure thought.

Thought takes many forms. It is at this vantage point in their return that souls begin to anticipate meeting others who wait for them. A few of these companions may have already been seen at the gateway, but most have not. Without exception, souls who wish to contact each other, espe-cially when on the move, do so by just thinking of the entity they want. Suddenly, the individual called will appear in the soul mind of the trav-eler. These telepathic communications by the energy of all spiritual enti-ties allow for a non-visual affinity, while two energy forms who actually come near one another provide a more direct connection. There is unifor-mity in the accounts of my subjects as to their manner of spiritual travel, routes, and destinations, although what they see along the way is distinc-tive with each person.

I searched through my case files to find a subject whose experiences along this route to an ultimate spiritual destination was both descriptive and yet representative of what many others have told me. I selected an insightful, forty-one-year-old graphic designer with a mature soul. This man's soul had traveled over this course many times between a long span of lives.

✦ Case 14 ✦

Dr. N: You are now ready to begin the final portion of your homeward journey toward the place where your soul belongs in the spirit world. On the count of three, all the details of this final leg of your travels will become clear to you. It will be easy for you to report on everything you see because you are familiar with the route. Are you ready?

S: Yes.

Dr. N: (raising my voice to a commanding tone) *One*—we are getting started. *Two*—your soul has now moved out of the area of orientation. *Three!* Quickly, what is your first impression?

S: Distances are ... unlimited ... endless space ... forever ...

Dr. N: So, are you telling me the spirit world is endless?

S: (long pause) To be honest—from where I am floating—it looks endless. But when I begin to really move it changes.

Dr. N: Changes how?

S: Well ... everything remains ... formless ... but when I am ... gliding faster ... I see I'm moving around inside a gigantic bowl—turned upside down. I don't know where the rims of the bowl are, or even if any exist.

Dr. N: Then movement gives you the sense of a spherical spirit world?

S: Yes, but it's only a feeling of ... enclosed uniformity ... when I am moving rapidly.

Dr. N: Why does rapid movement—your speed—give you the feeling of being in a bowl?

S: (long pause) It's strange. Although everything appears to go on straight when my soul is drifting—that changes to ... a feeling of roundness when I am moving fast on a line of contact.

Dr. N: What do you mean by a line of contact?

S: Towards a specific destination.

Dr. N: How does moving with speed on a given line of travel change your observational perceptions of the spirit world to a feeling it is round?

S: Because with speed the lines seem to ... bend. They curve in a more obvious direction for me and give me less freedom of movement.

Note: Other subjects, who are also disposed toward linear descriptions, speak of traveling along directional force lines which have the spatial properties of a grid system. One person called them "vibrational strings."

Dr. N: By less freedom, do you mean less personal control?

S: Yes.

Dr. N: Can you more precisely describe the movement of your soul along these curving contact lines?

S: It's just more purposeful—when my soul is being directed someplace on a line. It's like I'm in a current of white water—only not as thick as water—because the current is lighter than air.

Dr. N: Then, in this spiritual atmosphere, you don't have the sense of density such as in water?

S: No, I don't, but what I am trying to say is I'm being carried along as if I were in a current underwater.

Dr. N: Why do you think this is so?

S: Well, it's as if we are all swimming—being carried along—in a swift current which *we* can't control ... under somebody's direction ... up and down from each other in space ... with nothing solid around us.

Dr. N: Do you see other souls traveling in a purposeful way above and below you?

S: Yes, it's as if we start in a stream and then all of us returning from death are pulled into a great river together.

Dr. N: When do the numbers of returning souls seem the highest to you?

S: When the rivers converge into ... I can't describe it ...

Dr. N: Please try.

S: (pause) We are gathered into ... a sea ... where all of us swirl around ... in slow motion. Then, I feel as though I'm being pulled away to a small tributary again and it's quieter ... further from the thoughts of so many minds ... going to the ones I know.

Dr. N: Later, in your normal travels as a soul, is it the same as being propelled around in streams and rivers as you have just described?

S: No, not at all. This is different. We are like salmon going up to spawn—returning home. Once we get there we are not pushed about this way. Then we can drift.

Dr. N: Who is doing the pushing while you are being taken home?

S: Higher entities. The ones in charge of our movements to get us home.

Dr. N: Entities such as your guide?

S: Above him, I think.

Dr. N: What else are you feeling at this moment?

S: Peace. There is such peace you never want to leave again.

Dr. N: Anything more?

S: Oh, I have some anticipation, too, while moving slowly with the energy current.

Dr. N: All right, now I want you to continue to move further along with the current of energy closer to the area where you are supposed to go. Look around carefully and tell me what you see.

S: I see ... a variety of lights ... in patches ... separated from each other by ... galleries ...

Dr. N: By galleries, do you mean a series of enclosures?

S: Mmm ... more like a long ... corridor ... bulging out in places ... stretching out away from me into the distance.

Dr. N: And the lights?

S: They are people. The souls of people within the bulging galleries reflecting light outward to me. That's what I'm seeing—patches of lights bobbing around.

Dr. N: Are these clusters of people structurally separated from each other in the bulges along the corridor?

S: No, there are no walls here. Nothing is structural, with angles and corners. It's hard for me to explain, exactly …

Dr. N: You are doing fine. Now, I want you to tell me what separates the light clusters from each other along this corridor you are describing.

S: The people … are divided by … thin, wispy … filaments … making the light milky, like the transparency of frosted glass. There is an incandescent glow from their energy as I pass by.

Dr. N: How do you see individual souls within the clusters?

S: (pause) As light dots. I see masses of dots hanging in clumps … as hanging grapes, all lit up.

Dr. N: Do these clumps represent various groups of soul energy masses with space between them?

S: Yes … they are separated into small groups … I am going to my own clump.

Dr. N: What else do you feel about them as you pass by on the way to your cluster?

S: I can feel their thoughts reaching out … so varied … but together too … such harmony … but … (stops)

Dr. N: Go on.

S: I don't know the ones I'm passing now … it doesn't matter.

Dr. N: Okay, let's pass on by these clusters which seem to bulge out along a corridor. Give me an example of what the whole thing looks like to you from a distance.

S: (laughs) A long glow-worm, its sides bulging in and out … the movement is … rhythmic.

Dr. N: You mean the corridor itself appears to move?

S: Yes, parts of it … swaying as a ribbon in the breeze while I am going further away.

Dr. N: Continue floating and tell me what happens to you next.

S: (pause) I'm at the edge of another corridor … I'm slowing down.

Dr. N: Why?

S: (grows excited) Because … oh, good! I'm coming in towards the site where my friends are attached.

Dr. N: And how do you feel at this moment?

S: Fantastic! There is a familiar pulling of minds … reaching out to me … I'm catching the tail of their kite … joining them in thought … I'm *home!*

Dr. N: Is your particular cluster group of friends isolated from the other groups of souls living in other corridors?

S: No one is really isolated, although some of the younger ones may think so. I've been around a long time, though, and I have a lot of connections (said with modest confidence).

Dr. N: So you felt connections with those other corridors, even with spirits in them you might not know from past experience?

S: I do because of the connections I have had. There is a oneness here.

Dr. N: When you are moving around as a spirit, what is the major difference in your interactions with other souls, compared to being in human form on Earth?

S: Here no one is a stranger. There is a total lack of hostility toward anyone.

Dr. N: You mean every spirit is friendly to every other spirit, regardless of prior associations in many settings?

S: That's right, and it's more than just being friendly.

Dr. N: In what way?

S: We recognize a universal bond between us which makes us all the same. There is no suspicion toward each other.

Dr. N: How does this attitude manifest itself between souls who first meet?

S: By complete openness and acceptance.

Dr. N: Living on Earth must be difficult for souls, then?

S: It is, for the newer ones especially, because they go to Earth expecting to be treated fairly. When they aren't, it's a shock. For some, it takes quite a few lives to get used to the earth body.

Dr. N: And if the newer souls are struggling with these earth conditions, are they less efficient when working within the human mind?

S: I would have to say yes, because the brain drives a lot of fear and violence into our souls. It's hard for us, but that's why we come to Earth … to overcome …

Dr. N: In your opinion, might the newer souls tend to be more fragile and in need of group support upon returning to their cluster?

S: That's absolutely true. We all want to return home. Will you let me stop talking now, so I can meet with my friends?

I have touched on the commonality of word usage by different clients to describe spiritual phenomena. Case 14 offered us a few more. I regularly hear such water-words as currents and streams used to explain a flowing directional movement, where a sky-word like cloud denotes a freedom of motion associated with drifting. Visual images which call up expressions of energy mass and group clusters to indicate souls themselves are especially popular. I have adopted some of this spiritual language myself.

At the final debarkation zone for the incoming soul, waiting cluster groups of familiar entities may be large or small, depending upon the soul developmental level and other factors which I will take up as we get a little further along. By way of comparison with Case 14, the next case demonstrates a more insular perception of the spirit world from a soul with less maturity.

In Case 15, the transition of this soul from the staging area to her home cluster is fairly rapid in her mind. The case is informative because it presents attributes of propriety felt by this soul to a designated space, as well as deference toward those who manage the system. Because this subject is less experienced and a bit edgy over what she sees as a need for conformity, we are given another interpretation of spiritual guidelines for group placement.

➻ Case 15 ➻

Dr. N: I want to talk to you about your trip into the place where you normally stay in the spirit world. Your soul is now moving toward this destination. Explain what you see and feel.

S: (nervously) I'm ... going ... outward, somehow ...

Dr. N: Outward?

S: (puzzled) I am ... floating along ... in a chain of some kind. It's as though I'm weaving through a series of ... connecting links ... a foggy maze ... then ... it opens up ... *oh!*

Dr. N: What is it?

S: (with awe) I have come into ... a grand arena ... I see many others ... criss-crossing around me ... (subject grows uncomfortable)

Dr. N: Just relax—you are in the staging area now. Do you still see your guide?

S: (with hesitation) Yes ... nearby ... otherwise I would be lost ... it's so ... vast ...

Dr. N: (I place my hand on the subject's forehead) Continue to relax and remember you have been here before, although everything may seem new to you. What do you do now?

S: I'm ... carried forward ... rapidly ... straight past others ... then I'm in ... an empty space ... open ...

Dr. N: Does this void mean everything is black around you?

S: It's never black here ... the light ... just contracts to darker shades because of my speed. When I slow down things get brighter. (others confirm this observation)

Dr. N: Continue on and report back to me what you see next.

S: After a while I see ... nests of people ...

Dr. N: You mean groups of people?

S: Yes—like hives—I see them as bunches of moving lights ... fireflies ...

Dr. N: All right, keep moving and tell me what you feel?

S: Warmth … friendship … empathy … it's dreamy … hmm …?

Dr. N: What is it?

S: I have slowed way down—things are different.

Dr. N: How?

S: More clearly defined (pause)—I know this place.

Dr. N: Have you reached your own hive (cluster group)?

S: (long pause) Not yet, I guess …

Dr. N: Just look about you and report back to me exactly what you see and feel.

S: (subject begins to tremble) There are … bunches of people … together … off in the distance … but … *there!*

Dr. N: What do you see?

S: (fearfully) People I know … some of my family … off in the distance … but … (with anguish) *I don't seem to be able to reach them!*

Dr. N: Why?

S: (in tearful bewilderment) I don't know! God, don't they know I'm here? (subject begins to struggle in her chair and then extends her arm and open hand at my office wall) *I can't reach my father!*

Note: I briefly stop my questioning. This client's father had a great influence in her most immediate past life and she needs additional calming techniques. I also decide to reinforce her protective shield before continuing.

Dr. N: What do you think is the reason your father is off in the distance so you can't reach him?

S: (during a long pause I use the time to dry subject's face, which has become wet with tears and perspiration) I don't know …

Dr. N: (I place my hand on subject's forehead and command) Connect with your father—*now!*

S: (after a pause the subject relaxes) It's okay … he is telling me to be patient and everything will become clear to me … I want to go over there and be near him.

Dr. N: And what does he tell you about that?

S: (sadly) He says ... that he can always be in my mind if I need him and ... I will learn to do this better (think telepathically), but he has to stay where he is ...

Dr. N: What do you think is the basic reason for your father remaining in this other place?

S: (tearfully) He does not belong in my hive.

Dr. N: Anything else?

S: The ... directors ... they don't ... (crying again) I'm not sure ...

Note: Normally, I try to avoid too much intervention when subjects are describing their spiritual transitions. In this case, my client is confused and disoriented, so I offer a little guidance of my own.

Dr. N: Let's analyze why you can't reach your father's position right now. Could this separation be the result of higher entities believing this is a time for individual reflection on your part and that you should associate only with other souls at your own level of development?

S: (subject is more restored) Yes, those messages are coming through. I have to work things out for myself ... with others like me. The directors encourage us ... and my father is helping me understand, too.

Dr. N: Are you satisfied with this procedure?

S: (pause) Yes.

Dr. N: All right, please continue with your passage from the moment you see some of your family in the distance. What happens next?

S: Well, I'm still slowing down ... moving gradually ... I'm being taken along a course I have been on before. I'm passing some other bunches of people (group clusters). Then, I stop.

Note: The final transit inward is especially important for the younger souls. One client, upon awakening, described this scene as giving him the sense he was arriving back home at twilight after a long trip away. Having passed from the countryside into his town, he finally reached the proper street. The front windows of his neighbors' houses were lit, and he could see people inside as he drove slowly past before reaching the driveway of his own home. Although people in trance may use such words as "clumps" and "hives" to describe how their home spaces look from a distance, this view becomes more individualistic once they go into each cluster. Then the subjects' spiritual surroundings are associated with towns, schools, and other living areas identified with earthly landmarks of security and pleasure.

Dr. N: Now that you are stationary, what are your impressions?

S: It's … large … activity … there are a lot of people in the vicinity. Some are familiar to me, others are not.

Dr. N: Can we get a little closer to all of them?

S: (abruptly my subject raises her voice with indignation) You don't understand! I don't go over *there*. (points a finger toward my office wall)

Dr. N: What's the problem?

S: I'm not supposed to. You can't just go off anywhere.

Dr. N: But, you have reached your destination?

S: It doesn't matter. I don't go over there. (again points a finger at her mental picture)

Dr. N: Does this tie in with the messages you received about your father?

S: Yes, it does.

Dr. N: Are you saying to me your soul energy cannot arbitrarily float anywhere—such as outside your group?

S: (pointing outward) *They* are not in my group over there.

Dr. N: Define what you mean by over there?

S: (in a grave tone of voice) Those others nearby—that is *their* place. (points down to the floor) This is *our* place. We are here. (nods head to confirm her statement)

Dr. N: Who are they?

S: Well, the others, of course, people not in my group. (in a burst of nervous laughter) Oh, *look!* … my own people, it's wonderful to see them again. They are coming toward me!

Dr. N: (I act as though I am hearing this information for the first time, to encourage spontaneous answers) Really? This does sound wonderful. Are these the same people who were involved with your past life?

S: More than one life, I can tell you. (with pride) These are *my* people!

Dr. N: These people are entities who are members of your own group?

S: Of course, yes, I have been with them for so long. Oh, it's fun seeing them all again. (subject is overjoyed and I give her a few moments with this picture)

Dr. N: I see quite a change in your understanding in just the short time since we arrived here. Look off in the distance at the others around this space. What is it like where they live?

S: (agitated) I don't *want* to know. That is their business. Can't you see? I'm not attached to them. I'm too busy with the people I am supposed to be with here. People I know and love.

Dr. N: I do see, but a few minutes ago you were quite distressed at not being able to get close to your father.

S: I know now he has his own gathering place with people.

Dr. N: Why didn't you know that when we arrived here?

S: I'm not sure. I admit it was a shock at first. Now I know the way things are. It's all coming back to me.

Dr. N: Why wasn't your guide around to explain all this to you before you saw your father?

S: (long pause) I don't know.

Dr. N: Probably other people you have known and loved besides your father are also in these groups. Are you saying you have no contact with them now that you are in your proper place in the spirit world?

S: (upset with me) *No,* I have contact with my mind. Why are you being so difficult? I am supposed to *stay here.*

Dr. N: (I prod the subject once more to gain additional information) And you don't just drift over to those other groups for visits?

S: *No!* You don't do that! You don't go into *their* groups and interfere with their energy.

Dr. N: But mental contact offers no interference with their energy?

S: At the right time. When they are free to do this with me …

Dr. N: So, what you are telling me is that everyone here is located in their own group spaces and you don't go wandering around visiting or making too much mental contact at the wrong times?

S: (calming down) Yes, they are in their own spaces with instruction going on. It's the directors who move around mostly …

Dr. N: Thank you for clearing all this up for me. You want me to know that you and your group friends are especially careful about infringing upon others' spaces?

S: That's right. At least that's the way things are around my space.

Dr. N: And you don't feel confined by this custom?

S: Oh no, there are great expanses of space and such a sense of freedom here, as long as we pay attention to the rules.

Dr. N: And what if you don't? Who decides what is the proper location for each group of souls?

S: (pause) The teachers help us, otherwise we would be lost.

Dr. N: It seemed to me you were lost when we first arrived here?

S: (with uncertainty) I didn't connect … I wasn't mentally in tune … I messed up … I don't think you realize how big it is around here.

Dr. N: Look around you at all the occupied spaces. Isn't the spirit world crowded with souls?

S: (laughs) Sometimes we do get lost—that's our own fault—this place is big! That's why it never gets crowded.

The two cases in this chapter represent different reactions from a beginner and a more advanced soul recalling the final phase of their return passages back to the spirit world. Every participant has their own interpretation of the panoramic view from the staging area to the terminus in their cluster group. Some of my subjects find the transition from the gateway to group placement to be so rapid that they need time to adjust upon arrival.

When recalling their memories between homecoming and placement, my subjects sometimes express concern that an important individual was not present in light form or did not communicate with them telepathically. Often this is a parent or spouse in the life just completed. By the end of the transition stage, the reason usually becomes evident. Frequently it has to do with embodiment.

We have seen how the average returning soul is overwhelmed by pleasure. Familiar beings are clustered together in undulating masses of bright light. On occasion, resonating musical sounds with specific chords guide the incoming traveler. One subject remarked, "As I come near my place, there is a monotone of many voices sounding the letter A, like Aaaaa, for my recognition, and I can see them all vibrating fast as warm, bright energy, and I know these are the disembodied ones right now."

What this means is that those souls who are currently incarnated in one or more bodies at the moment may not be actively engaged with welcoming anybody back. Another subject explained, "It is as if they are sleeping on autopilot—we always know who is out and who is in." Those souls who are not totally discarnated radiate a dim light with low pulsating energy patterns and don't seem to communicate much with anyone. Even so, these souls are able to greet the returning soul in a quiet fashion within the group setting.

The sense of a barrier between various groups, as experienced by Case 15, has different versions among my subjects, depending upon the age of the soul. I will have another perspective about mobility in the next case. The average soul with a great deal of basic work to do describes the separation of their group from others as similar to being in different classrooms in the same schoolhouse. I have also had clients who felt they were entirely separated in their own schoolhouse. The analogy of spiritual schools directed by teacher-guides is used so often by people under hypnosis that it has become a habit for me to use the same terminology.

As I mentioned earlier, after souls arrive back into their soul groups, they are summoned to appear before a Council of Elders. While the Council is not prosecutorial, they do engage in direct examination of a soul's activities before returning them to their groups. It is not unusual for my subjects to have some difficulty providing me with full details of what transpires at these hearings, and I am sure these blocks are intentional.

Here is a report from one case. "After I meet with my friends, my guide Veronica (subject's younger teacher) takes me to another place to meet with my panel of Elders. She is at my side as an interpreter for what I don't understand and to provide support for explanations of my conduct in the last life. At times, she speaks on my behalf as a kind of defense advocate but Quazel (subject's senior guide who arrived before Veronica) carries the most weight with the panel. There are always the same six Elders in front of me who wear long white robes. Their faces are kindly, and they evaluate my perceptions of the life I have just lived and how I could have done better with my talents and what I did that was beneficial. I am freely allowed to express my frustrations and desires. All the Elders are familiar to me, especially two of them who address me more than the others and who look younger than the rest. I think I can distinguish appearances which are male or female. Each has a special aspect in the way they question me but they are honest and truthful, and I am always treated fairly. I can hide nothing from them, but sometimes I get lost when their thoughts are transmitted back and forth in the rapid communication between them. When it is more than I can handle, Veronica translates what they are saying about me, although I have the feeling she does not tell me everything. Before I return to Earth, they will want to see me a second time."

Souls consider themselves having finally arrived home when they rejoin familiar classmates in group settings. Their attendance here with certain other souls does resemble an educational placement system in form and function. The criteria for group admission is based upon knowledge and a given developmental level. As in any classroom situation, some students connect well with teachers and others less so. The next chapter will examine the sorting-out process for soul groups and how souls view themselves in their respective spiritual locations.

7

Placement

 MY impression of the people who believe we do have a soul is that they imagine all souls are probably mixed into one great congregation of space. Many of my subjects believe this too, before their sessions begin. After awakening, it is no wonder they express surprise with the knowledge that everyone has a designated place in the spirit world. When I began to study life in the spirit world with people under hypnosis, I was unprepared to hear about the existence of organized soul support groups. I had pictured spirits just floating around aimlessly by themselves after leaving Earth.

Group placement is determined by soul level. After physical death, a soul's journey back home ends with debarkation into the space reserved for their own colony, as long as they are not a very young soul or isolated for other reasons as mentioned in Chapter Four. The souls represented in these cluster groups are intimate old friends who have about the same awareness level.

When people in trance speak of being part of a soul cluster group, they are talking about a small primary unit of entities who have direct and frequent contact, such as we would see in a human family. Peer members have a sensitivity to each other which is far beyond our conception on Earth.

Secondary groups of souls are arranged in the form of a community support group which is much less intimate with one another. Larger secondary groups of entities are made up of giant sets of primary clusters as lily pads in one pond. Spiritual ponds appear to be endless. Within these ponds, I have never heard of a secondary group estimated at less than a thousand souls. The many primary group clusters which make up one secondary group seem to have sporadic relationships, or no contact at all between clusters. It is rare for me to find souls involved with each other in any meaningful way who are members of two different secondary groups, because the number of souls is so great it is not necessary.

The smaller sub-group primary clusters vary in number, containing anywhere from three to twenty-five souls. I am told the average assemblage is around fifteen, which is called the Inner Circle. Any working contact between members of different cluster groups is governed by the lessons to be learned during an incarnation. This may be due to a past life connection, or the particular identity trait of the souls involved. Soul acquaintanceships between members of different cluster groups usually involve peripheral roles in life on Earth. An example would be a high school classmate who was once a close friend, but who you now see only at class reunions.

Members of the same cluster group are closely united for all eternity. These tightly-knit clusters are often composed of like-minded souls with common objectives which they continually work out with each other. Usually they choose lives together as relatives and close friends during their incarnations on Earth.

It is much more common for me to find a subject's brother or sister from former lives in the same cluster group rather than souls who have been their parents. Parents can meet us at the gateway to the spirit world after a death on Earth, but we may not see much of their souls in the spirit world. This circumstance exists not for reasons of maturity, since a parent soul could be less developed than their human offspring. Rather, it is more a question of social learning between siblings who are contemporary in one time frame. Although parents are a child's primary identification figures for both good and bad karmic effects, it is frequently our relations with spouses, brothers, sisters, and selected close friends over a whole lifetime that most influences personal growth. This takes nothing away from the importance of parents, aunts, uncles, and grandparents who serve us in different ways from another generation.

Figures 1 and 2 (pages 89–90) represent a random spiritual setting of souls. In Figure 1, a soul in primary Group 1, located within the larger secondary Group A, would work closely with all other souls in Group 1. However, some souls in primary Groups 9 and 10 (detailed in Figure 2) could

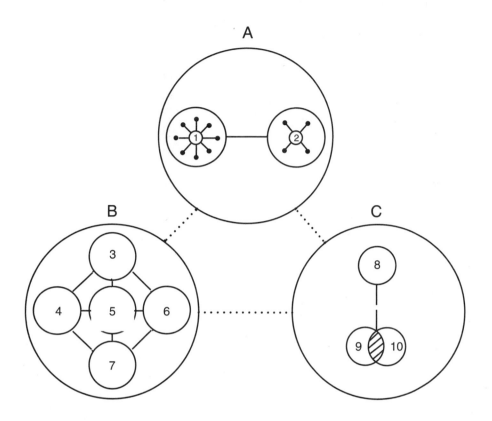

—————— Intense soul interaction within primary clusters.

— — Infrequent soul interaction between primary clusters within a secondary group.

········· Almost no soul interaction between secondary groups with less
advanced souls.

Figure 1—Social Interaction between Primary and Secondary
Soul Groups

This diagram illustrates the overall relationship between souls in primary
cluster groups (1–10) and their secondary groups (A, B, C). The total num-
ber of groups and soul members within these groups is hypothetical since the
scheme varies with each reporting subject's location in the spirit world.

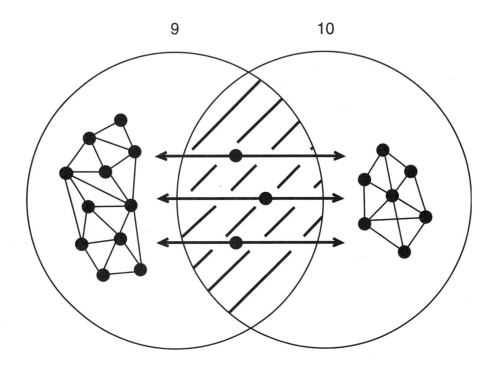

Figure 2—Social Interaction within a Primary Soul Group

This sociogram shows an enlargement of clusters 9 and 10 (from Figure 1) as an example of the less-common overlapping of two cluster groups. Here there is mutual contact between certain souls (within the shaded area) who selectively work with others from both groups.

also work together. The younger souls within secondary Groups A, B, and C would probably have little or no contact with each other in the spirit world or on Earth. Close association between souls depends on their assigned proximity to one another in cluster groups, where there is a similarity of knowledge and affinity brought about by shared earthly experiences.

The next case offers us an account of what it is like coming back to one's cluster group after physical death.

⊷ Case 16 ✈

Dr. N: Once you leave the staging area and have arrived in the spiritual space where you belong, what do you do then?

S: I go to school with my friends.

Dr. N: You mean you are in some kind of spiritual classroom?

S: Yes, where we study.

Dr. N: I want you to take me through this school from the time of your arrival so I can appreciate what is happening to you. Start by telling me what you see from the outside.

S: (with no hesitation) I see a perfectly square Greek temple with large sculptured columns—very beautiful. I recognize it because this is where I return after each cycle (life).

Dr. N: What is a classical Greek temple doing in the spirit world?

S: (shrugs) I don't know why it appears to me that way, except it seems natural ... since my lives in Greece.

Dr. N: All right, let's continue. Does anyone come to meet you?

S: (subject smiles broadly) My teacher Karla.

Dr. N: And how does she appear to you?

S: (confidently) I see her coming out of the entrance of the temple towards me ... as a goddess ... tall ... wearing long flowing robes ... one shoulder is bare ... her hair is piled up and fastened with a gold clasp ... she reaches out to me.

Dr. N: Look down at yourself. Are you dressed in the same garments?

S: We… all seem to be dressed the same … we shimmer with light… and we can change … Karla knows I like the way she looks.

Dr. N: Where are the others?

S: Karla has taken me inside my temple school. I see a large library. Small gatherings of people are speaking in quiet tones … at tables. It is … sedate … warm … a secure feeling which is so familiar to me.

Dr. N: Do all these people appear as adult men and women?

S: Yes, but there are more women in my group.

Dr. N: Why?

S: Because that's the valence they are most comfortable with right now.

Note: The word valence used by this subject to indicate gender preference is an odd choice, yet it does fit. Valences in chemistry are positive or negative properties which, when combined with other elements, give proportion. Souls in groups may be inclined toward male and female personages or mixed.

Dr. N: Okay, what do you do next?

S: Karla leads me to the nearest table and my friends immediately greet me. Oh, it's so good to be back.

Dr. N: Why are these particular people here with you in this temple?

S: Because we are all in the same study group. I can't tell you how happy I am to be with them once more. (subject becomes distracted with this scene and it takes me a minute to get her started again)

Dr. N: Tell me how many people are in this library with you?

S: (pauses while mentally counting) About twenty.

Dr. N: Are all twenty very close friends of yours?

S: We are all close—I've known them for ages. But five are my dearest friends.

Dr. N: Are every one of the twenty people at about the same level of learning?

S: Uh … almost. Some are a little further along than the rest.

Dr. N: Where would you place yourself in the group as far as knowledge?

S: Around the middle.

Dr. N: As to learning lessons, where are you in relation to your five closest friends?

S: Oh, we are about the same—we work together a lot.

Dr. N: What do you call them?

S: (chuckles) We have pet names for each other.

Dr. N: Why do you have nicknames?

S: Hmm … to define our essence. We see each other as representing earth things.

Dr. N: What is your pet name?

S: Thistle.

Dr. N: And this represents some personal attribute?

S: (pause) I … am known for sharp … reactions to new situations in my rotations (life cycles).

Dr. N: What is the entity you feel closest to called, and why?

S: (soft laughter) Spray. He goes flat out in his rotations … dispensing his energy so rapidly it splashes in all directions, just like the water he loves so much on Earth.

Dr. N: Your family group sounds very distinctive. Now would you explain to me what you and your friends actually do in this library setting?

S: I go to my table and we all look at the books.

Dr. N: Books? What sort of books?

S: The life books.

Dr. N: Describe them as best you can for me.

S: They are picture books—thick white edges—two or three inches thick—quite large …

Dr. N: Open one of the life books for me and explain what you and your friends at the table see.

S: (pause, while the subject's hands come together and move apart as though she were opening a book) There is no writing. Everything we see is in live pictures.

Dr. N: Action pictures—different than photographs?

S: Yes, they are multi-dimensional. They move … shift … from a center of … crystal … which changes with reflected light.

Dr. N: So, the pictures are not flat, the moving light waves have depth?

S: That's right, they are alive.

Dr. N: Tell me how you and your friends use the books?

S: Well, at first it's always out of focus when the book is opened. Then we think of what we want, the crystal turns from dark to light and … gets into alignment. Then we can see … in miniature … our past lives and the alternatives.

Dr. N: How is time treated in these books?

S: By frames … pages … time is condensed by the life books.

Dr. N: I don't want to dwell on your past right now, but take a look at the book and just tell me the first thing you see.

S: A lack of self-discipline in my last life because this is what is on my mind. I see myself dying young, in a lover's quarrel—my ending was useless.

Dr. N: Do you see future lives in the life book?

S: We can look at future possibilities … in small bites only … in the form of lessons … mostly these options come later with the help of others. These books are intended to emphasize our past acts.

Dr. N: Would you give me your impression of the intent behind this library atmosphere with your cluster group?

S: Oh, we all help one another go over our mistakes during this cycle. Our teacher is in and out and so we do a lot of studying together and discuss the value of our choices.

Dr. N: Are there other rooms where people study in this building?

S: No, this is for our group. There are different buildings where various groups study near us.

Note: The reader may refer to Figure 1 (page 89), circle B, as an example of what is meant here. In the graph, clusters 3-7 represent infrequent group interaction, although they are in close proximity to each other in the spirit world.

Dr. N: Are the groups of people who study in these buildings more or less advanced than those in your group?

S: Both.

Dr. N: Are you allowed to visit these other buildings where souls study?

S: (long pause) There is one which we go to regularly.

Dr. N: Which one?

S: A place for the newer ones. We help them when their teacher is gone. It's nice to be needed.

Dr. N: Help them how?

S: (laughs) With their homework.

Dr. N: But don't the teacher-guides have that responsibility?

S: Well, you see the teachers are ... so much further along (in development) ... this group appreciates our assistance because we can relate to them easily.

Dr. N: Ah, so you do a little student teaching with this group?

S: Yes, but we don't do it anywhere else.

Dr. N: Why not? Why couldn't more advanced groups come to your library to assist you once in a while?

S: They don't because we are further along than the newer ones. And, we don't infringe on them either. If I want to connect with someone, I do it outside the study center.

Dr. N: Can you wander about anywhere as long as you don't bother other souls in their study areas?

S: (responds with some evasiveness) I like to stay around the vicinity of my temple, but I can reach out to anyone.

Dr. N: I get the impression that your soul energy is restricted to this spiritual space even though you can mentally reach out further.

S: I don't feel restricted … we have plenty of room to go about … but I'm not attracted to everyone.

The statement about non-restriction, cited by Case 16, seems contrary to those boundaries of spiritual space seen by the last case. When I initially bring subjects into the spirit world, their visions are spontaneous, particularly as to spiritual order and their place in a community of soul life. While the average subject may talk about having private spaces, as far as living and working, none sees the spirit world as confining. Once their superconscious recall gets rolling, most people are able to tell me about having freedom of movement and going to open spaces where souls of many learning levels gather in a recreational atmosphere.

In these communal areas, floating souls socially engage in many activities. Some are quite playful, as when I hear of older souls "teasing" the younger ones about what lies ahead for them. One subject put it this way, "We play tricks on each other like a bunch of kids. During hide-and-seek, some of the younger ones get lost and then we help them find themselves." I am also told "guests" can appear in soul groups at times to entertain and tell stories, similar to the troubadours of the Middle Ages. Another subject mentioned that her group loved to see an odd-looking character known as "Humor" show up and make them all laugh with his antics.

Frequently, people in hypnosis find it hard to clearly explain the strange meanings behind their intermingling as souls. One diversion I hear rather often is of souls forming a circle to more fully unify and project their thought energy. Always, a connection with a higher power is reported here. Some people have told me, "Thought rhythms are so harmonized they bring forth a form of singing." Gracefully subtle dancing can also take place when souls whirl around each other in a mixture of energy, blending and separating in exotic patterns of light and color. Physical things such as shrines, boats, animals, trees, or ocean beaches can be conjured up at the center of these dances as well. These images have special meaning to soul groups as planetary symbols which reinforce positive memories from former lives together. This sort of material replication apparently does not represent sadness by spirits who long to be in a physical state again, but rather a joyful communion with historical events that helped shape their individual identities. For me, these mythic expressions by souls are ceremonial in nature and yet they go far beyond basic ritual.

Although certain places in the spirit world are described as having the same function by subjects in superconscious, their images in each of these regions can vary. Thus, a study area described as a Greek temple in this case is represented as a modern school building by another person. Other statements may seem more contradictory. For instance, many subjects mentally traveling from one location to another in the spirit world will tell me the space around them is like a sphere, as we saw in the last chapter, but then they will add that the spirit world is not enclosed because it is "limitless."

I think what we have to keep in mind is that people tend to structure their frame of reference during a trance state with what their conscious mind sees and has experienced on Earth. Quite a few people who come out of trance tell me there is so much about the spirit world they were unable to describe in earthly terms. Each person translates abstract spiritual conditions of their experience into symbols of interpretation which make sense to them. Sometimes a subject will even express disbelief at their own visions when I first take them into a spiritual place. This is because the critical area of their conscious mind has not stopped dropping message units. People in trance soon adapt to what their unconscious mind is recording.

When I began to gather information about souls in groups, I based my assessments of where these souls belonged on the level of their knowledge. Using only this criterion of identification, it was difficult for me to swiftly place a client. Case 16 came to me early in my studies of life in the spirit world. It was a significant one, because during the session I was to learn about the recognition of souls by color.

Before this case, I listened to my subjects describing the colors they were seeing in the spirit world without appreciating the importance of this information in relation to souls themselves. My clients reported about shades of soul energy mass, but I didn't piece these observations together. I was not asking the right questions.

I was familiar with Kirlian photography and the studies in parapsychology at U.C.L.A., where research has indicated each living person projects their own colored aura. In human form, apparently we have an ionized energy field flowing out and around our physical bodies connected by a network of vital power points called chakras. Since spiritual energy has been described to me as a moving, living force, the amount of electromagnetic energy required to hold a soul on our physical plane could be another factor in producing different earthly colors.

It has also been said that a human aura reflects thoughts and emotions combined with the physical health of an individual. I wondered if these personal meridians projected by humans had a direct connection to what I was being told about the light emitted by souls in the spirit world.

With Case 16, I realized that radiated soul light visualized by spirits is not all white. In the minds of my subjects, every soul generates a specific color aura. I credit this case with helping me decipher the meaning of these manifestations of energy.

Dr. N: All right, let's float outside your temple of study. What do you see around you, or off in the distance?

S: People—large gatherings of people.

Dr. N: How many would you say?

S: Hmm ... in the distance ... I can't count ... hundreds and hundreds ... there are so many.

Dr. N: And do you identify with all these souls—are you associated with them?

S: Not really—I can't even see all of them—it's sort of ... fuzzy out there ... but my gang is near me.

Dr. N: If I could call your gang of about twenty souls your primary cluster group, are you associated with the larger secondary body of souls around you now?

S: We ... are all ... associated—but not directly. I don't know those others ...

Dr. N: Do you see the physical features of all these other souls in the same way as you did your own group in the temple?

S: No, that isn't necessary. It is more ... natural out here in the open. I see them all as spirits.

Dr. N: Look out in the distance from where you are now. How do you see all these spirits? What are they like?

S: Different lights—buzzing around as fireflies.

Dr. N: Can you tell if the souls who work with each other, such as teachers and students, stick together all the time?

S: People in my gang do, but the teachers kind of stick to themselves when they are not assisting in our lessons.

Dr. N: Do you see any teacher-guides from where we are now?

S: (pause) Some … yes … there are much fewer of them than us, of course. I can see Karla with two of her friends.

Dr. N: And you know they are guides, even without seeing any physical features? You can look out there at all the bright white lights and just mentally tell they are guides?

S: Sure, we can do that. But they are not all white.

Dr. N: You mean souls are not all absolutely white?

S: That's partially true—the intensity aspect of our energy can make us less brilliant.

Dr. N: So Karla and her two friends display different shades of white?

S: No, they aren't white at all.

Dr. N: I don't follow you.

S: She and her two friends are teachers.

Dr. N: What is the difference? Are you saying these guides radiate energy which is not white?

S: That's right.

Dr. N: Well, what color are they?

S: Yellow, of course.

Dr. N: Oh … so all guides radiate yellow energy?

S: No, they don't.

Dr. N: What?

S: Karla's teacher is Valairs. He is blue. We see him sometimes here. Nice guy. Very smart.

Dr. N: Blue? How did we get to blue?

S: Valairs shows a light blue.

Dr. N: I'm confused. You didn't say anything about another teacher called Valairs being part of your group.

S: You didn't ask me. Anyway, he is not *in* my group. Neither is Karla. They have their own groups.

Dr. N: And these guides have auras which are yellow and blue?

S: Yes.

Dr. N: How many other energy colors do you see floating around here?

S: None.

Dr. N: Why not red and green energy lights?

S: Some are reddish, but no green lights.

Dr. N: Why not?

S: I don't know, but sometimes when I look around, this place is lit up like a Christmas tree.

Dr. N: I'm curious about Valairs. Does every spiritual group have two teachers assigned to their cluster?

S: Hmm … it varies. Karla trains under Valairs, so we have two. We see little of him. He works with other groups besides us.

Dr. N: So, Karla herself is student teaching as a less advanced guide?

S: (somewhat indignantly) She is advanced enough for me!

Dr. N: Okay, but will you help me straighten out these color schemes? Why is Karla's energy radiating yellow and Valairs blue?

S: That's easy. Valairs … precedes all of us in knowledge and he gives off a darker intensity of light.

Dr. N: Does the shade of blue, compared to yellow or plain white, make a difference between souls?

S: I'm trying to tell you. Blue is deeper than yellow and yellow is more intense than white, depending on how far along you are.

Dr. N: Oh, then the luminosity of Valairs radiates less brightly than Karla and she is less brilliant than your energy because you are further down in development?

S: (laughs) Much further down. They both have a heavier, more steady light than me.

Dr. N: And how does Karla's yellow color vary from your whiteness in terms of where you are going with your own advancement?

S: (with pride) I'm turning into a reddish-white. Eventually, I'll have light gold. Recently I've noticed Karla turning a little darker yellow. I expected it. She is so knowledgeable and good.

Dr. N: Really, and then will she eventually take her energy level to dark blue in intensity?

S: No, to a light blue at first. It's always gradual, as our energy becomes more dense.

Dr. N: So, these three basic lights of white, yellow, and blue represent the development stages of souls and are visibly obvious to all spirits?

S: That's right, and the changes are very slow.

Dr. N: Look around again. Do you see all the energy colors equally represented by souls in this area?

S: Oh no! Mostly white, some yellows, and few blues.

Dr. N: Thank you for clarifying this for me.

I routinely question everyone about their color hues while they are in trance. Aside from the general whiteness of the spirit world itself, my subjects report seeing a majority of other souls displaying shades of white. Apparently, a neutral white or gray is the starting point of development. Spirit auras then mix the primary colors of red, yellow, and blue from a base of white. A few people see greenish hues mixed with yellow or blue.

To equate what I have heard about soul energy with the physical laws which govern the color spectrum we see in the heavens is just supposition. However, I have found some similarities. The energy of radiated light from cooler stars in the sky is a red-orange, while the hotter stars increase from yellow to blue-white. Temperature acts on light waves that are also visible vibrations of the spectrum with different frequencies. The human eye registers these waves as a band of light to dark colors.

The energy colors of souls probably have little to do with such elements as hydrogen and helium, but perhaps there is an association with a high energy field of electromagnetism. I suspect all soul light is influenced by vibrational motion in tune with a harmonious spiritual oneness of wisdom. Some aspects of quantum physics suggest the universe is made up of vibrational waves which influence masses of physical objects by an interaction of different frequencies. Light, motion, sound, and time are all interrelated in physical space. I was hearing these same relationships applied to spiritual matter from my cases.

Eventually, I concluded both our spiritual and physical consciousness project and receive light energy. I believe individual vibrational wave patterns represent each soul's aura. As souls, the density, color, and form of light we radiate is proportional to the power of our knowledge and perception as represented by increasing concentrations of light matter as we develop. Individual patterns of energy not only display who we are, but indicate the degree of ability to heal others and regenerate ourselves.

People in hypnosis speak of colors to describe how souls appear, especially from a distance, when they are shapeless. From my cases, I have learned the more advanced souls project masses of faster moving energy particles which are reported to be blue in color, with the highest concentrations being purple. In the visible spectrum on Earth, blue-violet has the shortest wavelength, with energy peaking in the invisible ultraviolet. If color density is a reflection of wisdom, then the lower wavelengths of white through yellow emanating from souls must represent lower concentrations of vibrational energy.

Figure 3 (page 103) is a chart I have designed for the classification of souls by color coding, as reported by my subjects. The first column lists the soul's spiritual state, or grade-level of learning. The last column shows our guide status and denotes our ability and readiness to serve in that capacity for others, which will be explained further in the next chapter. Learning begins with our creation as a soul and then accelerates with the first physical life assignment. With each incarnation, we grow in understanding, although we may slip back in certain lives before regaining our footing and advancing again. Nevertheless, from what I can determine, once a spiritual level is attained by the soul, it stays there.

Classification Model for Soul Development Levels

Learning Stage	Kinetic Color Range	Guide Status
Level I: Beginner	White (bright and homogeneous)	None
Level II: Lower Intermediate	Off-White (reddish shades, ultimately turning into traces of yellow)	None
Level III: Intermediate	Yellow (solid, with no traces of white)	None
Level IV: Upper Intermediate	Dark Yellow (a deep gold, ultimately turning into traces of blue)	Junior
Level V: Advanced	Light Blue (with no traces of yellow, ultimately turning into traces of purple)	Senior
Level VI: Highly Advanced	Dark Bluish-Purple (surrounded by radiant light)	Master

Figure 3

In Figure 3, I show six levels of incarnating souls. Although I generally place my subjects into the broad categories of beginner, intermediate, and advanced souls, there are subtle differences in between, at Levels II and IV. For example, to determine whether a soul is starting to move out of the beginner stage at Level I into Level II, I must not only know how much white energy remains, but analyze the subject's responses to questions which demonstrate learning. A genealogy of past life successes, future expectations, group associations, and conversations between my subjects and their guides, all form a profile of growth.

Some of my subjects object to my characterizing the spirit world as a place governed by societal structure and organizational management symbolized by Figure 3. On the other hand, I continually listen to these same subjects describe a planned and ordered process of self-development influenced by peers and teachers. If the spirit world does resemble one great schoolhouse with a multitude of classrooms under the direction of teacher-souls who monitor our progress—then it has structure. Figure 3 represents a basic working placement model for my own use. I know it has imperfections. I hope follow-up research by regression therapists in future years may build upon my conceptualizations with their own replications to measure soul maturity.

This chapter may give the reader the impression that souls are as segregated by light level in the spirit world as people are by class in communities on Earth. Societal conditions on Earth cannot be compared with the spirit world. The differences in light frequency measuring knowledge in souls all comes from the same energy source. Souls are fully integrated by thought. If all levels of performance in the spirit world were on one grade level, souls would have a poor system of training. The old one-room schoolhouse concept of education on Earth limited students of different ages. In spiritual peer groups, souls work at their own developmental level with others like them. Mature teacher-guides prepare succeeding generations of souls to take their places.

And so there are practical reasons why conditions exist in the spirit world for a system designed to measure learning and development. The system fosters enlightenment and ultimately the perfection of souls. It is important to understand that while we may suffer the consequences of bad choices in our educational tasks, we are always protected, supported, and directed within the system by master souls. I see this as the spiritual management of souls.

The whole idea of a hierarchy of souls has been part of both Eastern and Western cultures for many centuries. Plato spoke of the transformation of souls from childhood to adulthood passing through many stages of moral reason. The Greeks felt humankind moves from amoral, immature, and violent beings over many lives to people who are finally socialized with pity, patience, forgiveness, honesty, and love. In the second century AD, the new Christian theology was greatly influence by Polotinus, whose Neoplatonist cosmology involved souls having a hierarchy of degrees of being. The highest being was a transcendent One, or God-creator, out of which the soul-self was born which would occupy humans. Eventually, these lower-souls would return to complete reunion with the universal over-soul.

My classification of soul development is intended to be neither socially nor intellectually elitist. Souls in a high state of advancement are often found in humble circumstances on Earth. By the same token, people in the upper strata of influence in human society are by no means in a blissful state of soul maturity. Often, just the reverse is true.

In terms of placement by soul development, I cannot overemphasize the importance of our spiritual groups. Chapter Nine, on beginner souls (Levels I and II), will more closely examine how a soul group functions. Before going further, however, I want to summarize what I have learned about the basic principles of soul group assignments.

- Regardless of the relative time of creation after their novice status is completed, all beginner souls are assigned to a new group of souls at their level of understanding.

- Once a new soul support group is formed, no new members are added in the future.

- There appears to be a systematic selection procedure for homogeneous groupings of souls. Similarities of ego, cognitive awareness, expression, and desire are all considerations.

- Irrespective of size, cluster groups do not directly intermix with each other's energy, but souls can communicate with one another across primary and secondary group boundaries.

- Primary clusters in Levels I and II may split into smaller subgroups for study, but are not separated from the integrated whole within a single cluster of souls.

- Rates of learning vary among peer group members. Certain souls will advance faster than others in a cluster group, although these students may not be equally competent and effective in all areas of their curricula. Around the intermediate level of learning, souls demonstrating special talents (healing, teaching, creating, etc.) are permitted to participate in specialty groups for more advanced work while still remaining with their cluster group.

- At the point where a soul's needs, motives and performance abilities are judged to be fully at Level III in all areas of self-development, they are then loosely formed into an "independent studies" work group. Usually, their old guides continue to monitor them through one master teacher. Thus, a new pod of entities graduating into full Level III could be brought together from many clusters within one or more secondary groups.

- When they approach Level IV, souls are given more independence outside group activities. Although group size diminishes as souls advance, the intimate contact between original peer group members is never lost.

- Spirit guides have a wide variety of teaching methods and instructional personifications depending upon group composition.

8

Our Guides

I HAVE never worked with a subject in trance who did not have a personal guide. Some guides are more in evidence than others during hypnosis sessions. It is my custom to ask subjects if they see or feel a discarnate presence in the room. If they do, this third party is usually a protective guide. Often, a client will sense the presence of a discarnate figure before visualizing a face or hearing a voice. People who meditate a great deal are naturally more familiar with these visions than someone who has never called upon his or her guide.

The recognition of these spiritual teachers brings people into the company of a warm, loving creative power. Through our guides, we become more acutely aware of the continuity of life and our identity as a soul. Guides are figures of grace in our existence because they are part of the fulfillment of our destiny.

Guides are complex entities, especially when they are master guides. The awareness level of the soul determines to some extent the degree of advancement of the guide assigned to them. In fact, the maturity of a particular guide also has a bearing on whether these teachers have only one student or many under their direction. Guides at the senior level of ability and above usually work with an entire group of souls in the spirit world and on Earth. These guides have other entities who assist them. From what I can see, every soul group usually has one or more rather new teachers in training. As a result, some people may have more than one guide helping them.

The personal names my clients attach to their guides range from ordinary, whimsical, or quaint-sounding words, to the bizarre. Frequently, these names can be traced back to a specific past life a teacher spent with a student. Some clients are unable to verbalize their guide's name because the sound cannot be duplicated, even when they see them clearly while under hypnosis. I tell these people it is much more important that they understand the purpose of why certain guides are assigned to them, rather than possessing their names. A subject may simply use a general designation for their guide such as: director, advisor, instructor, or just "my friend."

One has to be careful how the word *friend* is interpreted. Usually, when a person in trance talks about a spiritual friend, they are referring to a soulmate or peer group associate rather than a guide. Entities who are our friends exist on levels not much higher or lower than ourselves. These friends are able to offer mental encouragement from the spirit world while we are on Earth, and they can be with us as incarnated human companions while we walk the roads of life.

One of the most important aspects of my therapeutic work with clients is assisting them, on a conscious level, with appreciating the role their guides play in life. These teacher entities edify all of us with their skillful instruction techniques. Ideas we claim as our own may be generated by a concerned guide. Guides also comfort us during the trying periods in our lives, especially when we are children in need of solace. I remember a charming remark made by a subject after I asked when she began seeing her guide in this life. "Oh, when I was daydreaming," she said. "I remember my guide was with me on my first day of school when I was really scared. She sat on top of my desk to keep me company and then showed me the way to the bathroom when I was too afraid to ask the teacher."

The concept of personalized spiritual beings goes far back in antiquity to our earliest origins as thinking human beings. Anthropological studies at the sites of prehistoric people suggest their totemic symbols evoked individual protection. Later, some 5,000 years ago as city-states arose, official deities became identified with state religions. These gods were more remote and even generated fear. Thus, personal and family deities assumed great importance in the day-to-day life of people for protection. A personal soul deity served as a guardian angel to each person or family, and could be called upon for divine help during a crisis. This tradition has been carried down into our cultures of today.

We have two examples at opposite ends of the United States. Aumakua is a personal god to Hawaiians. The Polynesians believe one's ancestors can assume a personal god relationship (as humans, animals, or fish) to living family members. In visions and dreams, Aumakua can either assist or reprimand an individual. In northeastern America, the Iroquois believe a human's own inner spiritual power is called Orenda, which is connected to a higher personal Orenda spirit. This guardian is able to resist the powers of harm and evil directed at an individual. The concept of soul watchers who function as guides is part of the belief system of many Native American cultures. The Zuni tribes of the Southwest have oral traditions in their mythology of god-like beings with personal existences. They are called "the makers and holders of life paths" and are considered the caretakers of souls. There are other cultures around the world which also believe someone other than God is watching over them to personally intercede on their behalf.

I think human beings have always needed anthropomorphic figures below a supreme God to portray the spiritual forces around them. When people pray or meditate, they want to reach out to an entity with whom they are acquainted for inspiration. It is easier to ask for aid from a figure which can be clearly identified in the human mind. There is a lack of imagery with a supreme God which hinders a direct connection for many people. Regardless of our diverse religious preferences and degrees of faith, people also feel if there is a supreme God, this divinity is too busy to bother about their individual problems. People often express an unworthiness for a direct association with God. As a result, the world's major religions have used prophets who once lived on Earth to serve as our intermediaries with God.

Possibly because some of these prophets have been elevated to divine status themselves, they are not personal enough anymore. I say this without diminishing the vital spiritual influence all the great prophets have had on their followers. Millions of people derive benefit from the teachings of these powerful souls who incarnated on Earth as prophets in our historical past. And yet, people know in their hearts—as they have always known—that someone, some personal entity *i ndividual to them*—is there, waiting to be reached.

I have the theory that guides appear to people who are very religious as figures of their faith. There was a case on a national television show where the child of a devout Christian family suffered a near-death experience and said she saw Jesus. When asked to draw with crayons what she saw, the little girl drew a featureless blue man standing within a halo of light.

My subjects have shown me how much they depend upon and make use of their spiritual guides during life. I have come to believe we are their direct responsibility—not God's. These learned teachers remain with us over thousands of earth years to assist in our trials before, during, and after countless lives. I notice that, unlike people walking around in a conscious state, subjects in trance do not blame God for their misfortunes in life. More often than not, when we are in the soul state, it is our personal guide who takes the brunt of any dissatisfaction.

I am often asked if teacher-guides are matched to us or just picked at random. This is a difficult question to answer. Guides do appear to be assigned to us in the spirit world in an orderly fashion. I have come to believe their individual teaching styles and management techniques support and beautifully integrate with our permanent soul identity.

For instance, I have heard about younger guides, whose past lives included overcoming particularly difficult negative traits, being assigned to souls with the same behavior patterns. It seems these empathetic guides are graded on how well they do in their assignments to affect positive change.

All guides have compassion for their students, but teaching approaches vary. I find some guides constantly helping their students on Earth, while others demand their charges work out lessons with little overt encouragement. The maturity of the soul is, of course, a factor. Certainly graduate students get less help than freshmen. Aside from the developmental level, I look at the intensity of individual desire as another consideration in the frequency of appearance and form of assistance one receives from his or her guide during a life.

As to gender assignments, I find no consistent correlation of male and female subjects to masculine or feminine appearing guides. On the whole, people accept the gender portrayed by their guide as quite natural. It could be argued that this is because they have become used to them over eons of relative time as males or females rather than the assumption that one sex is more effective than another between specific students and teachers. Some guides appear as mixed genders, which lends support to souls being truly androgynous. One client told me, "My guide is sometimes Alexis or Alex, dropping in and out of both sexes, depending on my need for male or female advice."

From what I can determine, the procedure for teacher selection is carefully managed in the spirit world. Every human being has at least one senior, or a higher master guide, assigned to their soul since the soul was first created. Many of us inherit a newer, secondary guide later in our existence, such as Karla, in the previous chapter. For want of a better term, I have called these student teachers junior guides.

Aspiring junior guides can anticipate the beginning of their training near the end of Level III, as they progress into the upper intermediate stages of development. Actually, we begin our training as subordinate guides long before attaining Level IV. In the lower stages of development we help others in life as friends and between lives assist our peer group associates with counseling. Junior and senior teaching assignments appear to reflect the will of master guides, who form a kind of governing body, similar to a trusteeship, over the younger guides of the spirit world. We will see examples of how the process of guide development works in Chapters Ten and Eleven, which cover cases of more advanced souls.

Do all guides have the same teaching abilities, and does this affect the size of the group to which we are assigned in the spirit world? The following passage is from the case file of an experienced soul who discussed this question with me.

⊷ Case 17 ➜

Dr. N: I'm curious about teacher assignments in the spirit world in relation to their abilities to help undeveloped souls. When souls progress as guides, are they given quite a few souls to work with?

S: Only the more practiced ones.

Dr. N: I would imagine large groups of souls needing guides could become quite a responsibility for one advanced guide—even with an assistant.

S: They can handle it. Size doesn't matter.

Dr. N: Why not?

S: Once you attain competency and success as a teacher, the number of souls you are given doesn't matter. Some sections (clusters) have lots of souls and others don't.

Dr. N: So, if you are a senior in the blue light aura, class size has no relation to assignments, because you have the ability to handle large numbers of souls?

S: I didn't exactly say that. Much depends upon the types of souls in a section and the experience of the leaders. In the larger sections they have help too, you know.

Dr. N: Who does?

S: The guides you are calling seniors.

Dr. N: Well, who helps them?

S: The overseers. Now, they are the real pros.

Dr. N: I have heard them also called master teachers.

S: That's not a bad description for them.

Dr. N: What energy color do they project to you?

S: It's … purplish.

Note: As signified in Figure 3 in the last chapter, the lower ranges of a Level V radiate a sky-blue energy. With advancing maturity this aura grows more dense, first to a muted midnight blue and finally to deep purple, representing the total integration of a Level VI ascended master.

Dr. N: Since guides seem to have different approaches to teaching, what do they all have in common?

S: They wouldn't be teachers if they didn't have a love of training and a desire to help us join them.

Dr. N: Then define for me why souls are selected as guides. Take a typical guide and tell me what qualities that advanced soul possesses.

S: They must be compassionate without being too easy on you. They aren't judgmental. You don't have to do things their way. They don't restrain by imposing their values on you.

Dr. N: Okay, those are things guides don't do. If they don't over-direct souls, what are the important things they do, as you see it?

S: Uh … they build morale in their sections and instill confidence—we all know they have been through a lot themselves. We are accepted for who we are as individuals with the right to make our own mistakes.

Dr. N: I must say, I have found souls very loyal to their guides.

S: That's why—because they never give up on you.

Dr. N: What would you say is the most important attribute of any guide?

S: (without hesitation) The ability to motivate you and instill courage.

My next case provides an example of the actions of a still-incarnating guide. This guide is called Owa, and he represents the qualities of a devoted teacher reported by the last case. Evidently, his early assignments as a guide involved looking after the subject in Case 18 in a direct fashion, and his methods apparently have not changed. My client was stunned once she recognized her guide's latest incarnation.

Owa made his first appearance as a guide in my client's past about 50 BC. He was described as an old man living in a Judean village which had been overrun by Roman soldiers. Case 18 was then a young girl, orphaned by a Roman raid against local dissidents. In the opening scene of this past life, she spoke about working in a tavern as a virtual slave. As a serving girl, she was constantly beaten by the owner and occasionally raped by Roman customers. She died at age twenty-six of overwork, mistreatment, and despair. This subject made the following statement from her subconscious mind about an old man in her village: "I worked day and night and felt numb with pain and humiliation. He was the only person who was kind to me—who taught me to trust in myself—to have faith in something higher and finer than the cruel people around me."

Later in the superconscious state, this client detailed parts of other difficult lives where Owa appeared as a trusted friend, and once as a brother. In this state she saw these people were all the same entity and was able to name this soul as Owa, her guide. There were many lives when Owa did not appear, and sometimes his physical contact was only fleeting when he came to help her. Abruptly, I asked if Owa might possibly be in her life now? After a moment of hesitation, my subject began to shake uncontrollably. Tears came to her eyes and she cried out from the vision in her mind.

⇥ Case 18 ⇥

S: *Oh, Lord—I knew it!* I knew there was something different about him.

Dr. N: About who?

S: My son! *Owa is my son Brandon.*

Dr. N: Your son is actually Owa?

S: *Yes, yes!* (laughing and crying at the same time) *I knew it!* I felt it right from the day I delivered him—something wonderfully familiar and special to me—more than just a helpless baby ... oh ...

Dr. N: What did you know the day he was born?

S: I didn't really know—I felt it inside—something more than the excitement a mother feels at the time of her firstborn. I felt he came here—to help me—don't you see? Oh, it's so fantastic—it's true—it's *him!*

Dr. N: (I work on calming my client before continuing, because her excited wiggling around is about to carry her over the side of the office recliner) Why do you think Owa is here as your baby son Brandon?

S: (quieter now, but still crying softly) To get me through this bad time … with hard people who won't accept me. He must have known I was in for a long period of trouble and decided to come to me as my son. We didn't talk about doing this before I was born … what a wonderful surprise …

Note: At the time of this session, my client was struggling to gain recognition in a highly competitive business. She was also having marital difficulties at home, partly due to being the major wage earner. I have since learned she is divorced.

Dr. N: Did you sense something unusual about your baby after you took him home?

S: Yes, it started at the hospital and this feeling never left me. When I look into his eyes he … soothes me. Sometimes I come home so worn out—so tired and beat down—I am short-tempered with him when the baby-sitter leaves. But he is so patient with me. I don't even need to hold him. The way he looks at me is … so wise. I didn't fully understand what this meant until now. Now, I *know!* Oh, what a blessing. I wasn't sure if I should even have the baby—now I see it all.

Dr. N: What do you see?

S: (in a firm voice) As I try to advance in my profession, people are getting … harder … not accepting what I know and can do. My husband and I are having trouble. He puts me down for pushing too hard … wanting to achieve. Owa—Brandon—is here to keep me strong so I can overcome …

Dr. N: And do you think it is all right we discovered your guide is with you as Brandon in this life?

S: Yes, if Owa didn't want me to know that he decided to come into my life, I wouldn't have come to see you—it wouldn't have been on my mind.

This exceptional case represents the emotional intoxication a subject feels when an in-life contact is made with their guide. Notice the role Owa chose did not infringe upon the most typical role usually taken by a soulmate. He did not come through as her spouse, and never has, in any of her past lives. Certainly, soulmates take other roles besides spouses, but an incarnating guide does not normally take a role which might transgress between two soulmates working on their lives together. This client's soulmate happens to be an old flame from high school.

Based upon all the information I was able to gather, Owa seems to have moved into the level of a junior guide in the last two-thousand years. He may possibly graduate into the blue level of a senior guide before this client is qualified herself to rise from white to a yellow energy aura. Regardless of the number of centuries this takes, Owa will remain as her guide, even though he may never incarnate again with her in a life.

Do we ever catch up to our guides in development? Eventually, perhaps, but I can say I have not seen any evidence of this in my cases. Souls who develop relatively fast are gifted, but so are the guides who assist them.

It is not uncommon to find guides working in pairs with people on Earth, each with their own approaches to teaching. In these cases one is dominant, although the more experienced senior guide may actually be less evident in day-to-day activities of their charges. The reason for this spiritual arrangement in tandem is because one of the pair is either in training (such as a junior guide under a senior), or the association is so long-standing between the two guides (as with a senior to a master) that a permanent relationship has evolved. The senior guide may have acquired his or her own cluster of souls, which is still monitored by a master overseeing a number of soul groups.

Teams of guides do not interfere with each other in or out of the spirit world. I have a close friend whose guides illustrate how two teachers working together complement each other. Using this individual's case is appropriate, because I have observed the way this person's two guides interact in various life circumstances. My friend's junior guide appears in the form of a kindly, nurturing Native American medicine woman called Quan. Dressed simply in a deerskin sheath, her long hair pulled back, Quan's soft face is bathed in vivid light during her appearances. When she is called,

Quan provides a vehicle for insight and understanding events and the individuals associated with those events, which are troubling to my friend.

Quan's desire to lighten the load of the rather difficult life my friend has chosen is tempered by a challenging male figure called Giles. Giles is clearly a senior guide who may be close to being a master in the spirit world. In this capacity, he does not appear nearly as often as Quan. When Giles does come into my friend's higher consciousness, he does so abruptly. Here is a sample of how a senior guide operates differently from one of junior status.

⤛ Case 19 ⤜

Dr. N: When you are in deep reflection over a serious problem, how does Giles come to you?

S: (laughs) Not the same as Quan—I can tell you. Usually, he likes to ... hide a little ... at first ... behind a shadow of ... blue vapor. I hear him chuckling before I see him.

Dr. N: You mean he appears first as a blue energy form?

S: Yes ... to hide himself a bit—he likes to be secretive, but it doesn't last long.

Dr. N: Why?

S: I don't know—to make sure I really want him, I guess.

Dr. N: Well, when he shows himself, what does Giles look like to you?

S: An Irish Leprechaun.

Dr. N: Oh, then he is a small man?

S: (laughs again) An elf figure—tangled hair all over his wrinkled face—he looks a mess and moves constantly in all directions.

Dr. N: Why does he do that?

S: Giles is a slippery character—impatient, too—he frowns a lot while he paces back and forth in front of me with his arms clasped in back of him.

Dr. N: And how would you interpret this behavior?

S: Giles is not dignified like some (guides) ... but he is very clever ... crafty.

Dr. N: Could you be more specific as to how this conduct relates to you?

S: (strained) Giles has made me look upon my lives as a chess game with the Earth as the board. Certain moves bring certain results and there are no easy solutions. I plan, and then things go wrong during the game in my life. I sometimes think he lays traps for me to work through on the board.

Dr. N: Do you prosper with this technique of your advanced guide? Has Giles been a help to your problem-solving during the game of life?

S: (pause) … More afterward … here (in the spirit world) … but, he makes me work so damn hard on Earth.

Dr. N: Could you get rid of him and just work with Quan?

S: (smiles ruefully) It doesn't work that way here. Besides, he is brilliant.

Dr. N: So, we don't get to choose our guides?

S: No way. They choose you.

Dr. N: Do you have any idea why you have two guides who approach your problems so differently in the way they help you?

S: No, I don't, but I consider myself very fortunate. Quan … is gentle … and steady with her support.

Note: The embodiments of Native Americans who once lived in North America make powerful spiritual guides for those of us who have followed them to live in this land. The large number of Americans who report having such guides lends support to my belief that souls are attracted to geographical settings they have known during earlier incarnations.

Dr. N: What do you like most about Giles' teaching methods?

S: (pensively) Oh, the way he—well, trifles with me—almost mocking me to do better during the game and stop feeling sorry for myself. When things get especially rough he prods me and keeps me going … insisting I use all my abilities. There is nothing soft about Giles.

Dr. N: And you feel this coaching on Earth, even when you and I are not working together?

S: Yes, when I meditate and go inside myself ... or during my dreams.

Dr. N: And Giles comes when you want him?

S: (after some hesitation) No ... although it seems as though I have been with him forever. Quan does come to me more. I can't just grab hold of Giles in any situation I want, unless what I have going on is really serious. He is elusive.

Dr. N: Sum up your feelings about Quan and Giles for me.

S: I love Quan as a mother, but I wouldn't be where I am without Giles' discipline. They are both skillful because they allow me to benefit from my mistakes.

These two guides are a cooperating team of instructors, which is standard procedure for those people who have two guides. In this case, Giles enjoys teaching karmic lessons by the Socratic method. Providing no clues in advance, he makes sure problem-solving on major issues is never easy for my friend. Quan, on the other hand, provides comfort and gentle encouragement.

When my friend comes to me for a hypnosis session, I am aware that Quan remains in the background when Giles is on-board and active. Giles is a caring guide, as all guides are, but without a trace of indulgence. Adversity is allowed to build to the absolute limits of my friend's ability to cope before solutions suddenly begin to unfold. To be honest, I see Giles as a wicked taskmaster. This view is not really shared by my friend, who is grateful for the challenges offered by this complex teacher.

What is the average spiritual guide like? In my experience, no two guides are the same. These dedicated higher entities give me the impression of having attitudinal swings toward me from one session to the next, and even within the same session with a client. They can be cooperative or obstructive, tolerant or disobliging, evasive or revealing, or just flat out unconcerned with anything I do with a subject. I have great respect for guides because these powerful figures play such an important part in our destiny, but I must admit they can frustrate my inquiries. I find them enigmatic because they are unpredictable in their relations with me as a facilitator.

Early in this century, it was common for mediums working with people in hypnosis to call any discarnate entity in the room a "control," because they acted as the director of communications on the spiritual side for the subject. It was recognized that a spiritual control (whether a guide or not) had energy patterns which were in emotional, intellectual, and spiritual attunement with the subject. The importance of a harmonious energy pattern between facilitator and these entities was also known.

If a control is blocking my investigations with a client, I search for the reason why this is happening. With some blocking guides I must fight for every scrap of information, while others give me a great deal of latitude in a session. I never forget that guides have every right to block my approach to problems with souls under their care. After all, I have their people as my subjects for only a short while. Frankly, I would much rather have no contact with a client's guide than work with one who might assist me at one point and then block the rhythm of memory in the next portion of a session.

I believe a guide's motivation for blocking information goes far beyond resisting the immediate psychological direction a therapy session is taking. I am constantly searching for new data on the spirit world. A guide who lends support to a free flow of past life memories from one of my subjects may balk at my far-reaching questions about life on other planets, the structure of the spirit world, or creation itself. This is why I am only able to collect these spiritual secrets in fragments from a large body of client information reflecting the discretion of many guides. I also feel that I am receiving assistance from my own spiritual guide during communications with subjects and their guides.

Occasionally, a subject will express dissatisfaction with his or her particular guide. This is usually temporary. At any time, people are capable of believing their guides are too difficult and not working in their best interests, or just not paying enough attention to them. A subject once told me that he had tried for a long time to be assigned another guide. He said, "My guide is stonewalling me, she doesn't give enough of herself." The man told me his desire for a change in guides was not honored. I observed that he spent considerable time alone, without much group interaction after his last two lives, because he refused to deal with his issues. He projected anger toward his guide for not rescuing him from bad situations.

Our teachers really don't get perturbed with us to the point of alienation, but I notice they have a way of making themselves scarce when disgruntled students avoid real problem-solving. Guides only want the best for us and sometimes this means they must watch us endure much pain to reach certain objectives. Guides cannot assist in our progress until we are ready to make the necessary changes in order to take full advantage of life's opportunities.

Do we have reason to be fearful of our guides? In Chapter Five, with Case 13, we saw an obviously younger soul who expressed some trepidation right after death about meeting the guide Clodees for debriefing. Typically, this concern does not last. We may feel chagrined over having to explain to our guides why goals were not attained, but they understand. They want us to interpret our past lives so we will have the benefit of assisting in the analysis of mistakes.

My clients express all sorts of sentiments about their guides, but fear is not among them. On the contrary, people are more worried about being abandoned by spiritual advisors during difficult periods in their lives. Our relationship with guides is one of students and teachers rather than defendants and judges. Our personal guides help us cope with the separateness and isolation which every soul inherits at physical birth, regardless of the degree of love extended by our family. Guides give us an affirmation of Self in a crowded world.

People want to know if their guides always come whenever they call for help. Guides are not consistent in the manner in which they choose to assist us, because they carefully evaluate how badly they are needed. I am also asked if hypnosis is the best way to get in contact with one's guide. Naturally, I lean toward hypnosis, because I know how potent and effective this medium can be to obtain detailed spiritual information. However, hypnosis by a trained facilitator is not convenient on a daily basis, where meditation, prayer, and perhaps channeling with another person would be. Self-hypnosis, as a form of deep meditation, is an excellent alternative and may be preferred by those who have a fear of being hypnotized by others, or don't want the interference of a second party in their spiritual life.

Regardless of the method used, we all have the capacity to send out far-reaching thought waves from our higher consciousness. Every person's thoughts represent a mental fingerprint to guides marking who and where we are. During our lives, especially in periods of great stress, most people feel the presence of someone watching out for them. We may not be able to describe this power, but it is there nonetheless.

Reaching our soul is the first step on the ladder of finding our higher power. All lines of mental communication we use to reach a God-head are monitored by our guides on this step. They, too, have their guides further up the ladder. The entire ladder serves as one unbroken conduit to the source of all intelligent energy, with each rung being part of the whole. It is essential for people to have faith that a prayer for help will be answered by their *own* higher power. This is why guides are vitally important to our spiritual and temporal lives. If we are relaxed and in a state of concentrated focus, an inner voice speaks to us. And, even if we didn't initiate the message, we should trust what we hear.

National surveys by psychologists indicate one person in ten admits to hearing voices which are frequently positive and instructional in nature. It is a relief for many people to learn their inner voices are not the hallucinations associated with the mentally ill. Rather than something to be worried about, an inner voice is like having your own resident counselor on call. More often than not, these voices are those of our guides.

Guides assigned to different souls do work together relaying urgent mental messages for each other. People unable to help themselves in critical situations may find counselors, friends, and even strangers coming to their aid at just the right moment.

The inner strength which comes to us in our daily lives does not arrive as much by a visual picture of actually seeing our guides, as from the feelings and emotions which convince us we are not alone. People who listen and encourage their inner voice through quiet contemplation say they feel a personal connection with an energy beyond themselves which offers support and reassurance. If you prefer to call this internal guidance system inspiration or intuition, that is fine, because the system which aids us is an aspect of ourselves as well as higher powers.

During troublesome times in our lives, we have the tendency to ask for guidance to immediately set things right. When they are in trance, my clients see that their guides don't help them solve all their problems at once, rather they illuminate pathways by the use of clues. This is one reason why I am cautious about client-blocking during hypnosis. Insight is best revealed with a controlled pace relative to each person. A concerned teacher may not want all aspects of a problem uncovered at a given point in time for his or her student. We vary in our ability to handle revelations.

When asking for help from your higher spiritual power, I think it is best not to demand immediate change. Our success in life is predicated on planning, but we do have alternative paths to choose from to reach certain goals. When seeking guidance, I suggest requesting help with just the next step in your life. When you do this, be prepared for unexpected possibilities. Have the faith and humility to open yourself up to a variety of paths toward solutions.

After death we do not experience sadness as souls with the same emotional definition as grief felt in physical form. Yet, as we have already seen, souls are not detached beings without feelings. I have learned those powers who watch over us also feel what I call a spiritual sorrow when they see us making poor choices in life and going through pain. Certainly, our soulmates and peers suffer distress when we are tormented, but so do our guides. Guides may not show sorrow in orientation conferences and during soul group discussions between lives, but they keenly feel their responsibilities toward us as teachers.

In Chapter Eleven, we will get the perspective of a guide at Level V. I have never found a person who is a living grade VI, or master guide, as a subject. I suspect we don't have a whole lot of these advanced souls on Earth at any one time. Most Level VI's are much too involved with planning and directing from the spirit world to incarnate any longer. From the reports of the Level V's I have had, it would seem the Level VI has no new lessons to learn, but I have a hunch a still-incarnating soul at Level V may not know all the esoteric tasks involved with master level entities.

Once in a while during a session with a more advanced soul, I hear references to an even higher level of soul than Level VI. These entities, to whom even the masters report, are in the darkest purple range of energy. These superior beings must be getting close to the creator. I am told these shadowy figures are elusive, but highly venerated beings in the spirit world.

The average client doesn't know if spiritual guides should be placed in a less than divine category, or considered lesser gods because of their advancement. There is nothing wrong with any spiritual concept, as long as it provides comfort, is uplifting, and makes sense to each individual. Although some of my clients have the tendency to consider guides god-like—they are not God. In my opinion, guides are no more or less divine than we are, which is why they are seen as personal beings. In all my cases God is never seen. People in hypnosis say they feel the presence of a supreme power directing the spirit world, but they are uncomfortable using the word "God" to describe a creator. Perhaps the philosopher Spinoza said it best with these words: "God is not He who is, but That which is."

Every soul has a spiritual higher power linked to its existence. All souls are part of the same divine essence generated from one oversoul. This intelligent energy is universal in scope and so *we all share in divine status*. If our soul reflects a small portion of the oversoul we call God, then our guides provide the mirror by which we are able to see ourselves connected to this creator.

9

The Beginner Soul

THERE are two types of beginner souls: souls who are truly young in terms of exposure to an existence out of the spirit world, and souls who have been reincarnating on Earth for a long period of relative time, but still remain immature. I find beginner souls of both types in Levels I and II.

I believe almost three-quarters of all souls who inhabit human bodies on Earth today are still in the early stages of development. I know this is a grossly discouraging statement because it means most of our human population is operating at the lower end of their training. On the other hand, when I consider a world population beset by so much negative cross-cultural misunderstanding and violence, I am not inclined to change my opinion about the high percentage of lower level souls on Earth. However, I do think each century brings improvement of awareness in all humans.

Over a number of years, I have maintained a statistical count of client soul levels in my case files. Undoubtedly, the figures are weighted to some extent at the lower levels because these subjects were not selected at random. My cases could be over-represented by souls at the lower levels of development because they are the very people who require assistance in life and might come to me seeking information.

For those who are curious, the percentages by soul level of all my cases are as follows: Level I, 42%; Level II, 31%; Level III, 17%; Level IV, 9%; and Level V, 1%. Projecting these figures into a world population of five billion souls would be unreliable, using my small sample. Nevertheless, I see the possibility we may have only a few hundred thousand people on Earth at Level V.

My subjects state that souls end their incarnations on Earth when they reach full maturity. What is significant about the high percentage of souls in the early stages of development is our rapidly multiplying population and the urgency babies have for available souls. We are increasing by 260,000 children per day. This human necessity for souls means they must normally be drawn from a spiritual pool of less advanced entities who require more incarnations to progress and are, therefore, more available to return to another life.

I am sensitive to the feelings of clients whom I know to be in the early stages of development. I cannot count the number of times a new client has come into my office and said, "I know I am an old soul, but I seem to have problems coping with life." We all want to be advanced souls because most people hate to be considered a beginner in anything. Every case is unique. There are many variables within each soul's character, individual development rate, and the qualities of the guides assigned to them. I see my task as offering interpretations of what subjects report to me about the progression of their souls.

I have had many cases where a client has been incarnating for up to 30,000 years on Earth and is still in the lower levels of I and II. The reverse is also true with a few people, although rapid acceleration in spiritual development is uncommon. As with any educational model, students find certain lessons more difficult than others. One of my clients has not been able to conquer envy for 850 years in numerous lives, but she did not have too much trouble overcoming bigotry by the end of this same period. Another has spent nearly 1700 years off-and-on seeking some sort of authoritative power over others. However, he has gained compassion.

The next case represents an absolute beginner soul. This novice shows no evidence of having a spiritual group assignment as yet, because she has lived too few past lives. In her first life she was killed in 1260 AD in Northern Syria by a Mongol invasion. Her name was Shabez, and her settlement was sacked, resulting in a terrible massacre of the inhabitants when she was five years old.

↤ Case 20 ↦

Dr. N: Shabez, now that you have died and returned to the spirit world, tell me what you feel?

S: (shouts) *Cheated!* That life was so *cruel!* I couldn't stay. I was only a little girl unable to help anybody. What a mistake!

Dr. N: Who made this mistake?

S: (in a conspiratorial tone) My leader. I trusted his judgment, but he was wrong to send me into that cruel life to be killed before my life got started.

Dr. N: But you did agree to come into the body of Shabez?

S: (upset) I didn't know Earth would be such an awful place full of terror—I wasn't given all the facts—the whole stupid life was a mistake and my leader is responsible.

Dr. N: Didn't you learn anything from this life?

S: (pause) I started to learn to love … yes, that was wonderful … my brother … parents … but it was so short …

Dr. N: Did anything good come out of this life?

S: My brother Ahmed … to be with him …

Dr. N: Is Ahmed in your present life?

S: (suddenly my subject rises out of her chair) *I can't believe it!* Ahmed is my husband Bill—the same person—how can …?

Dr. N: (after calming subject, I explain the process of soul transference to a new body and then continue) Do you see Ahmed on your return to the spirit world after dying as Shabez?

S: Yes, our leader brings us together here … where we stay.

Dr. N: Does Ahmed emit the same energy color as yourself or are there differences?

S: (pause) We … are all white.

Dr. N: Describe what you do here.

S: While our leader comes and goes, Ahmed and I … just work together.

Dr. N: Doing what?

S: We search out what we think about ourselves—our experience on Earth. I'm still sore about us being killed so soon … but there was happiness … walking in the sun … breathing the air of Earth … love.

Dr. N: Go back further to the time before you and Ahmed had your life together, perhaps when you were alone. What was it like being created?

S: (disturbed) I don't know … I was just here … with thought …

Dr. N: Do you remember during your own creation when you first began to think as an intelligent being?

S: I realized … I existed … but I didn't know myself as myself until I was moved into this quiet place alone with Ahmed.

Dr. N: Are you saying your individual identity came more into focus when you began interacting with another soul entity besides your guide?

S: Yes, with Ahmed.

Dr. N: Keep to the time before Ahmed. What was it like for you then?

S: Warm … nurturing … my mind opening … she was with me then.

Dr. N: She? I thought your leader displayed a male gender to you?

S: I don't mean him … someone was around me with the presence of a … mother and father … mostly mother …

Dr. N: What presence?

S: I don't know … a soft light … changing features … I can't grasp it … loving messages … encouragement …

Dr. N: This was at the time of your creation as a soul?

S: Yes … it's all hazy … there were others … helpers … when I was born.

Dr. N: What else can you tell me about the place of your creation?

S: (long pause) Others … love me … in a nursery … then we left … and I was with Ahmed and our leader.

Dr. N: Who actually created you and Ahmed?

S: The One.

I have learned there seems to be a kind of spirit world maternity ward for newborn souls. One client told me, "This place is where infantile light is arranged in a honeycomb fashion as unhatched eggs, ready to be used." In Chapter Four, on displaced souls, we saw how damaged souls can be "remodeled." My conjecture is these creation centers described by Shabez have the same function. In the next chapter, Case 22 will explain more about spiritual areas of ego creation where raw, undefined energy can be manipulated into a genesis of Self.

Case 20 has some obvious traits of the immature soul. The subject is a sixty-seven-year-old woman who has had a lifetime of getting into disastrous ruts. She does not demonstrate a generosity of spirit toward others, nor does she take much personal responsibility for her actions. This client came to me searching for answers as to why life had "cheated me out of happiness." In our session we learned Ahmed was her first husband, Bill. She left him long ago for another man, whom she also divorced, because of her inability to bond with people. She does not feel close to any of her children.

The beginner soul may live a number of lives in a state of confusion and ineffectiveness, influenced by an Earth curriculum which is different from the coherence and supportive harmony of the spirit world. Less developed souls are inclined to surrender their will to the controlling aspects of human society, with a socio-economic structure which causes a large proportion of people to be subordinate to others. The inexperienced soul tends to be stifled by a lack of independent thinking. They also lean towards being self-centered and don't easily accept others for who they are.

It is not my intention to paint a totally bleak portrait of souls who comprise so much of our world population—if my estimates of the high numbers of this category of soul are accurate. Lower level souls are also able to lead lives which have many positive elements. Otherwise, no one would advance. No stigma should be attached to these souls, since every soul was once a beginner.

If we become angry, resentful, and confused by our life situations, this does not necessarily mean we possess an underdeveloped spirit. Soul development is a complex matter where we all progress by degrees in a variety of areas in an uneven manner. The important thing is to recognize our faults, avoid self-denial, and have the courage and self-sufficiency to make constant adjustments in our lives.

One of the clear indications that souls are coming out of novice status is when they leave their spiritual existence of relative isolation. They are removed from small family cocoons with other novices and placed in a larger group of beginner souls. At this stage they are less dependent upon close supervision and special nurturing from their guides.

For the younger souls, the first realization that they are part of a substantial group of spirits like themselves is a source of delight. Generally, I find this important spiritual event has occurred by the end of a fifth life on Earth, regardless of the relative length of time the novice soul was in semi-isolation. Some of the entities of these new spiritual groups are the souls of relatives and friends with whom the young soul was associated in their few past lives on Earth. What is especially significant about the formation of a new cluster group is that other peer group members are also newer souls who find themselves together for the first time.

In Chapter Seven on placement, we saw how a soul group appeared when Case 16 rejoined them, and the manner in which life experiences were studied through pictorial scenes, as reported by this subject. Case 21 will offer a more detailed account of spiritual group dynamics and how members impact on each other. The capacity of souls to learn certain lessons may be stronger or weaker between one another depending upon inclination, motivation, and prior incarnation experience. Cluster groups are carefully designed to give peer support through a sensitivity of identity traits between all members. This cohesiveness is far beyond what we know on Earth.

Although the next case is presented from the perspective of one group member, his superconscious mind provides an objectivity into the process of what goes on in groups. My subject will describe a grandiose, male-oriented spiritual group. The raucous entities of this group are linked by exhibitionism which could be labeled narcissistic. The common approaches these souls use in finding personal value is one indication why they are working together.

The extravagant behavior modes of these souls is offset, to some extent, by their spiritual prescience. Since the complete truth is known by all group members about each other in a telepathic world, humor is indispensible. Some readers may find it hard to accept that souls do joke with each other about their failings, but humor is the basis upon which self-deception and hypocrisy are exposed.

Ego defenses are so well understood by everyone in spiritual groups that evidence of a mastery of oneself among peers is a strong incentive for change. Spiritual "therapy" occurs because of honest peer feedback, mutual trust, and the desire to advance with others over eons of time. Souls can hurt, and they need caring entities around them. The curative power of spiritual group interaction is quite remarkable.

Soul members network by the use of criticism and acclaim as each strives toward common goals. Some of the best help I am able to give my clients comes from information I receive about their soul group. Spiritual groups are a primary means of soul instruction. Learning appears to come as much from one's peers as from the skill of guides who monitor these groups.

In the case which follows, my client has finished reliving his last past life as a Dutch artist living in Amsterdam. He died of pneumonia at a young age in 1841, about the time he was gaining recognition for his painting. We have just rejoined his spiritual group when my subject bursts out laughing.

⤝ Case 21 ⤞

Dr. N: Why are you laughing?

S: I'm back with my friends and they are giving me a hard time.

Dr. N: Why?

S: Because I'm wearing my fancy buckled shoes and the bright green velvet jacket—with yellow piping down the sides—I'm flashing them my big floppy painter's hat.

Dr. N: They are kidding you about projecting yourself wearing these clothes?

S: You know it! I was so vain about clothes and I cut a really fine figure as an artist in Amsterdam cafe society. I enjoyed this role and played it well. I don't want it to end.

Dr. N: What happens next?

S: My old friends are around me and we are talking about the foolishness of life. We rib each other about how dramatic it all is down there on Earth and how seriously we all take our lives.

Dr. N: You and your friends don't think it is important to take life on Earth seriously?

S: Look, Earth is one big stage play—we all know that.

Dr. N: And your group is united in this feeling?

S: Sure, we see ourselves as actors in a gigantic stage production.

Dr. N: How many entities are in your particular cluster group in the spirit world?

S: (pause) Well, we work with … some others … but there are five of us who are close.

Dr. N: By what name do they call you?

S: L … Lemm—no that's not right—it's Allum … that's me.

Dr. N: All right, Allum, tell me about your close friends.

S: (laughs) Norcross … he is the funniest … at least he is the most boisterous.

Dr. N: Is Norcross the leader of your group?

S: No, he is just the loudest. We are all equal here, but we have our differences. Norcross is blunt and opinionated.

Dr. N: Really, then how would you characterize his Earth behavior?

S: Oh, as being rather unscrupulous—but not dangerous.

Dr. N: Who is the quietest and most unassuming member of your group?

S: (quizzical) How did you guess—it's Vilo.

Dr. N: Does this attribute make Vilo the least effective contributing member of your group?

S: Where did you get that idea? Vilo comes up with some interesting thoughts about the rest of us.

Dr. N: Give me an example.

S: In my life in Holland—the old Dutch couple who adopted me after my parents died—they had a beautiful garden. Vilo reminds me of my debt to them—that the garden triggered my painting—to see life as an artist … and what I didn't do with my talent.

Dr. N: Does Vilo convey any other thoughts to you about this?

S: (sadly) That I should have done less drinking and strutting around and painted more. That my art was … reaching the point of touching people … (subject pulls his shoulders back) but I wasn't going to stay cooped up painting all the time!

Dr. N: Do you have respect for Vilo's opinions?

S: (with a deep sigh) Yes, we know he is our conscience.

Dr. N: So, what do you say to him?

S: I say, "Innkeeper, mind your own business—you were having fun, too."

Dr. N: Vilo was an innkeeper?

S: Yes, in Holland. Engaged in a business for profit, I might add.

Dr. N: Do you feel this was wrong of Vilo?

S: (contrite) No ... not really ... we all know he took losses to help those poor people on the road who needed food and shelter. His life was beneficial to others.

Dr. N: I would guess telepathic communication makes it hard to sustain your arguments when the complete truth is known by everyone?

S: Yes, we all know Vilo is progressing—*damn!*

Dr. N: Does it bother you that Vilo may be advancing faster than the rest of you?

S: Yes ... we have had such fun ... (subject then recalls an earlier life with Vilo where they traveled together as brothers in India)

Dr. N: What will happen to Vilo?

S: He is going to leave us soon—we all know that—to have associations with the others who have also gone.

Dr. N: How many souls have left your original group, Allum?

S: (A long pause, and then ruefully) Oh ... a couple have moved on ... we will eventually catch up to them ... but not for a while. They haven't disappeared—we just don't see their energy as much.

Dr. N: Name the others of your immediate group for me besides Vilo and Norcross.

S: (brightening) Dubri and Trinian—now those two know how to have a good time!

Dr. N: What is the most obvious identifying characteristic of your group?

S: (with relish) *Adventure! Excitement!* We have some real pioneer types around here. (subject rushes on happily) Dubri just came off a wild life as a sea captain. Norcross was a free-wheeling trading merchant. We live life to its fullest because we are talented at taking what life has to offer.

Dr. N: I'm hearing a lot of self-gratification here, Allum.

S: (defensively) And what's wrong with that? Our group is not made up of shrinking violets, you know!

Dr. N: What's the story on Trinian's last life?

S: (reacts boisterously) He was a Bishop! Can you believe it? What hypocrisy.

Dr. N: In what way?

S: What self-deception! Norcross, Dubri, and I tell Trinian his choice to be a churchman had nothing to do with goodness, charity, or spirituality.

Dr. N: And what does Trinian's soul mentally project to you in self-defense?

S: He tells us he gave solace to many people.

Dr. N: What do you, Norcross and Dubri, tell him in response?

S: That he is going soft. Norcross tells him he wanted money or otherwise he would have been a simple priest. Ha—that's telling him—and I'm saying the same thing. You can guess what Dubri thinks about all this!

Dr. N: No, tell me.

S: Humph—that Trinian picked a large city with a rich cathedral—spilling a ton of money into Trinian's fat pockets.

Dr. N: And what do you tell Trinian yourself?

S: Oh, I'm attracted to the fancy robes he wore—bright red—the finest of cloth—his Bishop's ring which he loved—and all the gold and silver around. I also mention his desire to bask in adulation from his flock. Trinian can hide nothing from us—he wanted an easy, cushy life where he was well-fed.

Dr. N: Does he try to explain his motivations for choosing this life?

S: Yes, but Norcross reproaches him. He confronts Trinian on seducing a young girl in the vestry. (jovially) Yes, it actually happened! ... So much for providing solace to parishioners. We know Trinian for who he really is—an outright rogue!

Dr. N: Does Trinian offer any excuses to the group for his conduct?

S: (subject becomes quieter) Oh, the usual. He got carried away with the girl's need for him—she had no family—he was lonely in his choice of a celibate church life. He says he was trying to get away from the customary lives we all choose by going into the church—that he fell in love with the girl.

Dr. N: And how do you, Norcross and Dubri, feel about Trinian now?

S: (severely) We think he is trying to follow Vilo (as an advancing soul), but he failed. His pious intentions just didn't work for him.

Dr. N: Allum, you sound rather cynical about Trinian's attempts to improve himself and make changes. Tell me honestly, how do you feel about Trinian?

S: Oh, we are just teasing him ... after all...

Dr. N: Your amusement sounds as if you are scornful over what may have been Trinian's good intentions.

S: (sadly) You're right ... and we all know that ... but, you see ... Norcross, Dubri, and I ... well, we don't want to lose him from the group, too ...

Dr. N: What does Vilo say about Trinian?

S: He defends Trinian's original good intentions and tells him that he fell into a trap of self-gratification during this life in the church. Trinian wants too much admiration and attention.

Dr. N: Forgive me for passing judgment on your group, Allum, but it seems to me this is something you all want, except perhaps Vilo?

S: Hey, Vilo can be pretty smug. Let me tell you, his problem is conceit and Dubri tells him that in no uncertain terms.

Dr. N: And does Vilo deny it?

S: No, he doesn't ... he says at least he is working on it.

Dr. N: Who among you is the most sensitive to criticism?

S: (pause) Oh, I guess it would be Norcross, but it's hard for all of us to accept our faults.

Dr. N: Level with me, Allum. Does it bother the members of your soul group when things can't be hidden from the others—when all your shortcomings in a past life are revealed?

S: (pause) We are sensitive about it—but not morbid. There is great understanding here among us. I wanted to give artistic pleasure to people and grow through the meaning of art. So, what did I do? I ran around the Amsterdam canals a lot at night and got caught up in the fun and games. My original purpose was pushed aside.

Dr. N: If you admit all this to the group, what kind of feedback do you get? For example, how do you and Norcross regard each other?

S: Norcross often points out I hate to take responsibility for myself and others. With Norcross it's wealth … he loves power … but we are both selfish … except that I am more vain. Neither of us gets many gold stars.

Dr. N: How does Dubri fit into your group with his faults?

S: He enjoys controlling others by leadership. He is a natural leader, more than the rest of us. He was a sea captain—a pirate—one tough individual. You wouldn't want to cross him.

Dr. N: Was he cruel?

S: No, just hard. He was respected as a captain. Dubri was merciless against his opponents in sea battles, but he took care of his own men.

Dr. N: You have told me that Vilo assisted people who were in need on the road, but you haven't said much about the positive side of your lives. Is anyone in your group given any gold stars for un-selfish acts?

S: (intently) There is something else about Dubri …

Dr. N: What is that?

S: He did one outstanding thing. Once, during heavy seas, a sailor fell off the mast into the ocean and was drowning. Dubri tied a line around his waist and dove off the deck. He risked his life and saved a shipmate.

Dr. N: When this incident is discussed in your group, how do you all respond to Dubri?

S: We praise him for what he did with admiration in our minds. We came to the same conclusion that none of us could match this single act of courage in our last lives.

Dr. N: I see. Yet, Vilo's life at the inn, feeding and housing people who could not pay him, may represent acts of unselfishness for a longer term and therefore is more praiseworthy?

S: Granted, and we give him that. (laughs) He gets more gold stars than Dubri.

Dr. N: Do you get any strokes from the group for your last life?

S: (pause) I had to scramble for patrons to survive as a painter, but I was good to people … it wasn't much … I enjoyed giving pleasure. My group recognizes I had a good heart.

Every one of my clients has special attachments to their soul group, regardless of character makeup. People tend to think of souls in the free state as being without human deficiencies. Actually, I think there are many similarities between groups of souls close to each other and human family systems. For instance, I see Norcross as the rebellious scapegoat for this group of souls, while he and Allum are the inventory takers for everyone's shortcomings. Allum said Norcross is usually the first to openly scrutinize any rationalizations or self-serving justifications of past life failures offered by the other members. He appears to have the least self-doubt and emotional investment over standards of conduct. This may define his own insecurity, because Norcross is probably fighting the hardest to keep up with the advancing group.

I suspect Allum himself could be the group's mascot (often the youngest child in human families), with all his clowning around, preening, and making light of serious issues. Some souls in spiritual groups do seem to me to be more fragile and protected than other group members. Vilo's conduct demonstrates he is the current hero (or eldest family member), with his drive for excellence. I have the impression from Allum that Vilo is the least defiant of the group, partly because he has the best record of achievement in recent past lives. Just as in human family systems, the roles of spiritual group members can be switched around, but I was told Vilo's kinetic energy is turning pink, signaling his growth into Level II.

I attach human labels on ethereal spirits because, after all, souls who come to Earth do show themselves through human characteristics. However, I don't see hatred, suspicion, and disrespect in soul groups. In a climate of compassion, there are no power struggles for control among these peer groups whose members are unable to manipulate each other or keep secrets. Souls distrust themselves, not each other. I do see fortitude, desire, and the will to keep trying in their new physical lives. In an effort to confirm some of my observations about the social dynamics among spiritual group members in this case, I ask Allum a few more questions.

Dr. N: Allum, do you believe your criticism of each other is always constructive?

S: Sure, there is no real hostility. We have fun at each other's expense—I admit that—but it's just a form of … acknowledgement of who we really are, and where we should be going.

Dr. N: Is any member of your soul group ever made to feel shame or guilt about a past life?

S: Those are … human weapons … and too narrow for what we feel.

Dr. N: Well, let me approach your feelings as a soul in another way. Do you feel safer getting feedback from one of your group members more than another?

S: No, I don't. We all respect each other immensely. The greatest criticism comes from within ourselves.

Dr. N: Do you have any regrets for your conduct in any past life?

S: (long pause) Yes … I feel sorry if I have hurt someone … and … then have everyone here know all about my mistakes. But we learn.

Dr. N: And what do you do about this knowledge?

S: Talk among ourselves … and try to make amends the next time.

Dr. N: From what you told me earlier, I had the idea that you, Norcross, and Dubri might be releasing some pent-up feelings over your own shortcomings by dumping on each other.

S: (thoughtfully) We make cynical remarks, but it's not like being human anymore. Without our bodies we take criticism a little different ferently. We see each other for who we are without resentment or jealousy.

Dr. N: I don't want to put words in your mouth, but I just wondered if all this flamboyance exhibited by your group might indicate underlying feelings of unworthiness?

S: Oh, that's something else again. Yes, we do get discouraged as souls, and feel unworthy about our abilities ... to meet the confidence placed in us to improve.

Dr. N: So, while you have self-doubts about yourselves, it's okay to make cynical remarks about each other's motivations?

S: Of course, but we want to be recognized by one another for being sincere in working on our individual programs. Sometimes self-pride gets in the way and we use each other to move past this.

In the next passage of dialogue, I introduce another spiritual phenomenon relating to group healing. I have heard a number of variations about this activity which are supported by the interpretations of Case 21.

Dr. N: Now Allum, as long as we are discussing how your group members relate to each other, I want you to describe the spiritual energy by which you all are assisted in this process.

S: (hesitant) I'm not sure I can tell you ...

Dr. N: Think carefully. Isn't there another means by which your group is brought into harmony with each other with intelligent energy?

S: (long pause) Ah ... you mean from the cones?

Dr. N: (the word "cone" is new to me, but I know I'm on the right track) Yes, the cones. Explain what you know about them relative to your group.

S: (slowly) Well, the cones do assist us.

Dr. N: Please continue, and tell me what the cone does. I think I have heard about this before, but I want your version.

S: It's shaped to go around us, you know.

Dr. N: Shaped in what way? Try to be more explicit.

S: It is cylindrical—very bright—it is above and all around us. The cone is small at the top and wide at the bottom, so it fits over all of us—like getting under a great white cap—we can float under the cone in order to use it.

Dr. N: Are you sure this isn't the shower of healing you experienced right after your return to the spirit world?

S: Oh no, that was more individual purification—to repair Earth damage. I thought you knew …

Dr. N: I do. I want you to explain how the cone is different from the shower of healing.

S: The top funnels energy down as a waterfall in a spreading circle around all of us and allows us to really concentrate on our mental sameness as a group.

Dr. N: And what do you feel when you are under the cone?

S: We can feel all our thoughts being expanded … then drawn up … and returned back … with more knowledge added.

Dr. N: Does this intelligent energy help your unity as a group in terms of more focused thinking?

S: Yes, it does.

Dr. N: (deliberately confrontational) To be frank with you, Allum, I wonder if this cone is brainwashing your original thoughts? After all, the arguments and disagreements between you and the others of your group are what make you individuals.

S: (laughs) We aren't brainwashed! Don't you know anything about the afterlife? It gives us more collective insight to work together.

Dr. N: Is the cone always available?

S: It is there when we need it.

Dr. N: Who operates the cone?

S: Those who watch over us.

Dr. N: Your guide?

S: (bursts out laughing) Shato? I think he is too busy traveling around on his circuit.

Dr. N: What do you mean?

S: We think of him as a circus master—a stage manager—of our group.

Dr. N: Does Shato take an active part in your group deliberations?

S: (shakes head) Not really—guides are above a lot of this stuff. We are left on our own quite a bit, and that's fine.

Dr. N: Do you think there is one specific reason for the absences of Shato?

S: (pause) Oh, he probably gets bored with our lack of progress. He loves to show off as the master of ceremonies though.

Dr. N: In what way?

S: (chuckling) Oh, to suddenly appear in front of us during one of our heated debates—throwing off blue sparks—looking like a wizard who is an all-powerful moderator!

Dr. N: A wizard?

S: (still laughing) Shato appears in long, sapphire-blue robes with a tall, pointed hat. With his flowing white beard he looks simply great, and we do admire him.

Dr. N: I get the picture of a spiritual Merlin.

S: An Oriental Merlin, if you will. Very inscrutable sometimes. He loves making a grand entrance in full costume, especially when we are about to choose another life. He knows how much we appreciate his act.

Dr. N: With all this stage management, I am curious if Shato has much emotional connection to your group as a serious guide.

S: (scoffing at me) Listen, he knows we are a wild bunch, and he plays to that as a non-conformist himself—but he is also very wise.

Dr. N: Is Shato indulgent with your group? He doesn't seem to limit your extravagance very much.

S: Shato gets results from us because he is not heavy-handed or preachy. That wouldn't sit well with our people. We respect him.

Dr. N: Do you see Shato as a consultant who comes only once in a while to observe, or as an active supervisor?

S: He will pop in unannounced to set up a problem for our discussions. Then he leaves, coming back later to listen to how we might solve certain things …

Dr. N: Give me an example of a major problem with your group.

S: (pause) Shato knows we identify too much as actors playing parts on Earth. He hits … on superficiality. He is trying to get us to cast ourselves from the inside out, rather than the reverse.

Dr. N: So Shato's instruction is serious, but he knows you all like to have fun along the way?

S: Yeah, that's why Shato is with us, I think. He knows we waste opportunities. He assists us in interpreting the predicaments we get into in order to get the best out of us.

Dr. N: From what you have told me, I have the impression that your spiritual group is run as a kind of workshop directed by your guide.

S: Yes, he builds up our morale and keeps us going.

Unlike educational classrooms or therapy groups on Earth, I have learned teacher-counselors in the spirit world are not confined as group activity leaders on a continuous basis. Although Shato and his students are a colorful family of souls, there is much here that is typical of all cluster groups. A guide's leadership is more parental than dictatorial. In this case, Shato is a directive counselor while not being possessive, nor does he pose a threat to the group. There is warm acceptance of these young souls by this empathic guide, who seems to cater to their masculine inclinations. I will close this case with a few final questions about the group as a spiritual unit.

Dr. N: Why is your group so male-oriented on Earth?

S: Earth is an action planet which rewards physical exertion. We are inclined to male roles so we can grab hold and mold events … to dominate our surroundings … to be recognized.

Dr. N: Women are also influential in society. How can your group hope to progress without more experience in female roles?

S: We know this, but we have such a fierce desire to be independent.

In fact, we often expend too much energy for too little return, but the female aspects don't interest us as much right now.

Dr. N: If you have no female counterparts in your immediate group, where do you go for those entities to complement your lives on Earth?

S: Nearby there are some who relate better to female roles. I get along with Josey—she has been with me in some of my lives—Trinian is attached to Nyala—and there are others ...

Dr. N: Allum, I would like to end our conversation about your spiritual associations by asking you what you know about the origin of your group.

S: (long pause) I ... can't tell you ... we just came together at one time.

Dr. N: Well, someone had to bring those of you with the same attributes together. Do you think it was God?

S: (puzzled) No, below the source ... the higher ones ...

Dr. N: Shato, or other guides like him?

S: No, higher, I think ... the planners ... I don't know any more.

Dr. N: A while back you told me some of your old friends were reducing their active participation in your group due to their development. Do you ever get new members?

S: Never.

Dr. N: Is this because a new member might have trouble assimilating with the rest of you?

S: (laughs) We aren't *that* bad! It's just we are too closely connected by thought for an outsider, and they would not have shared our past experiences.

Dr. N: During your discussions about these past lives together, does your group believe it contributes to the betterment of human society?

S: (pause) We want our presence in a community to challenge conventions—to question basic assumptions. I think we bring nerve into our physical lives—and laughter, too ...

Dr. N: And when your spiritual group has finished discussing what is necessary to further your aims, do you look forward to a new life?

S: (zestfully) Oh yeah! Every time I leave for a new role on Earth, I say goodbye with, "See you all back here A.D. (after death)."

This case is an example of like-minded souls with ego-inflating needs who support and validate each other's feelings and attitudes. Herein lies the key to understanding the formation of soul groups. I have learned that many spiritual clusters have sub-groups made up of entities whose identities are linked by similar issues blocking their advancement. Even so, these souls do have differences in strengths and weaknesses. Each group member contributes their best attributes toward advancing the goals of others in the family.

I do not want to leave the impression from case 21 that the few remaining souls in this inner circle of close friends represent the behavior traits of everyone in the original cluster. When a primary group of, say fifteen or twenty souls is formed, there are marked similarities in talent and interests. But a support group is also designed to have differences in disposition, feelings, and reactions. Typically, my subjects report a male-female oriented mixture of one or more of the following character types in their groups: 1) Courageous, resilient, a tenacious survivor. 2) Gentle, quiet, devoted, and rather innocent. 3) Fun-loving, humorous, a jokester and risk-taker. 4) Serious, dependable, cautious. 5) Flamboyant, enthusiastic, frank. 6) Patient, steady, perceptive. 7) Thoughtful, calculating, determined. 8) Innovative, resourceful, adaptable. These differences give a group balance. However, if an entire group displays a strong tendency toward flamboyance or daring, the most cautious member would appear less so to another group of souls.

There is no question that the souls in Case 21 are in for a long development period. Yet they do contribute to the vitality of Earth. Subsequent questioning of this subject revealed the paths of these souls continue to cross in the twentieth century. For instance, Allum is a graphic designer and part-time professional guitar player involved with Josey, who is a singer. The fact that the closely-knit souls in this case were so male-oriented in their physical lives does not take away from their ability to associate with young souls with predominantly female preferences. Cluster groups are gender-mixed. As I have mentioned, truly advanced souls have balanced gender preferences in their physical life choices.

The desire for expression of self-identity is an important motivating factor for souls choosing to come to Earth to learn practical lessons. Sometimes a reason for discomfort with the lower level soul is the discrepancy in perception of Self in their free soul state, compared to how they act in human bodies. Souls can get confused with who they are in life. Case 21 did not seem to exhibit any conflict in this area, but I question the rate of growth achieved by Allum in recent past lives. However, the basic experience of living a life may compensate, to some extent, for the lack of insight gained from that life.

Our shortcomings and moral conflicts are recognized as faults far more in the spirit world than on Earth. We have seen how the nuances of decision-making are dissected and analyzed in spiritual groups. Cluster members have worked together for such a long time in earth years that entities become accountable to each other and the group as a whole. This fosters a great sense of belonging in all spiritual groups, and can give the appearance of thought barriers between clusters, especially with souls in the lower levels. Nevertheless, while rejection and loneliness is part of every soul's life in human form, in the spirit world our individual ego-identity is contantly enhanced by warm peer group socialization.

The social structure of soul groups is not the same as groups of people on Earth. Although there is some evidence of paired friendships, I don't hear about cliques, stars of attraction, or isolated souls within clusters. I am told souls do spend time alone in the silence of personal reflection when attached to a group. Souls are intimate entities in their family relationships on Earth and engagement in group community life in the spirit world. And yet, souls do learn much from solitude.

I understand from my white-light subjects that souls at the beginning levels are frequently separated from their groups to individually work on simple energy projects. One rather young soul recalled being alone in an enclosure trying to put together a "moving puzzle" of dissembled geometric shapes of cylinders, spheres, cubes and squares with self-produced energy. It was described as being "multi-dimensional, colorful, and holographic" in nature. He said, "We have to learn to intensify our energy to bring the diffused and jumbled into focus to give it some kind of basic shape." Another subject added, "These tests give the Watchers information about our imagination, creativity, and ingenuity, and they offer us encouragement rather than being judgmental."

Souls on all levels engage in another important activity when they are alone. They are expected to spend time mentally concentrating on helping those on Earth (or other physical worlds) whom they have known and cared about. From what I can gather, they go to a space some call the place of protection. Here they enter an "interdimensional field of floating, silvery-blue energy," and project outward to geographical area of their choosing. I am told this is a mental exercise in "holding and releasing positive vibrational energy to create a territory." This means souls ride on their thought waves to specific people, buildings, or a given area of land in an attempt to comfort or effect change.

10

The Intermediate Soul

ONCE our souls advance past Level II into the intermediate ranges of development, group cluster activity is considerably reduced. This does not mean we return to the kind of isolation we saw with the novice soul. Souls evolving into the middle development levels have less association with primary groups because they have acquired the maturity and experience for operating more independently. These souls are also reducing the number of their incarnations.

Within Levels III and IV we are at last ready for more serious responsibilities. The relationship we have with our guides now changes from teacher-student to one of colleagues working together. Since our old guides have acquired new student groups, it is now our turn to develop teaching skills which will eventually qualify us for the responsibilities of being a guide to someone else.

I have said the transitional stages of Levels II and IV are particularly difficult for me in pinpointing a soul's development. For instance, some Level IV souls begin targeting themselves toward primary cluster teacher training while still in Level III, while other subjects who are clearly Level IV's find they are unsuited to be effective guides.

Despite their high standards of morality and conduct, entities who have reached the intermediate levels of maturity are modest about their achievements. Naturally, each case is different, but I notice more composure with clients in this stage and above. I see trust rather than suspicion toward the motives of others on both a conscious and subconscious level. These people demonstrate a forward-looking attitude of faith and confidence for the future of humanity, which encourages those around them.

My questions to the more mature soul are directed to esoteric ideas of purpose and creation. I admit to taking advantage of the higher knowledge possessed by these souls for the sort of spiritual information others lack. There have been clients who have told me they felt I pushed them rather hard in drawing out their spiritual memories and I know they are right. The more advanced souls of this world possess remarkable comprehension of a universal life plan. I want to learn as much as possible from them.

My next case falls into the upper portion of Level III development, radiating a yellow energy devoid of any reddish tones. This client was a small, nondescript man nearly fifty years old. His demeanor was quietly courteous towards me when we met, and I thought him a trifle solemn. I felt his unassuming detachment was somewhat studied, almost as a cover for stronger emotions. The most striking feature about him was his dark, morose eyes, which grew more intense as he began to talk about himself in a direct and persuasive manner.

He told me he worked for a charitable organization dispensing food to the homeless, and that he had once been a journalist. This client had traveled quite some distance to discuss with me his concern over a decline in enthusiasm for his work. He said he was tired and wanted to spend the rest of his life quietly alone. His first session involved a review of the highlights of many past lives so we could better evaluate a proper course for the remainder of his current life.

I began by regressing the subject rapidly through a series of early lives starting from his first life as a Cro-Magnon man in a Stone Age culture some 30,000 years ago. As we moved forward in time, I noted a consistency of lone-wolf behavior patterns as opposed to normal tribal integration. From about 3,000 BC to 500 BC, my client lived a number of lives in the Middle East during the rise of the early city states in Sumerian, Babylonian, and Egyptian cultures. Nevertheless, even in lives as a woman, this subject often avoided family ties, including having no children. As a man, he showed a preference for nomadism.

By the time we reached a life in Europe during the Dark Ages, I was becoming accustomed to a rebellious soul resisting tyrannical societies. During his lives, my subject worked to uplift people from fear, while remaining non-aligned to opposing factions. Suffering hardships and many setbacks, he continued as a wanderer with an obsession for freedom of movement.

Some lives were not too productive, but during the twelfth century I found him in Central America in the body of an Aztec, organizing a band of Indians against the oppressions of a high priest. He was killed in this setting as a virtual outcast, while promoting non-violent relations between tribes who were traditional enemies.

In the fourteenth century, this soul was a European chronicler, traveling the silk road to Cathay to gain understanding of the peoples of Asia. Always facile with languages (as he is today), my client died in Asia as an old man happily living in a peasant village. In Japan, at the beginning of the seventeenth century, he was a member of the clan of the Bleeding Crane. These men were respected, independent Samurai mercenaries. At the end of this life my subject was living in seclusion from the ruling Tokugawa shoguns, because he had advised their weaker opponents on battle strategy.

Frequently the outsider, always an explorer searching for truth across many lands, this soul continued to seek a rational meaning to life while giving aid to those he met along the way. I was surprised when he popped up as the wife of an American farmer on the frontier in the nineteenth century. The farmer died soon after their marriage. I learned my subject had deliberately incarnated to be a widow with children, tied to a piece of property, as an exercise in the loss of mobility.

When this part of his session ended I knew I was working with a more advanced, older soul, even though he had a great many lives we did not review. Since this soul is approaching Level IV, I would not have been surprised if his first appearance on Earth had gone back 70,000 years rather than half that amount of time. However, as I have mentioned, it is not an absolute prerequisite that souls have hundreds of physical lives in order to advance. I once had a client who entered into a Level III state of awareness after only 4,000 years—an outstanding performance.

I talked to my client about his current life and his customary methods of learning in previous lives. He explained he had never been married, and that social non-alignments worked best for him. I suggested a few alternatives for his consideration. Primarily, I felt his lack of intimacy with people in too many lives was obstructing his progress. When this session ended, he was anxious that we explore his mind further for perceptions about the spirit world in another session. Upon his arrival the next day, I placed him in a superconscious state and we went back to work.

↔ Case 22 ↠

Dr. N: By what name are you called in the spirit world?

S: I am called Nenthum.

Dr. N: Nenthum, do you have spirits around you right now or are you alone?

S: (pause) I am with two of my long-time companions.

Dr. N: What are their names?

S: Raoul and Senji.

Dr. N: And are the three of you part of a larger spiritual group of souls working together?

S: We were … but now the three of us work … more by ourselves.

Dr. N: What are the three of you doing at this moment?

S: We are discussing the best ways to help each other during our incarnations.

Dr. N: Tell me what you do for each other.

S: I help Senji to forgive herself for mistakes and appreciate her own worth. She needs to stop being a mother-figure all the time on Earth.

Dr. N: How does she assist you?

S: To … see my lack of a sense of belonging.

Dr. N: Give me an example of Senji's actions to assist you with this issue.

S: Well, she was my wife in Japan after my days as a warrior were over. (something is troubling Nenthum, and after a pause he adds the following) Raoul likes to pair with Senji and I am usually alone.

Dr. N: What about Raoul, how do you two help each other?

S: I help him with patience and he helps me with my tendency to avoid community life.

Dr. N: Are you always two males and a female in your incarnations on Earth?

S: No, we can change—and do—but this is comfortable for us.

Dr. N: Why are the three of you working independently from the rest of your spiritual group?

S: (pause) Oh, we see them here ... some have not gone forward with us ... a few others are further ahead of us in their tasks.

Dr. N: Do you have a guide or teacher?

S: (in a soft tone) She is Idis.

Dr. N: It sounds to me as if you have a high regard for her. Do you communicate well with Idis?

S: Yes I do—not that we don't have our disagreements.

Dr. N: What is the main area of conflict between the two of you?

S: She doesn't reincarnate much, and I tell her she should have more direct exposure to current conditions on Earth.

Dr. N: Are you mentally in tune with Idis to such an extent that you know all about her background training as a guide?

S: (shakes head while pondering) It isn't that we can't ask questions ... but we can only question what we know. Idis reveals to me what she thinks is relevant to my own experience.

Dr. N: Are guides able to screen their thoughts so you can't read their minds completely?

S: Yes, the older ones get proficient at that—knowing how to filter things we don't need to know because this knowledge would confuse us.

Dr. N: Will you learn to filter images?

S: I already have ... a little.

Dr. N: This must be why I have had many people tell me they have not been given definitive answers by their guides to all their questions.

S: Yes, and the intent of the question is important ... when it was asked and why. Perhaps it was not in their best interests to be given certain information which might disrupt them.

Dr. N: Aside from her teaching techniques, are you fond of Idis in terms of her identity?

S: Yes … I just wish she would agree to come with me … once.

Dr. N: Oh, you would like to actually have an Earth incarnation with her?

S: (grins mischievously) I have told her we might relate better here if she would consent to come to Earth sometime and mate with me.

Dr. N: And what does Idis say to that suggestion?

S: She laughs and says she will think about it—if I can prove to her that it would be productive.

At this junction I ask Nenthum how long Idis has been associated with him and learn she was assigned these three entities when they moved into Level III. Nenthum, Raoul, and Senji are also under the tutelage of a beloved older master guide who has been with them since the beginning of their existence. It would be inaccurate to assume that more advanced spirits lead lonely spiritual lives. This subject told me he was in contact with many souls. Raoul and Senji were simply his closest friends.

Levels III and IV are significant stages for souls in their development because now they are given increased responsibilities for younger souls. The status of a guide is not given to us all at once, however. As with many other aspects of soul life, we are carefully tested. The intermediate levels are trial periods for potential teachers. While our aura is still yellow, our mentors assign us a soul to look after, and then evaluate our leadership performance both in and out of physical incarnations.

Only if this preliminary training is successful are we allowed to function even at the level of a junior guide. Not everyone is suited for teaching, but this does not keep us from becoming an advanced soul in the blue section. Guides, like everyone else, have different abilities and talents, as well as shortcomings. By the time we reach Level V, our soul aptitudes are well known in the spirit world. We are given occupational duties commensurate with our abilities, which I will go into later in this chapter. Different avenues of approach to learning eventually bring all of us to the same end in acquiring spiritual wholeness. The richness of diversity is part of a master plan for the advancement of every soul, and I am interested in how Case 22 is progressing in Level III.

Dr. N: Nenthum, can you tell me if Idis is preparing you to be a guide, assuming you have an interest in that activity?

S: (quick response) I do have an interest.

Dr. N: Oh, then are you developing as a guide yourself?

S: (modestly) Don't make too much of it. I'm really no more than a caretaker … helping Idis and taking directions.

Dr. N: Do you try and imitate her teaching style?

S: No, we are different. As an apprentice—a caretaker—I couldn't do what she is able to accomplish, anyway.

Dr. N: When did you know you were ready to be a caretaker and begin assisting others spiritually?

S: It's an … awareness which comes over you after a great number of lives … that you are more in balance with yourself than previously, and are able to aid people as a spirit and in the flesh.

Dr. N: Are you operating in or out of the spirit world as a caretaker at this time?

S: (has difficulty in forming a response) I'm out … in two lives.

Dr. N: Are you living in two parallel lives now?

S: Yes, I am.

Dr. N: Where are you living in this other life?

S: Canada.

Dr. N: Is geography important to your Canadian assignment?

S: Yes, I picked a poor family in a rural community where I would be more indispensable. I'm in a small mountain town.

Dr. N: Give me the details of this Canadian life and your responsibilities.

S: (slowly) I'm … taking care of my brother Billy. His face and hands were horribly burned by a flash fire from a kitchen stove when he was four years old. I was ten when it happened.

Dr. N: Are you the same age in the Canadian life as you are now in your American one?

S: About the same.

Dr. N: And your prime assignment in the Canadian life?

S: To care for Billy. To help him see the world past his pain. He is almost blind and his facial disfigurement causes him to be rejected by the community. I try to open him to an acceptance of life and to know who he really is from the inside. I read to him and go for walks in the forest holding his arm. I don't hold his hands because they are so damaged.

Dr. N: What about your Canadian parents?

S: (without boasting) I am the parent. My father left after the fire and never came back. He was a weak man who was not kind to the family even before the fire. My mother's soul is not very … capable in her body. They need someone with seasoning.

Dr. N: Someone physically strong?

S: (laughing) No, I'm a woman in Canada. I'm Billy's sister. My mother and brother require someone mentally tough to hold the family together and give them a course to follow.

Dr. N: How do you provide for the family?

S: I am a baker and I'll never marry, because I can't leave them.

Dr. N: What is your brother's major lesson?

S: To acquire humility without being crushed by a life of little self-gratification.

Dr. N: Why didn't you take the role of your burned brother? Wouldn't that scenario provide you with the more difficult challenge?

S: (grimacing) Hmm—I've already been through that one!

Note: This subject has been physically injured in a number of past lives.

Dr. N: Yes, I suppose you have. I wonder if Billy's soul was ever involved with physically hurting you in one of your past lives?

S: As a matter of fact, he did in one of them. When I was the sufferer another caretaker stayed with me and I was a grateful receiver. Now it is Billy's turn and I am here for him.

Dr. N: Did you know in advance your brother was going to be incapacitated before you came into the Canadian life?

S: Sure, Idis and I discussed the whole situation. She said Billy's soul would require a caretaker, and since I had negative contact with this soul before in another life, I welcomed the job.

Dr. N: Besides the karmic lesson for Billy's soul, there are some for you too, in terms of your being in the role of a woman who is tied down. You can't just take off and roam around as you often do in your lives.

S: That's true. The degree of difficulty in a life is measured by how challenging the situation is for *you*, not others. For me, being Billy's caretaker is harder than when I was on the receiving end with another soul as my caretaker.

Dr. N: Give me the most difficult factor of this assignment for you as a caretaker.

S: To sustain a child ... through their helplessness ... to adulthood ... to teach a child to confront torment with courage.

Dr. N: Billy's life is an extreme example, but it does seem Earth's children have much physical and emotional pain to go through.

S: Without addressing and overcoming pain you can never really connect with who you are and build on that. I must tell you, the more pain and adversity which come to you as a child, the more opportunity to expand your potential.

Dr. N: And how are things working out for you as a caretaker in Canada?

S: There is a more difficult set of choices to be made in the Canadian family—unlike my American life. But, I have confidence in myself ... to put my comprehension to practical use.

Dr. N: Did Idis encourage or discourage your wanting to accelerate development by living parallel lives?

S: She is always open about this ... I haven't done it too much in the past.

Dr. N: Why not?

S: Life combinations can be tiring and divisive. The effort may become counter-productive with diminished returns for both lives.

Dr. N: Well, I see that you are helping people in both your lives today, but have you ever lived contrasting lives where you did poorly in one life and better in another at the same time?

S: Yes, although that was a long time ago on Earth. This is one of the advantages of life combinations. One life can offset the other. Still, doing this can be rough going.

Dr. N: Then why do the guides permit parallel lives?

S: (scowling at me) Souls are not in a rigid bureaucratic environment. We are allowed to make mistakes in judgement and learn from them.

Dr. N: I have the impression you think the average soul is better off living one life at a time.

S: I would say yes, in most instances, but there are other motivations to cause us to speed up incarnations.

Dr. N: Such as ... ?

S: (amused) The rewards for bunching up lives can allow for more reflection out of incarnation.

Dr. N: You mean the rest periods between lives might last longer for us after concurrent lives?

S: (smiles) Sure, it takes longer to reflect on two lives than one.

Dr. N: Nenthum, I just have a couple more questions on the mechanics of soul-splitting. How do you see the manner in which you divide your soul energy into various parts?

S: We are ... as particles ... of energized units. We originated out of one unit.

Dr. N: What was the original unit.

S: The maker.

Dr. N: Does each part of your soul remain intact, complete within itself?

S: Yes, it does.

Dr. N: Do all parts of our soul energy go out of the spirit world when we incarnate?

S: Part of us never leaves, since we do not totally separate from the maker.

Dr. N: What does the part that remains in the spirit world do while we are on Earth in one or more bodies?

S: It is ... more dormant ... waiting to be rejoined to the rest of our energy.

Most of my colleagues who work with past life clients have listened to overlapping time chronologies from people living on Earth in two places at once. Occasionally, there are three or more parallel lives. Souls in almost any stage of development are capable of living multiple physical lives, but I really don't see much of this in my cases.

Many people feel the idea of souls having the capacity to divide in the spirit world and then attaching to two or more human bodies is against all their preconceptions of a singular, individualized spirit. I confess that I too felt uncomfortable the first time a client told me about having parallel lives. I can understand why some people find the concept of soul duality perplexing, especially when faced with the further proposition that one soul may even be capable of living in different dimensions during the same relative time. What we must appreciate is, if our souls are all part of one great oversoul energy force which divides, or extends itself to create our souls, then why shouldn't the offspring of this intelligent soul energy have the same capacity to detach and then recombine?

Collecting information about spiritual activity from souls who are in the higher stages of development is sometimes frustrating. This is because the complex nature of memory and knowledge at these levels can make it difficult to sift out what these people recognize and won't tell me, from what they really don't know. Case 22 was both knowledgeable and open to my questions. This case is compatible with other accounts in my files about the diversity of soul training in the spirit world.

Dr. N: Nenthum, I want to turn now to your activities in the spirit world when you are not so busy with Earth incarnations, interacting in souls groups and learning to be a guide. Can you tell me of other spiritual areas in which you are occupied?

S: (long pause) Yes, there are other areas ... I know of them ...

Dr. N: How many?

S: (cautiously) I can think of four.

Dr. N: What would you call these areas of activity?

S: The World Without Ego, the World of All Knowing, the World of Creation and Non-creation, and the World of Altered Time.

Dr. N: Are they worlds which exist in our physical universe?

S: One does, the rest are non-dimensional spheres of attention.

Dr. N: All right, let's start with the non-dimensional spheres. Are these three areas in the spirit world for the use of souls?

S: Yes.

Dr. N: Why do you call all these spiritual areas worlds?

S: I see them as … habitations for spiritual life.

Dr. N: So, three of them are mental worlds?

S: Yes, that's what they are.

Dr. N: What is the World Without Ego?

S: It's the place of learning to be.

Dr. N: I have heard of it, expressed in different ways. Doesn't it involve the beginners?

S: Yes, the newly created soul is there to learn who they are. It's the place of origin.

Dr. N: Are the ego-identities passed out at random, or is there a choice for beginner souls?

S: The new soul is not capable of choice. You acquire your character based upon the way your energy is … combined … put together for you.

Dr. N: Is there some sort of spiritual inventory of characteristics that are assigned to souls—so much of one type, so much of another?

S: (long pause) I think many factors are considered in the allocations of that which makes us who we are. What I do know is, once given, ego becomes a covenant between oneself and the givers.

Dr. N: What does that mean?

S: To do the best I can with who I am.

Dr. N: So, the purpose of this world is the distribution of soul identity by advanced beings?

S: Yes, the new soul is pure energy with no real Self yet. The World Without Ego provides you with a signature.

Dr. N: Then why do you call it the World *Without* Ego?

S: Because the newly created souls arrive with no ego. The idea of Self has not come into the new soul's consciousness. It is here where the soul is offered meaning to its existence.

Dr. N: And does the creation of souls with personhood go on continually?

S: As far as I know, yes.

Dr. N: I want you to answer this next question carefully for me. When you acquired your particular identity as a soul, did that automatically mean you were slated for Earth incarnations in human form?

S: Not specifically, no. Planets don't last forever.

Dr. N: I wondered if certain types of souls have an affinity for specific forms of physical life in the universe?

S: (pause) I won't argue against that.

Dr. N: In your beginnings, Nenthum, were you given the opportunity to choose other planetary hosts besides humans on Earth?

S: Ah ... as a new soul ... the guides assist in those selections. I was drawn to human beings.

Dr. N: Were you given other choices?

S: (long pause) Yes ... but it's not very clear at the moment. They usually start you on an easy world or two, without much to do. Then I was offered service on this severe planet.

Dr. N: Earth is considered severe?

S: Yes. On some worlds you must overcome physical discomforts—even suffering. Others lean toward mental contests. Earth has both.

We get kudos for doing well on the hard worlds. (smiling) We are called the adventurous ones by those who don't travel much.

Dr. N: What really appeals to you about Earth?

S: The kinship humans have for each other while they struggle against one another ... competing and collaborating at the same time.

Dr. N: Isn't that a contradiction?

S: (laughs) That's what appeals to me—mediating quarrels of a fallible race which has so much pride and need of self-respect. The human brain is rather unique, you know.

Dr. N: How?

S: Humans are egocentric but vulnerable. They can make their character mean and yet have a great capacity for kindness. There is weak and courageous behavior on Earth. It's always a push-me pull-you tug-of-war going on with human values. This diversity suits my soul.

Dr. N: What are some of the other things about human hosts which might appeal to the souls who are sent to Earth?

S: Hmm ... those of us developing on Earth have ... a sanction to help humans know of the infinite beyond their life and to assist them in expressing true benevolence through their passion. Having a *passion* to fight for life—that's what is so worthwhile about humanity.

Dr. N: Humans also have a great capacity for malevolence.

S: That's part of the passion. But it's evolving too, and when humans experience trouble, they can be at their best and are ... quite noble.

Dr. N: Perhaps it is the soul which fosters the positive characteristics you suggested?

S: We try to enhance what is already there.

Dr. N: Does any soul ever go back to the World Without Ego after they have once been there and acquired identity?

S: (uncomfortable) Yes ... but I don't want to get into that ...

Dr. N: Well, then we won't, but I have been told some souls do return if their conduct during physical assignments is consistently irregular. I have the impression they are considered defective and are returned to the factory for a kind of spiritual prefrontal lobotomy?

S: (subject shakes his head with annoyance) I am offended by that description. Where did you get such a notion? Those souls who have developed severe obstacles to improvement are mended by the restoration of positive energy.

Dr. N: Is this procedure just for Earth souls?

S: No, young souls from everywhere may require restoration as a last resort.

Dr. N: Are these restored spirits then allowed to return to their respective groups and eventually go back to incarnating on physical worlds?

S: (sighs deeply) Yes.

Dr. N: How would you compare the World Without Ego to the World of All Knowing?

S: They are opposites. This world is not for young souls.

Dr. N: Have you been to the World of All Knowing?

S: No, I'm not ready. I am only aware of it as a place we strive for.

Dr. N: What do you know about this spiritual area?

S: (long pause) It is a place of contemplation ... the ultimate mental world of planning and design. I can tell you little about this sphere except it is the final destination of all thought. The senses of all living things are coordinated here.

Dr. N: Then the World of All Knowing is abstract in the highest form?

S: Yes, it's about blending content with form—the rational with ideals. It is a dimension where the realization of all our hopes and dreams is possible.

Dr. N: Well, if you can't go there yet, how come you know about it?

S: We get ... glimpses ... as an incentive to encourage us to make that final effort to finish our work and join the masters.

The foundation of the spirit world is a place of knowing and has been alluded to under different names by clients. I am given only bare references to this universal absolute, because even my advanced subjects have no direct experience there. All souls are anxious to reach and be absorbed by this nucleus, especially as they draw closer and are enticed by what little they can see. I'm afraid the World of All Knowing can only be fully understood by a non-reincarnating soul above Level V.

> **Dr. N:** If the World Without Ego and the World of All Knowing are at opposite ends of a soul's experience, then where does the World of Altered Time fall?

> **S:** This sphere is available to all souls because it represents their own physical world. In my case, it is Earth.

> **Dr. N:** Oh, this must be the physical dimension you told me about?

> **S:** No, the sphere of Earth is only simulated for my use.

> **Dr. N:** Then all souls in the spirit world wouldn't study the same simulated world?

> **S:** No, each of us studies our own geographical planet, where we incarnate. They are physically real … temporarily.

> **Dr. N:** And you don't physically live on this simulated world which appears as Earth—you only use it?

> **S:** Yes, that's right—for training purposes.

> **Dr. N:** Why do you call this third sphere the World of Altered Time?

> **S:** Because we can change time sequences to study specific events.

> **Dr. N:** What is the basic purpose of doing this?

> **S:** To improve my decisions for life. This study makes me more discriminating and prepares me for the World of All Knowing.

Note: Subjects frequently use the term "world" to describe non-physical spatial work areas. These regions can be tiny or indescribably large in relation to the soul and may involve different dimensions. I believe there are separate realities for different learning experiences outside the restrictions of time. The coexistence of past, present, and future time in spiritual settings suggested by this case will be explored further in the next two chapters with Cases 23 and 25.

Dr. N: We haven't talked about the World of Creation and Non-creation. This must be the three-dimensional physical world you spoke of earlier.

S: Yes, and we enjoy using it as well.

Dr. N: Is this world intended for the use of all souls?

S: No, it is not. I'm just starting to apply myself there. I am considered a newcomer.

Dr. N: Well, before we get into that, I want to ask if this physical world is the same as Earth.

S: No, it is a little different. It's larger and somewhat colder. There is less water—fewer oceans, but similar.

Dr. N: Is this planet further from its sun than Earth is from our sun?

S: Yes.

Dr. N: If I could call this physical world Earth II, since it seems to be geographically similar to the Earth we know, would it be near Earth I in the sky?

S: No.

Dr. N: Where is Earth II in relation to Earth I?

S: (pause) I can't tell you.

Dr. N: Is Earth II in our Milky Way galaxy?

S: (long pause) No, I think it's further away.

Dr. N: Could I see the galaxy Earth II is located in with a telescope from my backyard?

S: I … would think so.

Dr. N: Would you say the galaxy containing this physical world is shaped like a spiral as our galaxy, or is it elliptical? How would it look in a telescope from a long way off?

S: … as a great extended … chain … (with a troubled expression) I can't tell you more.

Note: As an amateur stargazer who uses a large reflector telescope designed for deep sky objects, I am always inquisitive when a session takes an astronomical turn. Client responses to these kinds of questions usually fall short of my expectations. I am never sure if this is due to blocking by guides or the subject's lack of a physical frame of reference between Earth and the rest of our universe.

Dr. N: (I throw out a leading question) I suppose you go to Earth II to reincarnate with some sort of intelligent being?

S: (loudly) No! That's just what we don't want to do there.

Dr. N: When do you go to Earth II?

S: Between my lives on this Earth.

Dr. N: Why do you go to Earth II?

S: We go there to create and just enjoy ourselves as free spirits.

Dr. N: And you don't bother the inhabitants of Earth II?

S: (enthusiastically) There are *no* people … it's so peaceful … we roam among the forests, the deserts, and over oceans with no responsibilities.

Dr. N: What is the highest form of life on Earth II?

S: (evasive) Oh … small animals … without much intelligence.

Dr. N: N. Do animals have souls?

S: Yes, all living things do—but they have very simple fragments of mind energy.

Dr. N: Has your soul, and that of your friends, evolved from using lower forms of physical life on Earth I after your creation?

S: We don't know for sure, but none of us thinks so.

Dr. N: Why not?

S: Because intelligent energy is arranged by … a precedence of life. Plants, insects, reptiles—each is in a family of souls.

Dr. N: And all categories of living things are separated from each other?

S: No. The maker's energy joins the units of every living thing in existence.

Dr. N: Are you involved with this element of creation?

S: (startled) Oh, *no!*

Dr. N: Well, who is selected to visit Earth II?

S: Those of us who are connected with Earth come here. This is a vacation spot compared to Earth.

Dr. N: Why?

S: There is no fighting, bickering, or striving for supremacy. There is a pristine atmosphere and all life is … quiet. This place gives us an incentive to return to Earth and make it more peaceful, too.

Dr. N: Well, I do see how this Garden of Eden would allow you to rest and be carefree, but you also said you come here to create.

S: Yes, we do.

Dr. N: It is no accident then that souls from Earth come to a world that is so similar geographically?

S: That's right.

Dr. N: Do other souls, who are not earthbound, go to physical worlds which resemble those planets where they incarnate?

S: Yes … younger worlds with simpler organisms … to learn to create without any intelligent life around.

Dr. N: Go on.

S: We can experiment with creation and see it developing here. It's as if you were in a lab where you can form physical things from your energy.

Dr. N: Do these physical things resemble what you might see on Earth I?

S: Yes, only on Earth. That's why I am here.

Dr. N: Start with your arrival on Earth II and explain to me what your soul does first.

S: (balks at my question and then finally says) I'm … not very good.

Note: Since this subject is experiencing resistance, I take a few minutes for reconditioning and end with the following: "On the count of three you will feel more relaxed about telling me what you and Idis consider appropriate for my knowledge. *One, two, three!*" I repeat my question.

S: I look to see what I am supposed to make on the ground in front of me. Then I mold the object in my mind and try and create the same thing with small doses of energy. The teachers assist us with … control. I'm supposed to see my mistakes and make corrections.

Dr. N: Who are the teachers?

S: Idis and Mulcafgil (subject's highly advanced guide) … and there are other instructors around … I don't know them very well.

Dr. N: Try to be as clear as possible. What exactly are you doing?

S: We … form things …

Dr. N: Living things?

S: I'm not ready for that yet. I experiment with the basic elements— you know, hydrogen and oxygen—to create planetary substance … rocks, air, water … keeping everything very small.

Dr. N: Do you actually create the basic elements of our universe?

S: No, I just use the elements available.

Dr. N: In what way?

S: I take the basic elements and charge them with impulses from my energy … and they can change.

Dr. N: Change into what?

S: (simply) I'm good with rocks …

Dr. N: How do you form rocks with your energy?

S: Oh … by learning to heat and cool … dust … to make it hard.

Dr. N: Do you make the minerals in the dust?

S: They do that for you … the teachers give us that stuff … gas vapors for water making … and so on …

Dr. N: I want to understand this clearly. Your work consists of learning to create by causing heat, pressure, and cooling from your energy flow?

S: That's about right—by alternating our currents of energy radiation.

Dr. N: So, you don't actually produce the substance of rock and water in some chemical way?

S: No, like I told you, my job is to transform things by … mixing what I am given. I play with the frequency and dosages of my energy—it's tricky, but not too complicated …

Dr. N: Not complicated! I thought nature did those things?

S: (laughs) Who do you think nature is?

Dr. N: Well, who creates the basic elements of your experiments—the primary substances of physical matter?

S: The maker … and those creating on a grander scale than me.

Dr. N: Well, in a sense you are creating inanimate objects such as rocks.

S: Hmm … it's more our trying to copy what we see in front of us … what we know. (as an afterthought) I'm getting into plants … but I can't do them yet.

Dr. N: And you start small, experimenting until you get better?

S: That's it. We copy things and compare them against the original so we can make larger models.

Dr. N: This all sounds like souls playing as children in a sandbox with toys.

S: (smiles) We *are* children. Directing an energy flow resembles the sculpturing of clay.

Dr. N: Are the other members of this creative training class from your original cluster group?

S: Some are. Most come from all over (the spirit world), but they have all incarnated on Earth.

Dr. N: Does everyone make the same things as you do?

S: Well, of course, some of us are better with certain things, but we help each other. The teachers come around and give us tips and advice on how to improve … but … (stops)

Dr. N: But, what?

S: (sheepishly) If I am clumsy and do a bad job, I disassemble some creations without showing them to Idis.

Dr. N: Give me an example.

S: Plants … I don't apply my energy delicately enough to produce the proper chemical conversions.

Dr. N: You are not good with the formation of plant life?

S: No, so I undo my abominations.

Dr. N: Is this what you mean by uncreation? You can destroy energy?

S: Energy can't be destroyed. We reassemble it and start over using different combinations.

Dr. N: I don't see why the creator needs your help in creating.

S: For our benefit. We participate in these exercises so that when our work is judged to be of quality, hopefully we can make real contributions to life.

Dr. N: If we are all working up the ladder of development as souls, Nenthum, I am left with the impression the spirit world is one huge organizational pyramid with a supreme authority of power at the top.

S: (sighs) No, you are wrong. It is not a pyramid. We are all threads in the same long piece of fabric. We are all woven into it.

Dr. N: It's hard for me to visualize fabric when there are so many levels of competency for souls.

S: Think of it as a moving continuum rather than souls being in brackets of highs and lows.

Dr. N: I always think of souls moving up in their existence.

S: I know you do, but consider us moving across …

Dr. N: Give me something I can picture in my mind.

S: It's as if we are all part of a universal train on a flat track of existence. Most of the souls on Earth are in one car moving along the track.

Dr. N: Are all other souls in different cars?

S: Yes, but all on the same track.

Dr. N: Where are the conductors such as Idis?

S: They move back and forth between the connected cars, but sit closer to the engine.

Dr. N: Where is the engine?

S: The maker? Up front, naturally.

Dr. N: Can you see the engine from your car?

S: (laughs at me) No, but I can smell the smoke. I can feel the engine rumbling along and I can hear the motor.

Dr. N: It would be nice if all of us were closer to the engine.

S: Ultimately, we will be.

From what I am able to determine, souls are expected to begin familiarizing themselves with the forces of creation by the time they are solidly established in Level III. Exposure to plant photosynthesis takes place before student souls work up the organic scale of life. I am told that early creation training consists of souls learning relationships between substances to develop the ability of unifying their energy with different values in the elements. The formation of inanimate to animate objects from the simple to the complex is a long, slow process. Students are encouraged to create miniature planetary microhabitats for a given set of organisms which can adapt to certain environmental conditions. With practice comes improvement, but not until they approach Level V do my clients begin to feel they might actually contribute to the development of living things. We will hear more about this with Case 23; however, many of my clients won't, or can't, talk about creation.

Some souls seem to have a natural gift for working with energy in their creation classes. My cases indicate ability in creation assignments does not mean a soul is at the same level of advancement in all other areas of the spiritual curricula. A soul may be a good technician in harnessing the forces of creation, but lack the subtle techniques of a competent guide. Perhaps this is why I have been given the impression that the highly advanced soul is allowed to specialize.

In the previous chapter, I explained some benefits of soul solitude and the last case gave us another example. Spiritual experience is not easily translated into human language. Case 22 talks about the World of Altered Time as a means of transient planetary study. To someone in trance, it is the timeless mental world that is true reality while all else is an illusion created for various benefits. Other subjects at about the same level call this sphere "the space of transformation" or simply "rooms of recreation." Here, I'm told, souls are able to meld their energy into animate and inamate objects created for learning and pleasure. One subject said to me, "I think of what I want and it happens. I know I'm being assisted. We can be anything familiar to our past experiences."

For instance, souls can become rocks to capture the essence of density, trees for serenity, water for a flowing cohesiveness, butterflies for freedom and beauty and whales for power and immensity. People deny these actions represent former earthly transmigrations. I have also learned souls may become amorphous without substance or texture and totally integrate into a particular feeling, such as compassion, to sharpen their sensitivity.

Some subjects tell of being mystical spirits of nature including figures I associate with folklore, such as elves, giants and mermaids. Personal contact with strange mythological beasts are mentioned as well. These accounts are so vivid it is hard for me to simply label them as metaphoric. Are the old folk tales of many races pure superstition, or manifestations of shared soul experience? I have the sense that many of our legends are the sympathetic memories of souls carried from other places to Earth long ago.

11

The Advanced Soul

 PEOPLE who possess souls which are both old and highly advanced are scarce. Although I haven't had the opportunity to regress many Blues in Level V, they are always stimulating to work with because of their comprehension and far-reaching spiritual consciousness. The fact is, a person whose maturity is this high doesn't seek out a regression therapist to resolve life-plan conflicts. In most cases, Level V's are here as incarnated guides. Having mastered the fundamental issues most of us wrestle with daily, the advanced soul is more interested in making small refinements toward specific tasks.

We may recognize them when they appear as public figures, such as a Mother Teresa; however, it is more usual for the advanced soul to go about their good works in a quiet, unassuming manner. Without displaying self-indulgence, their fulfillment comes from improving the lives of other people. They focus less on institutional matters and more on enhancing individual human values. Nevertheless, Level V's are also practical, and so they are likely to be found working in a cultural mainstream which allows them to influence people and events.

I have been asked if most people who are sensitive, aesthetic, and particularly right-brained have advanced souls since individuals with these characteristics often appear to be at odds with the wrongs of an imperfect world. I see no correlation here. Being emotional, appreciating beauty, or having extrasensory impressions—including psychic talent—does not necessarily denote an advanced soul.

The mark of an advanced spirit is one who has patience with society and shows extraordinary coping skills. Most prominent is their exceptional insight. This is not to say life has no karmic pitfalls for them, otherwise the Level V probably wouldn't be here at all. They may be found in all walks of life, but are frequently in the helping professions or combating social injustice in some fashion. The advanced soul radiates composure, kindness, and understanding toward others. Not being motivated by self-interest, they may disregard their own physical needs and live in reduced circumstances.

The individual I have chosen to represent the Level V soul is a woman in her mid-thirties who works for a large medical treatment facility specializing in chemical substance abuse. I was introduced to this woman by a colleague who told me of her skill in guiding recovering drug addicts into an improved state of self-awareness.

At our first meeting, I was struck by the woman's expression of serenity while surrounded by chaotic emergencies at her place of employment. She was tall and excessively thin, with flaming red hair which stuck out in all directions. Although warm and friendly, there was about her an air of impenetrability. Her clear, luminous gray eyes were those of one who sees small things unnoticed by ordinary folk. I felt she was looking into rather than at me.

My colleague suggested the three of us have lunch because this woman was interested in my studies of the spirit world. She told me that she had never been hypnotically regressed but there was the sense of a long spiritual genealogy through her own meditations. She thought our meeting was no accident on her own learning path and we came to an agreement to explore her spiritual knowledge. A few weeks later she arrived at my office. Clearly, this woman had no compelling desire for a long chronology of past life history. I decided to get a brief sketch of her earliest lives on Earth to use as a springboard into superconscious memories. She rapidly entered into a deep trance and made instant contact with her inner self.

Almost at once, I found this woman's span of incarnations staggering, going far back into the distant past of human life on Earth. Touching on her earliest memories, I came to the conclusion her first lives occurred at the beginning of the last warm interglacial period which lasted from 130,000 to 70,000 years ago, before the last great Ice Age spread over the planet. During the warmer climate of the middle Paleolithic period of Earth's history, my subject described living in moist, sub-tropical savannas near hunting, fishing, and plant-gathering areas. Later, some 50,000 years ago, when continental sheets of ice had again changed Earth's climate, she spoke of living in caves and enduring bitter cold.

Leaping rapidly over large blocks of time, I found her physical appearance changing from a slightly bent to a more erect posture. As we moved forward in time, I directed her to look into pools of water and feel her body while reporting back to me. Her sloping forehead became more vertical over thousands of years in different bodies. Supraorbital ridges above the eyes grew less pronounced as did body hair and the massive jaws of archaic man. In her many lives as both men and women, I was given enough information on habitat, the use of fire, tools, clothes, food, and ritualistic tribal practices for rough anthropological dating.

Paleontologists have estimated *Homo erectus*, an ape-like ancestor of modern humans, appeared at least 1.7 million years ago. Have souls been incarnating on Earth for this long, utilizing the bodies of these primitive bipeds we call hominids? A few of my more advanced clients declare that highly advanced souls who specialize in seeking out suitable hosts for young souls, evaluated life on Earth for over a million years. My impression is these examiner souls found the early hominid brain cavity and restricted voice box to be inadequate for soul development earlier than some 200,000 years ago.

Archaic *Homo sapiens*, whom we call humans, evolved several hundred thousand years ago. Within the last 100,000 years, we find two clear signs of spiritual consciousness and communication. These are burial practices and ritualistic art, as found in carved totems and rock drawings. There is no anthropological evidence that these practices existed on Earth before Neanderthal peoples. Souls eventually made us human, not the reverse.

One of my advanced subjects remarked, "Souls have seeded the Earth in different cycles." A composite of information collected from a wide range of clients suggests to me that the land masses we know today deviate from earlier continents, drowned, perhaps, by cataclysmic volcanic or magnetic upheavals. For instance, the Azores in the Atlantic Ocean have been said to represent the tops of mountains of the submerged continent of Atlantis. Indeed, I have had subjects discuss being in ancient lands on Earth that I cannot identify with modern geography.

Thus, it is possible souls existed in bodies more advanced than *Homo erectus*, who died out about a quarter of a million years ago, with the fossilized evidence hidden from us today by geological change. However, this hypothesis means the physical evolution of humans was an up, down, up affair, which I think is unlikely.

I now moved my subject into an African life around 9,000 years ago, which she said was an important milestone in her advancement. This was the last life she was to spend with her guide, Kumara. Kumara was an advanced soul herself at the time of this life, counseling a benevolent tribal chief as his influential wife. I tentatively located their land as the highlands of Ethiopia. Apparently, my subject had known Kumara in a number of earlier lives covering thousands of years during Kumara's final incarnations on Earth. Their association in human form ended when my subject died, saving Kumara's life on a river boat, by throwing herself in front of an enemy spear.

Full of love, Kumara still appears to this subject as a large woman, with skin of polished mahogany and a shock of white hair crowned by a head-dress of feathers. She is practically nude, except for a strip of animal hide around her ample middle. On Kumara's neck hangs a garish bunch of multi-colored stones, which she sometimes jiggles in my subject's ear to get her attention during dreams in the middle of the night.

Kumara teaches by a technique of flashing symbolistic memories of prior lessons already learned in past lives. Old solutions to problems are mixed with new hypothetical choices in the form of metaphoric picture puzzles. By these means, Kumara tests her student's considerable store-house of knowledge during meditations and dreams.

I glanced at my watch. There was no more time for background information if I was going to allow for exploration of this woman's after life experiences. Rapidly I took her into superconsciousness, anticipating some interesting spiritual disclosures. She would not disappoint me.

↞ Case 23 ↠

Dr. N: What is your spiritual name?

S: Thece.

Dr. N: And your spiritual guide kept her African name of Kumara?

S: For me, yes.

Dr. N: What do you look like in the spirit world?

S: A glowing fragment of light.

Dr. N: What exactly is the color of your energy?

S: Sky-blue.

Dr. N: Does your light have flecks of another color in it?

S: (pause) Some gold … not much.

Dr. N: How about Kumara's energy color?

S: It's violet.

Dr. N: How does light and color identify the quality of a soul's spiritual attainment?

S: The intensity of mental power increases with the darker phases of light.

Dr. N: Where does the highest intensity of intelligent light energy originate from?

S: The knowledge by which the energy of darker light is extended to us comes from the source. Our light is attached to the source.

Dr. N: When you say source—you mean God?

S: That word has been misused.

Dr. N: How?

S: By too much personalizing, which makes the source less than it is.

Dr. N: What's wrong with us doing that?

S: It takes the liberty of making the source too … human, although we are all part of its oneness.

Dr. N: Thece, I want you to reflect on the source as we talk about other aspects of soul life and the spirit world. Later, I will ask you more about this oneness. Now, let's go back to the energy manifestations of souls. Why do spirits display two black glowing cavities for eyes when not showing their human forms? It seems so spooky to me.

S: (laughs and is more relaxed) That's how Earth's legends of ghosts came about—from these memories. Our energy mass is not uniform. The eyes you speak of represent a more concentrated intensity of thought.

Dr. N: Well, if the myths about ghosts are not so fanciful after all, then these black eye sockets must be useful extensions of their energy.

S: Rather than eyes ... they are windows to old bodies ... and all the physical extensions of former selves. This blackness is a ... concentration of our presence. We communicate by absorbing the energy presence of each other.

Dr. N: When you return to the spirit world, do you have energy contact with other souls who may look like ghosts?

S: Yes, and appearance is a matter of individual preference. Of course there is always a multitude of thought waves around me—mingling with my returning energy, but I avoid too much contact.

Dr. N: Why?

S: It is not necessary for me to make attachments here. I will be alone for a while to contemplate and sort out any mistakes from my last incarnation, before talking to Kumara.

Note: This statement is typical of advanced souls returning to the spirit world, mentioned earlier in Case 9. However, this soul is so advanced she will have no deliberations with her guide until much later, and upon her request.

Dr. N: Perhaps we should talk about older souls for a minute. Does Kumara incarnate on Earth any more?

S: No, she doesn't.

Dr. N: Do you know others like Kumara who were here during the early times on Earth and don't come back any more?

S: (cautiously) A few ... yes ... many got on Earth early and got off before I came.

Dr. N: Did any stay?

S: What do you mean?

Dr. N: Advanced souls who keep coming back to life on Earth when they could stay in the spirit world.

S: Oh, you mean the Sages?

Dr. N: Yes, the Sages—tell me about them. (this is a new term for me, but I often pretend to know more than I do with advanced souls to elicit information)

S: (with admiration) They are the true watchers of Earth, you know … to be here and keep watch over what is going on.

Dr. N: As highly advanced souls who continue to incarnate?

S: Yes.

Dr. N: Don't the Sages get tired of still hanging around Earth?

S: They choose to stay and help people directly because they are dedicated to Earth.

Dr. N: Where are these Sages?

S: (wistfully) They live simple lives. I first came to know some of them thousands of years ago. Today it's hard to see them … they don't like cities much.

Dr. N: Are there many of them?

S: No, they live in small communities, or out in the open … in the deserts and mountains … in simple dwellings. They wander about, too …

Dr. N: How does one recognize them?

S: (sighs) Most people don't. They were known as the oracles of truth in earlier times on Earth.

Dr. N: I know this sounds pragmatic, but wouldn't these old, highly developed souls be more useful helping humankind in positions of international leadership rather than being hermits?

S: Who said they were hermits? They prefer to be with the common people who are most affected by the movers and shakers.

Dr. N: What is the feeling one gets when meeting a Sage on Earth?

S: Ah … you feel a special presence. Their power of understanding and the advice they give you is so wise. They do live simply. Material things mean nothing to them.

Dr. N: Are you interested in this sort of service, Thece?

S: Hmm … no, they are saints. I welcome the time when I can stop incarnating.

Dr. N: Perhaps the word Sage could also be applied to souls like Kumara, or even with the entities to whom she turns for knowledge?

S: (pause) No, they are different ... they are beyond the Sages. We call them the Old Ones.

Note: I would place these beings beyond Level VI.

Dr. N: Are there many Old Ones working with souls at Kumara's level and above?

S: I don't think so ... compared to the rest of us ... but we feel their influence.

Dr. N: What do you feel in their presence?

S: (pensive) A ... concentrated power of enlightenment ... and guidance ...

Dr. N: Could the Old Ones be embodiments of the source itself?

S: It is not for me to say, but I don't think so yet. They must be close to the source. The Old Ones represent the purest elements of thought ... engaging in the planning and arranging of ... substances.

Dr. N: Could you clarify a bit more what you mean by these highly placed souls being close to the source?

S: (vaguely) Only that they must be close to conjunction.

Dr. N: Does Kumara ever talk about these entities who help her?

S: To me—only a little. She aspires to be of them, as we all do.

Dr. N: Is she getting close to the Old Ones in knowledge?

S: (faintly) She ... approaches, as I approach her. It is slow assimilating with the source, because we are not complete.

Once the duties of a guide are fully established for the advancing soul, it is necessary for these entities to juggle two balls. Besides completing their own unfinished business with continued (though less frequent) incarnations, they must also help others while in a discarnated state. Thece talks to me about this aspect of her soul life.

Dr. N: When you are back in the spirit world and come out of your self-imposed isolation, what do you ordinarily do then?

S: I join with members of my company.

Dr. N: How many souls are in your company?

S: Nine.

Dr. N: (jumping to the next conclusion too quickly) Oh, so the ten of you are a group of souls under the leadership of Kumara?

S: No, they are *my* responsibility.

Dr. N: Then, these nine entities are students whom you teach?

S: Hmm … you could say that …

Dr. N: And they are all in one group (cluster)—which, I assume, is your company?

S: No, my company is made up of two different groups.

Dr. N: Why is that?

S: They are in … different progressions (levels).

Dr. N: And yet, you are the spiritual teacher for all nine?

S: I prefer to call myself a watcher. Three of my company are also watchers.

Dr. N: Well, who are the other six?

S: (matter-of-factly) People who don't watch.

Dr. N: I want to clarify this using my terms, if you will, Thece. If you are a senior watcher, three of your company must be what I would call junior guides?

S: Yes, but the words senior and junior—that portrays us as authoritarian, which we are not!

Dr. N: My intention is not to denote rank, for me it is just an easy identification of responsibility. Consider the word senior as meaning an advanced teacher. I would call Kumara a master teacher or possibly an educational director.

S: (shrugs) That's okay, I suppose, as long as director doesn't mean dictator.

Dr. N: It doesn't. Now, Thece, cast your mind to a place where you can see the energy colors of all your company. What do the six souls who are not watchers look like?

S: (smiles) Dirty snowballs!

Dr. N: If they are white in tone, what about the rest?

S: (pause) Well … two are rather yellowish.

Dr. N: We are one short. What about the ninth member?

S: That's An-ras. He is doing quite well.

Dr. N: Describe his energy color.

S: He is … turning bluish … an excellent watcher … he will be leaving me soon …

Dr. N: Let's go to the opposite end of your company. What member are you most concerned about and why?

S: Ojanowin. She has the conviction from many lives that love and trust only bring hurt. (musing) She has fine qualities which I want to bring out but this attitude is holding her back.

Dr. N: Ojanowin is developing more slowly than the rest?

S: (protectively) Don't misunderstand, I am proud of her effort. She has great sensitivity and integrity, which I like. She just requires more of my attention.

Dr. N: As a watcher-teacher, what is the one quality which An-ras has acquired which you want to see in Ojanowin?

S: (no hesitation) Adaptability to change.

Dr. N: I am curious if the nine members of your company advance in a rather uniform way together under your teaching.

S: That's totally unrealistic.

Dr. N: Why?

S: Because there are differences in character and integrity.

Dr. N: Well, if learning rates are different between souls because of character and integrity, how does this equate with the mental capabilities of the human brain a soul selects?

S: It doesn't. I was speaking of motivation. On Earth we use many variations of the physical brain in the course of our expansion. However, each soul is driven by its integrity.

Dr. N: Is this what you mean by a soul having character?

S: Yes, and intensity of desire is part of character.

Dr. N: If character is the identity of a soul, where does desire come in?

S: The drive to excel is internal to each soul, but this too can fluctuate between lives.

Dr. N: So where does a soul's integrity fit into this?

S: The extension of desire. Integrity is the desire to be honest about Self and motives to such an extent that full awareness of the path to the source is possible.

Dr. N: If all basic intelligent energy is the same, why are souls different in their character and integrity?

S: Because their experiences with physical life change them and this is intentional. By that change new ingredients are added to the collective intelligence of every soul.

Dr. N: And this is what incarnation on Earth is all about?

S: Incarnation is an important tool, yes. Some souls are driven more than others to expand and achieve their potential, but all of us will do so in the end. Being in many physical bodies and different settings expands the nature of our real self.

Dr. N: And this sort of self-actualization of the soul identity is the purpose of life on our world?

S: On any world.

Dr. N: Well, if each soul is preoccupied with Self, doesn't this explain why we have a world of self-centered people?

S: No, you misinterpret. Fulfillment is not cultivating Self for selfish means, but allowing for integration with others in life. That also shows character and integrity. This is ethical conduct.

Dr. N: Does Ojanowin have less honesty than An-ras?

S: (pause) I'm afraid she does engage in self-deception.

Dr. N: I wonder how you can function effectively as a spiritual guide for the nine members of your company and still incarnate on

Earth to finish your own lessons.

S: It used to affect my concentration to some extent, but now there is no conflict.

Dr. N: Do you have to separate your soul energy to accomplish this?

S: Yes, this capacity (of souls) allows for the management of both. Being on Earth also permits me to directly assist a member of my company and help myself at the same time.

Dr. N: The idea that souls can divide themselves is not an easy thing for me to conceptualize.

S: Your use of the term divide is not quite accurate. Every part of us is still whole. I'm only saying it does take some getting used to at first, since you manage more than one program at a time.

Dr. N: So your effectiveness as a teacher is not diminished by having multiple activities?

S: Not in the least.

Dr. N: Would you consider the major thrust of your instruction to be on Earth with your human body or in the spirit world as a free entity?

S: They are two different settings. My instruction is diversified but no less effective.

Dr. N: But your approach to a company member would be different depending upon the setting?

S: Yes, it would.

Dr. N: Wouldn't you say the spirit world is the main center for learning?

S: It is the center for evaluation and analysis, but souls do rest.

Dr. N: When your students are living on Earth, do they know you are their guide and are with them always?

S: (laughs) Some more than others, but they all sense my influence at one time or another.

Dr. N: Thece, you are on Earth with me right now as a woman. Are you also able to be in contact with members of your company?

S: I told you, yes.

Dr. N: What I am getting at is this—isn't teaching by example diffi- cult when your Earth visits are rather infrequent these days?

S: If I came too often and worked with them directly as one human being to another I would be interfering with their natural unfolding.

Dr. N: Do you have the same reservations about interference as a teacher operating from the spirit world in a discarnate state?

S: Yes, I do … although the techniques are different.

Dr. N: For mental contact?

S: Yes.

Dr. N: I would like to know more about the ability of spiritual teachers to contact their students. What exactly do you do from the spirit world to comfort or advise one of the nine company members on Earth?

S: (no answer).

Dr. N: (coaxing her) Do you know what I am asking? How do you implant ideas?

S: (finally) I'm unable to tell you.

Note: I suspect blocking here, but I can't complain. So far, Thece has been liberal with information and so has her guide. I decide to stop the session for a minute to appeal directly to Kumara. It is a speech I have given before.

Dr. N: Kumara, permit me to reason with you through Thece. My work here is intended for good. By questioning your disciple, I wish to add to my knowledge of healing and bring people closer to the higher creative power available within themselves. My larger mis- sion is to combat the fear of death by offering people understanding about the nature of their souls and their spiritual home. Will you aid me in this endeavor?

S: (Thece answers me in an odd tone of voice) We know who you are.

Dr. N: Then would you both assist me?

S: We will talk to you … at our discretion.

Note: This tells me if I exceed the undefined boundaries of these two guides with an intrusive question, it won't be answered.

Dr. N: All right, Thece, on the count of three you will feel more comfortable talking to me about how souls function as guides. Begin by telling me in what way a company member on Earth can signal to get your attention. *One, two, three!* (I snap my fingers for added effect)

S: (after a long pause) First, they have to calm their minds and focus attention away from their immediate surroundings.

Dr. N: How would they do this?

S: By silence ... reaching inward ... to fasten on their inner voice.

Dr. N: Is this how one calls for spiritual help?

S: Yes, at least to me. They must expand upon their inner consciousness to engage me on a central thought.

Dr. N: On you, or the specific problem which is bothering them?

S: They must reach out beyond what is troubling them in order to be receptive to me. That's difficult when they don't remain calm.

Dr. N: Do all nine company members have about the same abilities to reach you for help?

S: No, they don't.

Dr. N: Perhaps Ojanowin has the most problems?

S: Mmm, she is one of those that does ...

Dr. N: Why?

S: For me, getting the signals is easy. It's harder for people on Earth. The energy of directed thought must override human emotion.

Dr. N: Within a spirit world framework, how do you pick up the messages of just your company out of billions of souls who are sending out distress signals to other guides?

S: I know instantly. All watchers do because people send out their own individual patterns of thought.

Dr. N: Like a vibrational code in a field of thought particles?

S: (laughing) You could describe an energy pattern that way, I guess.

Dr. N: Okay, then how would you reach back to someone in need of guidance?

S: (grins) By whispering answers into their ear!

Dr. N: (lightly) Is that what a friendly spirit does with a troubled mind on Earth?

S: It depends ...

Dr. N: On what? Are teacher-spirits rather indifferent with the day-to-day problems of humans?

S: Not indifferent, or we wouldn't communicate. We gauge each situation. We know life is transitory. We are more ... detached because without human bodies we are unencumbered by the immediacy of human emotion.

Dr. N: But when the situation does call for spiritual guidance, what do you do?

S: (gravely) As watchers in the stillness, we recognize the amount of ... turbulence ... from the wake of troubled thought. Then we carefully merge with it and gently touch the mind.

Dr. N: Please describe this connection process further.

S: (pause) It's a slip-stream of thought which is usually turbulent rather than smooth, from someone in distress. I was awkward at first and I still don't have Kumara's skill. One must enter with subtlety ... to wait for the best receptivity.

Dr. N: How can a watcher be awkward, you have had thousands of years of experience?

S: Communicators are not all the same. Watchers too have a variety of abilities. If one of my company is in crisis—physically hurt, sad, anxious, resentful—they send out great amounts of uncontrolled negative energy which alerts me, but exhausts them. This is the challenge of a watcher, to know when and how to communicate. When people want immediate relief, they may not be in the proper mode for reflection.

Dr. N: Well, in terms of abilities, can you tell me how you were awkward as an inexperienced guide?

S: I wanted to rush in too fast to help without coordinating the patterns of thought we talked about. People can go numb. You don't get through to them when they have intense grief, for example. You are shut out of a cluttered mind when attentions are distracted and thought energy is scattered all about.

Dr. N: Do the nine members of your company sense your intrusion into their minds following a cry to you for help?

S: Watchers are not supposed to intrude. It's more of a ... soft coupling. I implant ideas—which they assume is inspiration—to try and give them peace.

Dr. N: What single thing do you have the most problem with during communications with people on Earth?

S: Fear.

Dr. N: Would you enlarge on that?

S: I have to be careful not to spoil my people by making life too easy for them ... to let them work out most of their difficulties without jumping right in. They only suffer more if a watcher moves in too quickly before this is done. Kumara is an expert at this ...

Dr. N: Is she ultimately responsible for you and your company?

S: Well yes, we are all under her influence.

Dr. N: Do you ever see any of your own peer members around? I'm thinking of associates at your level of attainment with whom you can confer about teaching methods.

S: Oh, you mean with those I grew up with here?

Dr. N: Yes.

S: Yes ... three in particular.

Dr. N: And do they lead company groups themselves?

S: Yes.

Dr. N: Are these more advanced souls responsible for about the same number of souls as you?

S: Uh ... yes, except Wa-roo. His company is more than double my own. He is good. Another company is being added to his work load.

Dr. N: How many superior entities do you and your friends who are company leaders go to for advice and direction?

S: One. We all go to Kumara to exchange observations and seek ways of improvement.

Dr. N: How many souls like you and Wa-roo does Kumara oversee?

S: Oh … I couldn't know that …

Dr. N: Try and give an estimate of the number.

S: (after reflection) At least fifty, probably more.

Additional inquiries into Kumara's spiritual activities were fruitless, so I turned next to Thece's creation training. Her experiences (which I have condensed) take us a little further than those training exercises described by Nenthum in the last chapter. To those readers with a scientific bent, I want to stress that when a subject is reporting to me about creation their frame of reference is really not grounded in earth science. I have to make the best interpretations I can from the information provided.

Dr. N: The curriculum for souls seems to have great variety, Thece. I want to go into another aspect of your training. Does your energy utilize the properties of light, heat, and motion in the creation of life?

S: (startled) Uh … you know about that …

Dr. N: What more can you tell me?

S: Only that I am familiar with this …

Dr. N: I don't want to talk about anything which will make you uncomfortable, but I would appreciate your confirmation of certain biological effects resulting from the actions of souls.

S: (hesitates) Oh … I don't think …

Dr. N: (I jump in quickly) What creation have you recently done which makes Kumara proud of you?

S: (without resistance) I am proficient with fish.

Dr. N: (I follow up with a deliberate exaggeration to keep her going) Oh, so you can create a whole fish with your mental energy?

S: (vexed) … You must be kidding?

Dr. N: Then where *do* you start?

S: With the embryos, of course. I thought you knew …

Dr. N: Just checking. When do you think you will be ready for mammals?

S: (no answer)

Dr. N: Look Thece, if you will try to cooperate with me for a few more minutes, I promise not to take long with my questions on this subject. Will you agree to that?

S: (pause) We will see …

Dr. N: Okay, as a means of basic clarification tell me what you actually do with your energy to develop life up to the stage of fish.

S: (reluctantly) We give instructions to … organisms … within the surrounding conditions …

Dr. N: Do you do this on one world or many in your training?

S: More than one. (would not elaborate except to say these planets were "earth types")

Dr. N: In what kind of environment are you working now?

S: In oceans.

Dr. N: With basic sea life such as algae and plankton?

S: When I started.

Dr. N: You mean before you worked up to the embryos of fish?

S: Yes.

Dr. N: Then when souls start to create forms of life, they begin with microorganisms?

S: … Small cells, yes, and this is very difficult to learn.

Dr. N: Why?

S: The cells of life… our energy cannot become proficient unless we can direct it to … alter molecules.

Dr. N: Then you are actually producing new chemical compounds by mixing the basic molecular elements of life by your energy flow?

S: (nods)

Dr. N: Can you be more explicit?

S: No, I can't.

Dr. N: Let me try and sum this up, and please tell me if I am on the wrong track. A soul who becomes proficient with actually creating life must be able to split cells and give DNA instructions, and you do this by sending particles of energy into protoplasm?

S: We must learn to do this, yes—coordinating it with a sun's energy.

Dr. N: Why?

S: Because each sun has different energy effects on the worlds around them.

Dr. N: Then why would you interfere with what a sun would naturally do with its own energy on a planet?

S: It is not interference. We examine new structures ... mutations ... to watch and see what is workable. We arrange substances for their most effective use with different suns.

Dr. N: When a species of life evolves on a planet, are the environmental conditions for selection and adaptation natural, or are intelligent soul-minds tinkering with what happens?

S: (evasively) Usually a planet hospitable to life has souls watching and whatever we do is natural.

Dr. N: How can souls watch and influence biological properties of growth evolving over millions of years on a primordial world?

S: Time is not in Earth years for us. We use it to suit our experiments.

Dr. N: Do you personally create suns in our universe?

S: A full scale sun? Oh no, that's way over my head ... and requires the powers of many. I generate only on a small scale.

Dr. N: What can you generate?

S: Ah ... small bundles of highly concentrated matter ... heated.

Dr. N: But what does your work look like when you are finished?

S: Small solar systems.

Dr. N: Are your miniature suns and planets the size of rocks, buildings, the moon—what are we talking about here?

S: (laughs) My suns are the size of basketballs and the planets … marbles … that's the best I can do.

Dr. N: Why do you do this on a small scale?

S: For practice, so I can make larger suns. After enough compression the atoms explode and condense, but I can't do anything really big alone.

Dr. N: What do you mean?

S: We must learn to work together to combine our energy for the best results.

Dr. N: Well, who does the full-sized thermonuclear explosions which create physical universes and space itself?

S: The source … the concentrated energy of the Old Ones.

Dr. N: Oh, so the source has help?

S: I think so …

Dr. N: Why is your energy striving to create universal matter and more complex life when Kumara and the entities above her are already proficient?

S: We are expected to join them, just as they wish to unite their accomplished energy with the Old Ones.

Creation questions always evoke the issue of First Cause. Was the exploding interstellar mass which caused the birth of our stars and planets an accident of nature or planned by an intelligent force? When I listen to subjects such as Thece, I ask myself why souls would be practicing the chain reactions of energy matter with models on a small scale if they were not intending to make larger celestial bodies. I have had no subjects in Levels VI and above to substantiate how they might carry the forces of creation further. It would seem if souls do progress, then entities at this level could be expected to involve themselves with the birthing of planets and the development of life forms capable of higher intelligence suitable for soul use.

After pondering why less-than-perfect souls are associated with creation at all, I came to the following conclusion. All souls are given the opportunity to participate in the development of lower forms of intelligent life in order to advance themselves. This principle could also be applied to the reason why souls incarnate in physical form. Thece suggested that the supreme intelligence she calls the source is made up of a combination of creators (the Old Ones) who fuse their energy to spawn universes. The thought has been expressed to me in different ways by other subjects when they describe the combined power of non-reincarnating old souls.

This concept is not new. For instance, the idea we have no single God-head is the philosophy of the Jainist sect in India. The Jains believe fully perfected souls, called Siddhas, are a group of universal creators. These souls are fully liberated from further transmigrations. Below them are the Arhats souls, advanced illuminators who still incarnate along with three more lower gradations of evolving souls. To the Jains, reality is uncreated and eternal. Thus, the Siddhas need no creator. Most Eastern philosophies deny this tenet of Jainism in favor of a divine board of directors created by a chairman. This conclusion is more palatable to the Western mind as well.

With certain subjects it is possible to pursue a wide range of topics in condensed periods. Earlier, Thece had alluded to intelligent life existing on other worlds when she talked about a soul's cosmic training. This brings up another aspect about soul life which may be hard for some of us to accept. A small percentage of my subjects, usually the older, advanced souls, are able to recall being in strange, non-human intelligent life-forms on other worlds. Their memories are rather fleeting and clouded about the circumstances of these lives, the physical details, and planetary location relative to our universe. I wondered if Thece had any such experiences long ago, so I opened up this line of inquiry for a few minutes to see where it might lead.

> **Dr. N:** A while back you remarked about other physical worlds besides Earth which are available to souls.
>
> **S:** (hesitant) Yes …
>
> **Dr. N:** (casually) And, I assume, some of these planets support intelligent life which are useful to souls wishing to incarnate?
>
> **S:** That's true, there are many schoolyards.
>
> **Dr. N:** Do you ever talk to other souls about their planetary schoolyards?
>
> **S:** (long pause) It's not my inclination to do so—I'm not attracted to them—the other schools.

Dr. N: Perhaps you could give me some idea of what they are like?

S: Oh, some are ... analytical schools. Others are basically mental worlds ... subtle places ...

Dr. N: What do you think of the Earth school by comparison?

S: The Earth school is insecure, still. It is filled with resentment of many people over being led and antagonism of the leaders toward each other. There is so much fear to overcome here. It is a world in conflict because there is too much diversity among too many people. Other worlds have low populations with more harmony. Earth's population has outpaced its mental development.

Dr. N: Would you rather be training on another planet, then?

S: No, for all Earth's quarreling and cruelty, there is passion and bravery here. I like working in crisis situations. To bring order out of disorder. We all know Earth is a difficult school.

Dr. N: So, the human body is not an easy host for souls?

S: ... There are easier life forms ... who are less in conflict with themselves ...

Dr. N: Well, how would you know this unless your soul had been in another life form?

After I had provided this suitable opening, Thece began talking about being a small flying creature in an alien environment on a dying world where it was hard to breathe. From her descriptions, the sun of this planet was apparently going into a nova stage. Her words were halting and came in short, rapid breaths.

Thece said she lived on this world in a humid jungle with a night sky so densely packed with stars there were no dark lanes in between. This gave me the impression she was located near the center of a galaxy, perhaps our own. She also said her brief time on this world was spent as a very young soul and Kumara was her mentor. After the world could no longer support life, they had come to Earth to continue working together. I was told there was a kinship in the mental evolution of life on Earth and what she had experienced before. This flying race of people began afraid, isolated, and dangerous to each other. Also, like Earth, family alliances were important, representing expressions of loyalty and devotion. While I was concluding this line of questioning, there was a further development.

Dr. N: Do you think there are other souls on Earth who also had physical lives on this now-dead world?

S: (pause, then unable to restrain herself) Actually, I have met one.

Dr. N: Under what circumstances?

S: (laughs) I met a man at a party a while ago. He recognized me, not physically, but with the mind. It was an odd meeting. I was caught off balance when he came up to me and took my hand. I thought he was pushy when he said he knew me.

Dr. N: Then what happened?

S: (softly) I was in a daze, which is unusual for me. I *knew* there was something between us. I thought it was sexual. Now, I can see it all clearly. It was … Ikak. (this name is spoken with a clacking noise from the back of her throat) He told me we were once together from a place far away and there were a couple of others here …

Dr. N: Did he say anything more about them?

S: (faintly) No … I wonder … I ought to know them …

Dr. N: Did Ikak say anything else about your former physical relationship on this world?

S: No. He saw I was confused. I didn't know what he was talking about then anyway.

Dr. N: How could he consciously know about this planet when you didn't?

S: (puzzled) He is … ahead of me … he knows Kumara. (then, more to herself than me) What is he doing here?

Dr. N: Why don't you finish telling me about him at the party?

S: (laughs again) I thought he was just trying to pick me up. It was awkward because I was drawn to him. He said I was very attractive, which is something men don't usually say to me. There were flashes in my mind that we had been together before … as fragments in a dream sequence.

Dr. N: How did your conversation end with this man?

S: He saw my discomfort. I guess he thought it best to have no further contact, because I haven't seen him since. I've thought about him though, and maybe we will see each other again …

I believe souls do come across time and space for each other. Recently, I had two subjects who were best friends and came to me at the same time for regression. Not only had they been soulmates in many former lives on Earth, but were also mated as fish-like intelligent beings in a beautiful water world. Both recalled the enjoyment of playing underwater with their strong appendages and coming up to the surface, "to peek." Neither subject could recall much about this planet or what happened to their race of sea creatures. Perhaps they were part of a failed Earth experiment long before a land mammal developed into the most promising species on Earth for souls. I suspect it was not Earth because I have had others who tell of living in an aquatic environment they know was unearthly. One of these subjects said, "My water world was very warm and clear because we had three suns overhead. The total lack of darkness underwater was comforting and made building our dwellings much easier." I have often wondered if the dreams we have at night about flying, breathing underwater, and performing other non-human physical feats relate to our earlier physical experiences in other environments.

In the early days of my studies of souls, I half-expected that those subjects who could recall other worlds would say they had lived in our galaxy within the neighborhood of the sun. This assumption was naive. Earth is in a sparse section of the Milky Way with only eight stars that are ten light years from the sun. We know our own galaxy has more than two-hundred billion stars within a universe currently speculated at one-hundred-billion galaxies. The worlds around the suns which might support life are staggering to the imagination. Consider, if only a small fraction of one percent of the stars in our galaxy had planets with intelligent life useful to souls, the number would still be in the millions.

From what I can gather from subjects willing and able to discuss former assignments, souls are sent to any world with suitable intelligent life forms. Out of all the stars which are known to us, only four percent are like our sun. Apparently this means nothing to souls. Their planetary incarnations are not linked to Earth-type worlds or with intelligent bipeds who walk on land. Souls who have been to other worlds tell me they have a fondness for certain ones and return to them (like Earth) periodically for a succession of lives. I have not had many subjects who are able to recall specific details about living on other worlds. This may be due to lack of experience, a suppression of memory, or blocks imposed by master guides to avoid any discomfort from flashbacks in non-earthly bodies.

Those subjects who are able to discuss their experiences on other worlds tell me that before coming to Earth, souls are frequently placed in the bodies of creatures with less intelligence than human beings (unlike Thece's case). However, once in a human body, souls are not sent back down the mental evolutionary ladder. Yet, physical contrasts can be stark and side trips away from Earth are not necessarily pleasant. One mid-level client of mine expressed it this way. "After a long series of human lives, I told my guide I needed a break from Earth for a while in another kind of environment. He warned me, 'You might not like this change right now because you have become so accustomed to the attributes of the human mind and body.'" My client persisted and was duly given life on what was described as, "A pastel world living among a race of small, thickly-set beings. They were a thoughtful but somber people with tiny chalk-white faces which never smiled. Without human laughter and physical flexibility, I was out of sync and made little progress." The assignment must have been particularly difficult for this individual when we consider that humor and laughter is such a hallmark of soul life in the spirit world.

I was now approaching the final phase of my session with Case 23. It was necessary to apply additional deepening techniques because I wanted Thece to reach into the highest recesses of her superconscious mind to talk with me about space-time and the source.

Dr. N: Thece, we are coming to the end of our time together and I want you to turn your mind once again to the source-creator. (pause) Will you do that for me?

S: Yes.

Dr. N: You said the ultimate objective of souls was to seek unification with the supreme source of creative energy—do you remember?

S: … The act of conjunction, yes.

Dr. N: Tell me, does the source dwell in some special central space in the spirit world?

S: The source *is* the spirit world.

Dr. N: Then why do souls speak of reaching a core of spiritual life?

S: When we are young spirits we sense power around us everywhere and yet we feel we … are on the edge of it. As we grow older there is an awareness of a concentrated power, but it is the same feeling.

Dr. N: Even though you have called this the place of the Old Ones?

S: Yes, they are part of the concentrated power of the source which sustains us as souls.

Dr. N: Well, lumping this power together as one energy source, can you describe the creator in more human terms?

S: As the ultimate selfless being which we strive to be.

Dr. N: If the source represents all the spirit world, how does this mental place differ from physical universes with stars, planets, and living things?

S: Universes are created—to live and die—for the use of the source. The place of spirits … is the source.

Dr. N: We seem to live in a universe which is expanding and may contract again and eventually die. Since we live in a space with time limitations, how can the spirit world itself be timeless?

S: Because here we live in non-space which is timeless … except in certain zones.

Dr. N: Please explain what these zones are.

S: They are … interconnecting doors … openings for us to pass through into a physical universe of time.

Dr. N: How can time-doors exist in non-space?

S: The openings exist as thresholds between realities.

Dr. N: Well, if the spirit world is non-dimensional, what kind of reality is that?

S: A constant reality state, as opposed to the shifting realities of dimensional worlds which are material and changing.

Dr. N: Do past, present, and future have any relevance for souls living in the spirit world?

S: Only as a means of understanding succession in physical form.

Living here … there is a … changelessness … for those of us not crossing thresholds into a universe of substance and time.

Note: A major application of time thresholds used by souls will be examined in the upcoming chapter on life selection.

Dr. N: You speak of universes in the plural. Are these other physical universes besides the one which contains Earth?

S: (vaguely) There are … differing realities to suit the source.

Dr. N: Are you saying souls can enter various rooms of different physical realities from spiritual doorways?

S: (nods) Yes, they can—and do.

Before concluding the session with this highly advanced subject, I should add that most people who are in deep hypnosis are able to see beyond an Earth reality of three-dimensional space, into alternate realities of timelessness. In the subconscious state, my subjects experience a chronology of time with their past and present lives which resembles what they perceive when conscious. There is a change when I take them into superconsciousness and the spirit world. Here they see the *now* of time as one homogeneous unit of past, present, and future. Seconds in the spirit world seem to represent years on Earth. When their sessions are over, clients will often express surprise at how time in the spirit world is unified.

Quantum mechanics is a modern branch of physics which investigates all subatomic movement in terms of electromagnetic energy levels where all things in life are thought to be ultimately non-solid and existing in a unified field. Going beyond Newton's physical laws of gravity, the elements of action on time are also considered to be unified by light wave frequency and kinetic energy. Since I show that souls do experience feelings of the passage of time in a chronological fashion in the spirit world, doesn't this contradict the concept of oneness for past, present, and future? No, it does not. My research indicates to me that the illusion of time progression is created and sustained for those souls coming to and from physical dimensions (who are used to such biological responses as aging), so they may more easily gauge their advancement. Thus, it makes sense to me when the quantum physicists hypothesize that time, rather than being an absolute of three phases, is only an expression of change.

When my subjects speak of traveling as souls on lines which curve, I think of the space-time theories of those astrophysicists who believe light and motion are a union of time and space curving back on itself. They say if space is bent severely enough, time stops. Indeed, when listening to my clients talk about time zones and tunnels of passage into different dimensions, I think about the similarities here to current astronomical theories of physical space being warped, or twisted, into cosmic loops creating "mouths" of hyperspace and black holes which may lead out of our three-dimensional universe. Perhaps the space-time concepts of astrophysics and metaphysics are edging closer together.

I have suggested to my subjects that if the spirit world seems round to them, and appears to curve when they travel rapidly as souls, this could represent a finite, enclosed sphere. They deny the idea of any dimensional boundaries yet offer me little else except metaphors. Case 23 says the spirit world itself is the source of creation. Some have called this place the heart, or breath, of God. Case 22 defined the space of souls as "fabric" and I have had other subjects give the spirit world a quality of "the folds of a seamless dress swishing back and forth." They sometimes feel the effects of a gently "rippling" motion from light energy which has been described as "waves (or rings) rolling outward from a disturbed pool of water." Normally, the geography of soul spaces has a smooth and open consistency to people in superconsciousness, without displaying the properties of gravity, temperature, pressure, matter, or a time clock associated with a chaotic physical universe. However, when I attempt to characterize the entire spirit world as a void, people in trance resist this notion.

Although my cases are unable to fully explain the place where their souls live, they are all outspoken about its ultimate reality for them. A subject in trance doesn't see the spirit world as being either near or far away from our physical universe. Nevertheless, in a curious way, they do portray spiritual *substance* as being light or heavy, thick or thin, and large or small, when comparing their experiences as souls to life on Earth.

While the absolute reality of the spirit world appears to remain constant in the minds of people in hypnosis, their references to other physical dimensions do not. I have the sense that universes other than our own are created for the purpose of providing environments suitable for the growth of souls with beings we can't even imagine. One advanced subject told me he had lived on a number of worlds in his long existence, never dividing his soul more than twice at one time. Some adult lives lasted only months in Earth time for him, due to local planetary conditions and short life spans of the dominant life form. While speaking of a "paradise planet," with few people and a quieter, simpler version of Earth, he added this world was not far from Earth. "Oh," I interrupted, "then it must only be a few light years from Earth?" He patiently explained that the planet was not in our universe, but closer to Earth than many planets in our own galaxy.

It is important for the reader to understand that when people do recall living on other worlds they seem not to be limited by the dimensional constraints of our universe. When souls travel to planets intergalactically or interdimensionally, they measure the trip by the time it takes them to reach their destinations through the tunnel effect from the spirit world. The size of the spatial region involved and the relative position of worlds to each other are also considerations. After listening to references about multiple dimensional realities from some of my subjects, I am left with the impression they believe there is a confluence of all these dimensional streams into one great river of the spirit world. If I could stand back and take apart all these alternate realities seated in the minds of my cases, it would be like peeling an artichoke of all its layers down to one heart at the core.

I had been questioning Thece for quite a while and I could see she was growing tired. Few subjects can sustain this level of spiritual receptivity for very long. I decided to end the session with a few questions about the genesis of all creation.

Dr. N: Thece, I want to close by asking you more about the source. You have been a soul for a long time, so how do you see yourself relating to the oneness of creation you told me about earlier?

S: (long pause) By sensations of movement. In the beginning there is an outward migration of our soul energy from the source. Afterward, our lives are spent moving inward … toward cohesion and the uniting …

Dr. N: You make this process seem as though a living organism was expanding and contracting.

S: … There is an explosive release … then a returning … yes, the source pulsates.

Dr. N: And you are moving toward the center of this energy source?

S: There really is no center. The source is all around us as if we were … inside a beating heart.

Dr. N: But, you did say you were moving back to a point of origin as your soul advanced in knowledge?

S: Yes, when I was thrust outward I was a child. Now I'm being drawn back as my adolescence fades ...

Dr. N: Back where?

S: Further inside the source.

Dr. N: Perhaps you could describe this energy source through the use of colors to explain soul movement and the scope of creation.

S: (sighs) It's as if souls are all part of a massive electrical explosion which produces ... a halo effect. In this ... circular halo is a dark purple light which flares out ... lightening to a whiteness at the edges. Our awareness begins at the edges of brilliant light and as we grow ... we become more engulfed in the darker light.

Dr. N: I find it hard to visualize a god of creation as cold, dark light.

S: That's because I am not close enough to conjunction to explain it well. The dark light is itself a ... covering, beyond which we feel an intense warmth ... full of a knowing presence which is everywhere for us and ... alive!

Dr. N: What was it like when you were first aware of your identity as a soul after being pushed out to the rim of this halo?

S: To be ... is the same as watching the first flower of spring open and the flower is you. And, as it opens more, you become aware of other flowers in a glorious field and there is ... unbounded joy.

Dr. N: If this explosive, multi-colored energy source collapses in on itself, will all the flowers eventually die?

S: Nothing is collapsing ... the source is endless. As souls we will never die—we know that, somehow. As we coalesce, our increasing wisdom makes the source stronger.

Dr. N: Is that the reason the source desires to perform this exercise?

S: Yes, to give life to us so we can arrive at a state of perfection.

Dr. N: Why does a source, who is ostensibly perfect already, need to create further intelligence which is *less* than perfect?

S: To help the creator create. In this way, by self-transformation and rising to higher plateaus of fulfillment, we add to the building blocks of life.

Dr. N: Were souls forced to break away from the source and come to places like Earth because of some sort of original sin or fall from grace in the spirit world?

S: That's nonsense. We came to be ... magnified ... in the beautiful variety of creation.

Dr. N: Thece, I want you to listen to me carefully. If the source needs to be made stronger, or more wise, by using a division of its divine energy to create lesser intelligence which it hopes will magnify—doesn't this suggest it lacks full perfection itself?

S: (pause) The source creates for fulfillment of itself.

Dr. N: That's my point. How can that which is absolute become more absolute unless something is lacking?

S: (hesitates) That which we see to be ... our source ... is all we can know, and we think what the creator desires is to *express* itself through us by ... birthing.

Dr. N: And do you think the source is actually made stronger by our existence as souls?

S: (long pause) I see the creator's perfection ... maintained and enriched ... by sharing the possibility of perfection with us and this is the ultimate extension of itself.

Dr. N: So the source starts out by deliberately creating imperfect souls and imperfect life forms for these souls and watches what happens in order to extend itself?

S: Yes, and we have to have faith in this decision and trust the process of returning to the origin of life. One has to be starving to appreciate food, to be cold to understand the blessings of warmth, and to be children to see the value of the parent. The transformation gives us purpose.

Dr. N: Do you want to be a parent of souls?

S: ... Participation in the conception of ourselves is ... a dream of mine.

Dr. N: If our spirits did not experience physical life, would we ever know of these things you are telling me about?

S: We would know of them, but not about them. It would be as if your spiritual energy were told to play piano scales with only one note.

Dr. N: And do you believe if the source didn't create souls to nurture and grow, its sublime energy would shrink from a lack of expression?

S: (sighs) Perhaps that is its purpose.

With this last prophetic statement by Thece, I ended the session. As I brought this subject out of her deep trance, it was as though she were returning to me from across time and space. As she sat quietly focusing her eyes around my office, I expressed my appreciation for the opportunity of working with her on such an advanced level. Smiling, the lady said if she had any idea of the grilling in store for her, she might well have refused to work with me.

As we said goodbye, I thought about her last statements concerning the source of life. In ancient Persia the Sufis had a saying that if the creator represents absolute good, and therefore absolute beauty, it is the nature of beauty to desire manifestation.

12

Life Selection

 THERE comes that time when the soul must once again leave the sanctuary of the spirit world for another trip to Earth. This decision is not an easy one. Souls must prepare to leave a world of total wisdom, where they exist in a blissful state of freedom, for the physical and mental demands of a human body.

We have seen how tired souls can be when reentering the spirit world. Many don't want to think about returning to Earth again. This is especially true when we have not come close to our goals at the end of a physical life. Once back in the spirit world, souls have misgivings about even temporarily leaving a world of self-understanding, comradeship, and compassion to go to a planetary environment of uncertainty and fear brought about by aggressive, competing humans. Despite having family and friends on Earth, many incarnated souls feel lonely and anonymous among large impersonal populations. I hope my cases show the opposite is true in the spirit world, where our souls are involved in the most intimate sharing on an everlasting basis. Our spiritual identity is known and appreciated by a multitude of other entities, whose support is never ending.

The rejuvenation of our energy and personal assessment of one's Self takes longer for some souls than others, but eventually the soul is motivated to start the process of incarnation. While our spiritual environment is hard to leave, as souls we also remember the physical pleasures of life on Earth with fondness and even nostalgia. When the wounds of a past life are healed and we are again totally at one with ourselves, we feel the pull of having a physical expression for our identity. Training sessions with our counselors and peer groups have provided a collaborative spiritual effort to prepare us for the next life. Our karma of past deeds towards humanity and our mistakes and achievements have all been evaluated with an eye toward the best course of future endeavors. The soul must now assimilate all this information and take purposeful action based upon three primary decisions:

- Am I ready for a new physical life?

- What specific lessons do I want to undertake to advance my learning and development?

- Where should I go, and who shall I be in my next life for the best opportunity to work on my goals?

Older souls incarnate less, regardless of the population demands of their assigned planets. When a world dies, those entities with unfinished business move on to another world which has a suitable life form for the kind of work they have been doing. Cycles of incarnation for the eternal soul seem to be regulated more by the internal desires of a particular soul, than by the urgency of host bodies evolving in a universe of planets.

Nevertheless, Earth certainly has an increasing need for souls. Today, we have over five billion people. Demographers vary in their calculations on how many individuals have lived on Earth in the last 200,000 years. The average estimate is some 50 billion people. This figure, which I think is low, does not signify the number of visitations by different souls. Bear in mind the same souls continue to reincarnate, and there are those who occupy more than one body at a time. There are reincarnationists who believe the number of people living on Earth today is close to the total number of souls who ever lived here. The frequency of incarnation on Earth by souls is uneven. Earth clearly has more need for souls today than in the past. Population estimates in 1 AD are around 200 million. By 1800, humans had quadrupled, and after only 170 more years, quadrupled again. Between 1970 and 2010, the world's population is expected to double once more.

When I study the incarnation chronology of a client, I find there is usually a long span of hundreds, even thousands, of years between their lives in Paleolithic nomadic cultures. With the introduction of agriculture and domesticated animals in the Neolithic Age, from 7,000 to 5,000 years ago, my subjects report living more frequent lives. Still, their lives are often spaced as much as 500 years apart. With the rise of cities, trade, and more available food, I see the incarnation schedules of souls increasing with a growing population. Between 1000 and 1500 AD, my clients live an average of once in two centuries. After 1700, this changes to once in a century. By the 1900s, living more than one life in a century is common among my cases.

It has been argued these increases in soul incarnations only appear to be so because past life recall improves as people in hypnosis get closer to their current lives. This may be true to some extent, but if a life is important it will be vividly remembered at any age in time. Without doubt, the enormous population increase on Earth is the basic cause for souls coming here more often. Is there a possibility that the inventory of souls slated for Earth could be strained by this surge in human reproduction?

When I ask clients about the inventory of available souls, they tell me I should worry more about our planet dying from over-population than exhausting the reserve of souls. There is the conviction that new souls are always available to fill any expanding population requirements. If our planet is just one example among all other intelligent populations which exist in this universe, the inventory of souls must truly be astronomical.

I have said souls do have the freedom to choose when, where, and who they want to be in their physical lives. Certain souls spend less time in the spirit world in order to accelerate development, while others are very reluctant to leave. There is no question but what our guides exert great influence in this matter. Just as we were given an intake interview in the orientation phase right after death, there are preparatory exit interviews by spiritual advisors to determine our readiness for rebirth. The case which follows illustrates a typical spiritual scene with a lower-level soul.

⇤ Case 24 ⇥

Dr. N: When do you first realize that you might be returning to Earth?

S: A soft voice comes into my mind and says, "It's about time, don't you think?"

Dr. N: Who is this voice?

S: My instructor. Some of us have to be given a push when they think we are ready again.

Dr. N: Do you feel you are about ready to return to Earth?

S: Yes, I think so … I have prepared for it. But my studies are going to take such a long time in earth years before I'm done. It's kind of overwhelming.

Dr. N: And do you think you will still be going to Earth when you near the end of your incarnations?

S: (long pause) Ah … maybe no … there is another world besides Earth … but with Earth people …

Dr. N: What does this mean?

S: Earth will have fewer people … less crowded … it's not clear to me.

Dr. N: Where do you think you might be then?

S: I'm getting the impression there is colonization someplace else— it's not clear to me.

Note: The opposite of past life regression is post life progression, which enables some subjects to see snatches of the future as incomplete scenes. For instance, some have told me Earth's population will be greatly reduced by the end of the twenty-second century, partially due to adverse soil and atmospheric changes. They also see people living in odd-looking domed buildings. Details about the future are always rather limited, due, I suspect, to built-in amnesia from karmic constraints. I'll have more to say about this with the next case.

Dr. N: Let's go back to what you were saying about the instructors giving people a push to leave the spirit world. Would you prefer that they not do this?

S: Oh … I'd like to stay … but the instructors don't want us hanging around here too long or we will get into a rut.

Dr. N: Could you insist on staying?

S: Well … yes … the instructors don't force you to leave because they are so gentle. (laughs) But they have their ways of … encouraging you when the time comes.

Dr. N: Do you know of anyone who didn't want to be reborn again on Earth for any reason?

S: Yes, my friend Mark. He said he had nothing to contribute anymore. He was sick of life on Earth and didn't want to go back.

Dr. N: Had he lived many lives?

S: No, not really. But he wasn't adjusting well in them.

Dr. N: What did the teachers do with him? Was he allowed to stay in the spirit world?

S: (reflectively) We choose to be reborn when it is decided we are ready. They don't force you to do anything. Mark was shown he did benefit others around him.

Dr. N: What happened to Mark?

S: After some more … indoctrination … Mark realized he had been wrong about his abilities and finally he went back to Earth.

Dr. N: Indoctrination! This makes me think of coercion.

S: (disturbed by my remark) It's not that way at all! Mark was just discouraged, and needed the confidence to keep trying.

Note: Case 10 in Chapter Four on displaced souls told us about how souls who had absorbed too much negative energy from Earth were "remodeled." Case 22 also mentioned the need for restoration with some damaged souls. These are more extreme alterations than the basic reframing apparently used on Mark's tired soul.

Dr. N: If the guides don't force you, could a soul absolutely refuse to be reborn?

S: (pause) Yes … I guess you could stay here and never be reborn if you hated it that much. But the instructors told Mark that without life in a body, his studies would take longer. If you lose having direct experience, you miss a great deal.

Dr. N: How about the reverse situation where a soul insists on returning to Earth immediately, say after an untimely death?

S: I have seen that, too. It's an impulsive reaction and does wear off after a while. The instructors get you to see that wanting to hurry back someplace as a new baby wouldn't change the circumstances of your death. It might be different if you could be reborn as an adult right away in the same situation. Eventually, everyone realizes they must rest and reflect.

Dr. N: Well, give me your final thoughts about the prospect of living again.

S: I'm excited about it. I would have no satisfaction without my physical lives.

Dr. N: When you are ready for a new incarnation, what do you do?

S: I go to a special place.

Once a soul has decided to incarnate again, the next stage in the return process is to be directed to the place of life selection. Souls consider when and where they want to go on Earth before making a decision on who they will be in their new life. Because of this spiritual practice, I have divided life selection and our final choice of a body into two chapters for ease of understanding.

The selection of a time and place for incarnation and who we want to be are not completely separate decisions. However, we start by having the opportunity of viewing how we might fit into certain environments in future time segments. Then our attention is directed to people living in these places. I was a little distracted by this procedure until I realized a soul is largely influenced by cultural conditions and events, as well as by the participants in these events, during a span of chronological time.

I have come to believe that the spirit world, as a whole, is not functionally uniform. All spiritual regions are seen by traveling souls as having the same ethereal properties, but with different applications. As an illustration, the space of orientation for incoming souls could be contrasted to the space of life selection for those who are leaving. Both involve life evaluations for souls in transit which include scenes from Earth, but there the resemblance ends. Orientation spaces are said to be small, intimate conference areas designed to make a newly arrived soul comfortable, but our mental attitude in this space can be somewhat defensive. This is because there is the feeling we might have done better with life. A guide is always directly interacting with us.

On the other hand, when we enter the space of life selection, we are full of hope, promise, and lofty expectations. Here souls are virtually alone, with their guides out of sight, while evaluating new life options. This hectic, stimulating place is described as being much larger than other spiritual study areas. Case 22 considered it a world unto itself, where transcendent energy alters time to allow for planetary study.

While some spiritual locales are difficult for my subjects to describe, most love to talk about the place of life selection, and they use remarkably similar descriptions. I am told it resembles a movie theater which allows souls to see themselves in the future, playing different roles in various settings. Before leaving, souls will have selected one scenario for themselves. Imagine being given a dress rehearsal before the actual performance of a new life. To tell us about it, I have picked a male subject who is well acquainted with the way his soul is assisted in making appropriate decisions.

⇤ Case 25 ⇥

Dr. N: After you have made the decision you want to come back to Earth, what happens next?

S: Well, when my trainer and I agree the time is right to accomplish things, I send out thoughts ...

Dr. N: Go on.

S: My messages are received by the coordinators.

Dr. N: Who are they? Doesn't your trainer-guide handle all the arrangements for incarnation?

S: Not exactly. He talks to the coordinators, who actually assist us in previewing our life possibilities at the Ring.

Dr. N: What is the Ring?

S: That's where I'm going. We call it the Ring of Destiny.

Dr. N: Is there just one place like it in the spirit world?

S: (pause) Oh, I think there must be many, but I don't see them.

Dr. N: All right, let's go to the Ring together on the count of three. When I am finished with my count you will have the capacity to remember all the details of this experience. Are you ready to go?

S: Yes.

Dr. N: *One, two, three!* Your soul is now moving toward the space of life selection. Explain what you see.

S: (long pause) I ... am floating towards the Ring ... it's circular ... a monster bubble ...

Dr. N: Keep going. What else can you tell me.

S: There is a … concentrated energy force … the light is so intense. I'm being sucked inward … through a funnel … it's a little darker.

Dr. N: Are you afraid?

S: Hmm … no, I've been here before, after all. It's going to be interesting. I'm excited at what's in store for me.

Dr. N: Okay, as you float inside the Ring, what are your first impressions?

S: (voice lowers) I … am a little apprehensive … but the energy relaxes me. I have an awareness of concern for me … caring … I don't feel alone … my trainer's presence is with me, too.

Dr. N: Continue to report everything. What do you see next?

S: The Ring is surrounded by banks of screens—I am looking at them.

Dr. N: Screens on walls?   .

S: They appear as walls themselves, but nothing is really solid … it's all … elastic … the screens curve around me … moving …

Dr. N: Tell me more about the screens.

S: They are blank … not reflecting anything yet … they shimmer as sheets of glass … mirrors.

Dr. N: What happens next?

S: (nervously) I feel a moment of quietness—it's always like this— then it's as if someone flipped a switch on the projector in a panorama movie theater. The screens come alive with images and there is color … action … full of light and sound.

Dr. N: Keep reporting to me. Where is your soul in relation to the screens?

S: I am hovering in the middle, watching the panorama of life all around me … places … people …(jauntily) I *know* this city!

Dr. N: What do you see?

S: New York.

Dr. N: Did you ask to see New York City?

S: We talked about my going back there … (absorbed) Gee—it's changed—more buildings … and the cars … it's as noisy as ever.

Dr. N: I'll come back to New York in a few minutes. Right now I want you to tell me what is expected of you in the Ring.

S: I'm going to mentally operate the panel.

Dr. N: What's that?

S: A scanning device in front of the screens. I see it as a mass of lights and buttons. It's as if I'm in the cockpit of an airplane.

Dr. N: And you see these mechanical objects in a spiritual setting?

S: I know it sounds crazy, but this is what is coming through to me so I can explain to you what I am doing.

Dr. N: That's fine, don't worry about it. Just tell me what you are supposed to do with the panel.

S: I will help the controllers change the images on the screens by operating the scanner with my mind.

Dr. N: Oh, you are going to operate the projector as if you were working in a movie theater?

S: (laughs) Not the projector, the scanner. Anyway, they aren't really movies. I am watching life actually going on in the streets of New York. My mind connects with the scanner to control the movement of the scenes I am watching.

Dr. N: Would you say this device resembles a computer?

S: Sort of … it works on a tracking system which … converts …

Dr. N: Converts what?

S: My commands … are registered on the panel so I can track the action.

Dr. N: Position yourself at the panel and become the operator while continuing to explain everything to me.

S: (pause) I have assumed control. I see … lines converging along various points in a series of scenes … I'm traveling through time now on the lines and watching the images on the screens change.

Dr. N: And the scenes are constantly moving around you?

S: Yes, then the points light up on the lines when I want the scene to stop.

Note: Lines of travel is a term we have heard before in other spiritual regions to describe soul transition (i.e., Case 14).

Dr. N: Why are you doing all this?

S: I'm scanning. The stops are major turning points on life's pathways involving important decisions … possibilities … events which make it necessary to consider alternate choices in time.

Dr. N: So, the lines mark the pathways through a series of events in time and space?

S: Yes, the track is controlled in the Ring and transmitted to me.

Dr. N: Do you create the scenes of life while you track?

S: Oh, no! I simply control their movement through time on the lines.

Dr. N: What else can you tell me about the lines?

S: The lines of energy are … roads with points of colored light as guideposts which I can move forward, backward, or stop.

Dr. N: As if you were running a video tape with start, fast-forward, stop, and rewind buttons?

S: (laughs) That's the idea.

Dr. N: All right, you are moving along the track, scanning scenes and you decide to stop. Tell me what you do then.

S: I suspend the scene on the screens so I can enter it.

Dr. N: What? Are you saying you become part of the scene yourself?

S: Yes, now I have direct access to the action.

Dr. N: In what way? Do you become a person in the scene, or does your soul hover overhead while people move around?

S: Both. I can experience what life is like with anyone in the scene, or just watch them from any vantage point.

Dr. N: How can you leave the panel and go into a scene on Earth while still monitoring the action in the Ring?

S: I know you probably won't understand this, but part of me stays at the controls so I can start up the scene again and stop it anytime.

Dr. N: Perhaps I do understand. Can you divide your energy?

S: Yes, and I can send thoughts back to myself. Of course, the controllers are helping too, as I go in and out of the screens.

Dr. N: So, essentially you can move time forward, backward, and stop it while tracking?

S: Yes … in the Ring.

Dr. N: Outside the Ring, does time co-exist for you in the spirit world, or is it progressive?

S: It co-exists here, but we can still see it progress on Earth.

Dr. N: It seems to me when souls are in the Ring of Destiny they use time almost like a tool.

S: As spirits, we do use time … subjectively. Things and events are moved around … and become objects in time … but to us time is uniform.

Dr. N: The paradox I have with time travel is that what is going to happen has already happened, so you could meet your own soul in some human being as you come and go in life scenes from the future.

S: (smiles enigmatically) When making contact the soul in residence is put on hold for a moment. It's relatively short. We don't disturb life cycles when tracking through time.

Dr. N: Well, if past, present, and future are not really separate while you are tracking, why do you stop scenes to consider choices when you can already see into the future?

S: I'm afraid you don't realize the real purpose of time use by the controllers of the Ring. Life is still conditional. Progressive time is created to test us. We are not shown all the possible endings to a scene. Parts of lives are obscured to us.

Dr. N: So, time is used as a catalyst for learning by viewing lives when you can't see everything that is going to happen?

S: Yes, to test our ability to find solutions. We gauge our abilities against the difficulty of the events. The Ring sets up different experiments to choose from. On Earth we will try to solve them.

Dr. N: In the Ring, can you look at life on planets besides Earth?

S: I can't because I'm programmed for tracking time on Earth.

Dr. N: Your being able to jump through time from the screens sounds like a ball!

S: (grins) Oh, it's stimulating—that's for sure—but we can't frolic around, because there are serious decisions to be made for the next life. I'll have to accept the consequences for any mistakes in my choices … if I am not able to handle a life well.

Dr. N: I still don't see how you could make many serious mistakes in your choices when you actually experience part of the life in which you plan to live.

S: My choices of life environments are not unlimited. As I said, I probably won't be able to see all of a scene in one time segment. Because of what they don't show you, there is risk attached to all body choices.

Dr. N: If one's future destiny is not fully preordained, as you say, why call this space the Ring of Destiny?

S: Oh, there is destiny, all right. The life cycles are in place. It's just that there are so many alternatives which are unclear.

When I take my subjects into the spatial area of life selection, they see a circle of past, present and future time—such as the Ring in this case. Sensing they are leaving spiritual *Now* time within the circle, souls apparently rotate back and forth on resonating waves during their observational runs. All aspects of time are presented to them as reoccurring realities ebbing and flowing together. Because parallel realities are superimposed upon one another, they too can be seen as possibilities for physical lives, especially by the more experienced souls.

I was puzzled why my subjects did not fully see the future under these conditions, as part of an all-knowing spiritual setting. In trying to sort this out, I finally came to the conclusion that the spirit world is designed to protect the interests of each soul. Generally, the people I work with are still incarnating younger souls. They may not clearly see significant events too far into the future because the further away these souls get from present probabilities, the higher the incidence of possible alternative realities which cloud their images. Although the same properties hold true for time in the distant past, there is one exception. A soul's own past lives are more easily identified. This is because a single reality, with a definite course of action, was previously established to train this soul, and thus is firmly imprinted on his memory.

In Chapter Five, Case 13 demonstrated how amnesia is imposed upon us when we come into a current life, so that past life experiences will not inhibit self-discovery in the present. The same condition holds true for souls examining future lives. Without knowing why, most people believe their life has a plan. Of course, they are right. Although amnesia does prevent having full conscious knowledge of this plan, the unconscious mind holds the key to spiritual memories of a general blueprint of each life. The vehicle of life selection provides a kind of time machine for souls, where they see some alternative routes to the main road. Although these paths are not fully exposed to us as souls, we carry some of the road map to Earth. A client once said to me, "Whenever I am confused about what to do in life, I quietly sit down and think about where I have been and compare this to where I might want to go in future. The answer to the next step just comes to me from inside myself."

Accepting what befalls us on the road of life as "acts of God" does not mean our existence should be locked into spiritual determinism where we must submit to an unalterable fate. If everything was preordained, there would be no purpose or justice to our struggle. When adversity strikes, it is not intended that we sit back with a fatalistic attitude and not fight to improve the situation by making on-site changes. During our lives all of us will experience opportunities for change which involve risk. These occasions may come at inconvenient times. We may not act upon them, but the challenge is there for us. The purpose of reincarnation is the exercise of free will. Without this ability, we would be impotent creatures indeed.

Thus, karmic destiny means we are not just caught up in events over which we have no control. This also means we have karmic lessons and responsibilities. The law of cause and effect for our actions always exists, which is why this case did not want to make a mistake in choosing a life unsuited to him. But whatever happens to us in life, it is important we understand that our happiness or pain does not reflect either blessings or betrayal on the part of a God-oversoul, our guides, or life selection coordinators. We are the masters of our destiny.

As I conclude my conversation with Case 25, it may strike the reader that the musical goals of this individual toward his next life are rather self-serving. Certainly his desire to be an admired musical talent has elements of personal compensation which would be less evident in a more advanced soul. However, it will also be seen that this soul wants to give a lot of himself.

> **Dr. N:** Now, I want to talk more about the scenes you are seeing of New York City. Prior to your coming into the Ring, were you given any preparation about selections based on geography?
>
> **S:** Oh, to some extent. My trainer and I talked about the fact that I had died young in New York in my last life. I wanted to go back to this dynamic city and study music.
>
> **Dr. N:** Did you also talk to your trainer about other souls—your friends, who might want to incarnate with you?
>
> **S:** Sure, that's part of it. Some of us begin staking out a new life by deciding what surroundings are best for all concerned. I made it known I wanted to start again in the same place where I was killed. My trainer and friends offered their suggestions.

Note: This subject came to America as a Russian immigrant in his past life. He was killed in a railway construction accident in New York at age twenty-two in 1898. His rebirth in the same city occurred in 1937.

> **Dr. N:** What suggestions?
>
> **S:** We talked about my wanting to be a classical pianist. I had played an accordion for extra pick-up change—you know, banquets, weddings—that kind of thing.
>
> **Dr. N:** And this experience is motivating your interest in the piano?
>
> **S:** Yes. When making ice deliveries on the streets of New York, I would pass by the concert hall. It was my goal to some day study music and make a name for myself in the big city. I hardly got started before I died.

Dr. N: Did you see your death as a young man in New York during your last visit to the Ring?

S: (sadly) Yes … and I accepted that … as a condition of the life. It was a good life—just short. Now I want to go back with a better start and make a name for myself in music.

Dr. N: Could you ask to go anywhere on Earth?

S: Hmm … it's fairly open. If we have preferences, they are weighed against what's available.

Dr. N: You mean, against what bodies are available?

S: Yes, in certain places.

Dr. N: When you said you wanted a better start in music, I assume this is another reason you want to go back to New York.

S: This city will give me the best opportunity to develop my desire to study the piano. I wanted a large, cosmopolitan city with music schools.

Dr. N: What's wrong with a city like Paris?

S: I wasn't offered a body in Paris.

Dr. N: I want to be clear on your selection options. When you start previewing life scenes in the Ring, are you primarily looking at people or locations?

S: We begin with locations.

Dr. N: Okay, and so you are looking at the streets of New York City at the moment?

S: Right, and it's wonderful because I am doing more than looking. I'm floating around smelling the food in the restaurants … I hear the honking of cars … I'm following people walking past the shops on Fifth Avenue … getting the feel of the place again.

Dr. N: At this point have you actually entered the minds of the people walking along the streets?

S: No, not yet.

Dr. N: What do you do next?

S: I go to other cities.

Dr. N: Oh, I guess I just assumed your body choices had to be in New York City.

S: I didn't tell you that. I also could go to Los Angeles, Buenos Aires, or Oslo.

Dr. N: I'm going to count to five and when I reach five you will scan these cities while we continue talking … *one … two … three … four … five!* Report what you are doing.

S: I'm going to concert halls and music academies and watching the students practice.

Dr. N: Do you just observe the general surroundings while floating around these students?

S: I do more. I go inside the heads of some of them to see how they … translate the music.

Dr. N: Do you need to be in a special place like the Ring to examine the mental processes of people?

S: For past and future events I do. Making contact with someone in the present on Earth can be done anywhere (from the spirit world).

Dr. N: Could you describe the way your soul makes contact with someone?

S: (pause) As … a light brush stroke.

Note: Souls are quite capable of sending and receiving messages from each other between spiritual and temporal worlds, as many of us have personally experienced. However, these temporary connections are made and broken quickly. The joining of a soul to a soulless baby for a lifetime is more difficult, and will be described further in Case 29.

Dr. N: As you look at these prospective lives, what year is it on Earth?

S: (hesitates) It's … 1956 now, and most of my prospects are in their teens. I'll check them out before and after this year … as much as the Ring will let me.

Dr. N: So the Ring gives you the opportunity to actually *be* various people who, in relative time on Earth, are not yet born?

S: Uh-huh, to see if I would fit in well—to check out their talent and parents   that sort of thing. (decisively) I want New York.

Dr. N: Do you think you have looked at the other cities carefully enough?

S: (impatiently) Yes, I did that, but I don't want them.

Dr. N: Wait a minute. What if you liked a music student in Oslo, but wanted to live in New York City?

S: (laughs) As a matter of fact, there is a promising girl in Los Angeles, but I still want New York.

Dr. N: All right, move forward. As your time in the Ring draws to a close, give me the details of your probable life selection.

S: I am going to New York to be a musician. I'm still trying to make up my mind between a couple of people, but I think I will choose (stops to laugh) a dumpy kid with a lot of talent. His body won't have the stamina of my last one, but I'll have the advantage of parents with some money who will encourage me to practice, practice, practice.

Dr. N: Money is important?

S: I know I sound … grasping … selfish … but there was no money in my last life. If I want to express the beauty of music and give pleasure to myself and others, I need proper training and supportive parents, otherwise I'll get sidetracked … I know myself.

Dr. N: If you didn't like any of the options presented to you in the Ring, could you ask for more places and people to look at?

S: It isn't necessary, at least for me. I'm offered enough.

Dr. N: Let me be more blunt. If you are supposed to select a life from only the selections shown you in the Ring, how do you know the coordinators aren't stacking the deck against you? Maybe they are programming you to make certain choices?

S: (pause) I don't think so, considering all the times I have come to the Ring. We don't go unless our minds are made up as to the type of life we want to live, and I've always had interesting choices based upon my own ideas.

Dr. N: Okay, after you are completely finished with reviewing lives in the Ring, what happens then?

S: The controllers … come into my mind to see if I am satisfied with what I have been shown.

Dr. N: Are they always the same entities?

S: I think so … as far back as I can remember.

Dr. N: Do they pressure you to make a decision before leaving the Ring?

S: Not at all. I float out and go back to talk to my companions before making up my mind.

Case 25 told us his choice of locations was confined to four cities. The number of scenes souls preview before a new life is, of course, different for each visit. Individual life offerings are selective, which indicates to me that other spiritual entities have been actively working on our behalf to set up location scenes before we arrive. The number of specialist spirits who assist souls at the space of life selection never seems to be large. They appear as rather vague apparitions to my subjects, although most believe members of their Council of Elders and personal guides are involved.

Early in human history, when the world was underpopulated, my clients recall lives where they were always born in sparse human settlements. In time, with the rise of villages and then larger centers of ancient civilizations, my cases report returning to the same areas. Life selections were geographically scattered again by the great migrations of people colonizing new lands, particularly in the last four hundred years. In this century of over-population, more souls are choosing to live in places where they have been before.

Does this tendency today mean souls want to return to the same countries because of race? Souls are not inclined toward life selections based on ethnicity or nationalism. These products of human separatism are taught in childhood. Aside from the comfortable familiarity of culture in a soul's choice (which is different from racial bias), we must also factor in the affinity many spirits have for deserts, mountains, or the sea. Souls may also have a preference for rural or urban living.

Are souls drawn back to the same geographic areas because they want a new life with the same family they had in their past life? The tradition among certain cultures, such as Native Americans, is that souls choose to stay within family bloodlines. A dying man is expected to come back as his own unborn grandchild. In my practice I rarely see souls repeating the same genetic choices in past lives because this would inhibit growth and opportunity.

Once in awhile I hear about a soul returning to the body of a relative in a former life under unusual karmic circumstances. For example, if a brother and sister had a close affinity for each other, and one were to die suddenly while still young, the soul of the dead sibling might want to return in the surviving sibling's child to restore this broken life connection to finish an important task.

What is even more common in my experience, are the souls of young children who die soon after birth and then return to the same parents as the soul of their next baby. These plans are all made in advance by the souls participating in tragic family events. They involve a maze of karmic issues. Not long ago, I had a case where my client had died from a birth defect early in his last life. I asked, "What was the purpose of your life ending when you were only a few days old?" He replied, "The lesson was for my parents, not me, and that's why I elected to come back for them as a filler." When souls return for a short life to help someone else rather than work on their own issues, because there isn't time, some call this "a filler life." In this case, the parents had abused and finally caused the death of another child when they were together in an earlier life. Although they were a loving young couple in the last life of my client, these parents evidently needed to experience the grief of having a child they desperately wanted taken away from them. Experiencing the anguish from this terrible loss gave the souls of these parents a deeper insight into the effects of severing a blood bond. I will have an example of this theme in Case 27.

Spirits do not routinely see their deaths in future lives. If souls choose a life where their death will be premature, they often see it in the place of life selection. I have found that souls essentially *volunteer* in advance for bodies who will have sudden fatal illnesses, are to be killed by someone, or come to an abrupt end of life with many others from a catastrophic event. Souls who become involved in these tragedies are not caught in the wrong place at the wrong time with a capricious God looking the other way. Every soul has a motive for the events in which it chooses to participate. One client told me his last life was planned in advance to end at seven years of age as an American Indian boy. He said, "I was looking for a short-burst lesson in humility and this life as a mistreated starving half-breed was enough."

Another, more graphic example of a soul volunteering for a terrible assignment was that of one of my subjects who elected in her last life to join (with three others of her soul group) the bodies of Jewish women taken from Munich into the death camp at Dachau in 1941. All were assigned to the same barracks (also prearranged) where my client died in 1943 at age 18 comforting the children and trying to help them survive. Her mission was accomplished with courage.

While events, race, culture, and geographic location often appear to come first in the selection process, they are not the most significant choices for the soul's next life. Aside from all other considerations, incarnation comes down to souls making that all-important decision of a specific body, and what can be learned by utilizing the brain of a certain human being. The next chapter is devoted to an analysis of why souls choose their bodies for various biological and psychological reasons.

13

Choosing a New Body

IN the place of life selection, our souls preview the life span of more than one human being within the same time cycle. When we leave this area, most souls are inclined toward one leading candidate presented to us for soul occupation. However, our spiritual advisors give us ample opportunity to reflect upon all we have seen in the future before making a final decision. This chapter is devoted to the many elements which go into that decision.

Our deliberations over body alternatives actually begin before we go to the place of life selection. Souls do this in order to adequately prepare themselves for viewing certain people in different cultural settings on Earth. I sense those souls who set up the screening room know in advance what to show us, because of these thoughts in our minds. Great care must be taken in choosing just the right body to serve us in the life to come. As I have said, guides and peer group members are part of this evaluation process prior to, and after, we visit the place of life selection.

When listening to my subjects describe all the preparations which go into picking a new physical body, I am constantly reminded of the fluidity of spiritual time. Our teachers use relative future time in the place of life selection to allow souls to measure human usefulness for working on unfinished lesson plans. Blueprints for the next life vary in the degree of difficulty the soul-mind sets for itself. If we have just come off an easy life, making little interpersonal progress, our soul might want to choose a person in the next time cycle who will face heartache and perhaps tragedy. It is not out of the ordinary for me to see someone who has skated through an unchallenging life overloading themselves with turmoil in the next one to catch up with their learning goals.

The soul-mind is far from infallible as it works in conjunction with a biological brain. Regardless of our soul level, being human means we will all make mistakes and have the necessity of engaging in midcourse corrections during our lives. This will be true with any body we select.

Before taking up the more complex mental factors in a soul's decision to join with the brain of a human baby, I will begin with the physical aspects of body choice. Despite the fact that our souls know in advance what they are going to look like, a national survey in the United States indicated 90 percent of both males and females were dissatisfied with the physical characteristics of their bodies. This is the power of conscious amnesia. Much unhappiness is created by society stereotyping an ideal appearance. Yet, this too is part of a soul's lesson plan.

How many times have we all looked in a mirror and said; "Is this the real me? Why do I appear this way? Am I in a body where I belong?" These questions are especially poignant when the type of body we have prevents us from doing those things we think we ought to be able to do in life. I have had a number of clients who came to me convinced their bodies prevented them from achieving satisfying lives.

Many handicapped people think if it were not for a genetic mistake, or being the victim of an accidental injury which damaged their body, their lives would be more fulfilled. As heartless as this may sound, my cases show few real accidents involving body damage which don't fall under the free will of souls. As souls, we choose our bodies for a reason. Living in a damaged body does not necessarily have to involve a karmic debt we are paying off because of past life responsibility for an injury to someone else. As my next case will demonstrate, when a soul is inside a damaged body, this choice can involve a learning path to another type of lesson.

It is difficult to tell a newly-injured person trying to cope with physical disablement that he or she has an opportunity to advance at a faster rate than those of us with healthy bodies and minds. This knowledge must come through self-discovery. The case histories of my clients convince me that the effort necessary to overcome a body impediment does accelerate advancement. Those of us whom society deems less-than-perfect suffer discrimination which makes the burden even heavier. Overcoming the obstacles of physical ailments and hurt makes us stronger for the ordeal.

Our bodies are an important part of the trial we set for ourselves in life. The freedom of choice we have with these bodies is based far more on psychological elements than from the estimated 100,000 genes inherited by each human being. However, I want to show in the opening case of this chapter why souls want certain bodies based largely on physical reasons without heavy psychological implications. The case exhibits the planning involved in the decision of a soul to be in contrasting physical bodies in different lives. After this case, we will examine why souls choose their bodies for other reasons.

Case 26 was a tall, well-proportioned woman who enjoyed participating in sports despite being bothered all her life with recurring leg pains. During her preliminary interview, I learned the pain was a dull ache in both legs, about midway down the thighbones. Over a period of years she had been to a number of doctors who could find no medical evidence of anything wrong with her legs. Clearly, she was worn down and willing to try anything for relief.

When I heard the doctors had concluded her discomfort was probably psychosomatic, I suspected the origin of this woman's pain might lie in a past life. Before going to the source of her problem, I decided to take my client through a couple of past lives to ascertain her motivations for body choices. When I asked her to tell me about a life in which she was the happiest with a human body she told of being in the body of a Viking called Leth around 800 AD. She said Leth was "a child of nature" who traveled by the Baltic Sea route into western Russia.

Leth was described as wearing a long, fur-lined cloak and soft, form-fitting animal skin pants with roped-up boots and a cap wrapped with metal. He carried an ax and a heavy, broad-bladed sword which he wielded easily in battle. My subject was intrigued by the picture in her mind of again being inside this magnificently proportioned warrior with "dirty strands of reddish-blond hair spilling over my shoulders." Standing well over six feet tall, he must have been a giant of his time, with enormous strength, a huge chest, and powerful limbs. A man of great endurance, Leth navigated with other Norsemen over long distances, sailing up rivers and hiking through thick, virgin forests, pillaging settlements along the way. Leth was killed during a raid while looting a village.

◂ Case 26 ▸

Dr. N: What was most important to you about this life you have just recalled as Leth the Viking?

S: To experience that magnificent body and the feeling of raw physical power. I have never had another body like that one in all my existences on Earth. I was fearless because my body did not react to pain even when wounded. In every respect it was flawless. I never got sick.

Dr. N: Was Leth ever mentally troubled by anything? Was there any emotional sensitivity for you in this life?

S: (bursts out laughing) Are you kidding? Never! I lived only for each day. My concerns were not getting enough fighting, plunder, food, drink, and sex. All my feelings were channeled into physical pursuits. What a body!

Dr. N: All right, let's analyze your decision to choose this great body in advance of Leth's life. At the time you made your choice in the spirit world did you request this body of good genetic stock or did your guide simply make the selection for you?

S: Counselors don't do that.

Dr. N: Then explain to me how this body came to be chosen by you.

S: I wanted one of the best physical specimens on Earth at the time and Leth was offered to me as a possibility.

Dr. N: You had only one choice?

S: No, I had two choices of people living in this time.

Dr. N: What if you didn't like any of the body choices presented to you for occupation in that time segment?

S: (thoughtfully) The alternatives of my choices always seem to match what I want to experience in my lives.

Dr. N: Do you have the sense the counselors know in advance which body selections are exactly right for you, or are they so harried it's just an indiscriminate grab bag of body choices?

S: Nothing here is careless. The counselors arrange everything.

Dr. N: I have wondered if the counselors might get mixed up once in a while. With all the new babies born could they ever assign two souls to one baby, or leave a baby without a soul for a while?

S: (laughing) We aren't in an assembly line. I told you they know what they are doing. They don't make mistakes like that.

Dr. N: I believe you. Now, as to your choices, I am curious if two bodies were sufficient for your examination in the place of life selection.

S: We don't need a lot of choices for lives once the counselors get their heads together about our desires. I already had some idea of the right body size and shape and the sex I wanted before being exposed to my two choices.

Dr. N: What was the body choice you rejected in favor of Leth?

S: (pause) That of a soldier from Rome … also with the strong body I wanted in that lifetime.

Dr. N: What was wrong with being an Italian soldier?

S: I didn't want … control over me by the state (subject shakes head from side to side) … too restrictive …

Dr. N: As I remember, by the ninth century much of Europe had fallen under the authority of Charlemagne's Holy Roman Empire.

S: That was the trouble with the soldier's life. As a Viking I answered to nobody. I was free. I could move around with my band of invaders in the wilderness without any governmental control.

Dr. N: Then freedom was also an issue in your choice?

S: Absolutely. The freedom of movement … the fury of battle … the use of my strength and uninhibited action. Life at sea and in the forests was robust and constant. I know the life was cruel, too, but it was a brutal time. I was no better or worse than the rest.

Dr. N: But what about other considerations, such as personality?

S: Nothing bothered me as long as I was able to physically express myself to the fullest.

Dr. N: Did you have a mate—children?

S: (shrugs) Too restrictive. I was on the move. I possessed many women—some willing—others not—and this pleasure added to my expression of physical power. I didn't want to be tied down in any way.

Dr. N: So, the body of Leth was your preference as a pure physical extension of sensual feeling?

S: Yes, I wanted to experience all body senses to the fullest, nothing more.

I felt my subject was now ready to go to work on her current problem. After bringing her out of superconscious into a subconscious state, I asked her to go directly to a life which may have involved leg pain.

Almost at once the woman dropped into her most recent past life and became a six-year-old girl named Ashley living in New England in the year 1871. Ashley was riding in a fully loaded, horse-drawn carriage when suddenly she opened the door and tumbled out under the vehicle. When she hit the cobblestone street, one of the heavy rear carriage wheels rolled over her legs at the same point above both knees, crushing the bones. My subject reexperienced a sharp pain in her legs while describing the fall.

Despite efforts from local physicians and the prolonged use of wood splints, Ashley's leg bones did not heal properly. She was never able to stand or walk again and poor circulation caused repeated swelling in her legs for the rest of a rather short life. Ashley died in 1912 after a productive period of years as a writer and tutor of disadvantaged children. When the narration of Ashley's life ended, I returned my subject to the spirit world.

Dr. N: In your history of body choices why did you wait a thousand years between being a physically strong man and a crippled woman?

S: Well, of course, I developed a better sense of who I was during the lives in between. I chose to be crippled to gain intellectual concentration.

Dr. N: You chose a broken body for this?

S: Yes, you see, being unable to walk made me read and study more. I developed my mind … and listened to my mind. I learned to communicate well and to write with skill because I wasn't distracted. I was always in bed.

Dr. N: Was any characteristic about your soul particularly evident in both Ashley and Leth the Viking?

S: That part of me which craves fiery expression was in both bodies.

Dr. N: I want you to go to the moment you were in the process of choosing the life of Ashley. Tell me how you decided on this particular damaged body.

S: I picked a family in a well-established, settled part of America. I wanted a place with libraries and to be taken care of by loving parents so I could devote myself to scholarship. I constantly wrote to many unhappy people and became a good teacher.

Dr. N: As Ashley, what did you do for this loving family who took care of you?

S: It always works two ways—the benefits and liabilities. I chose this family because they needed the intensity of love with someone totally dependent upon them all their lives. We were very close as a family because they were lonely before I was born. I came late, as their only child. They wanted a daughter who would not marry and leave them to be lonely again.

Dr. N: So it was a trade-off?

S: Most definitely.

Dr. N: Then let's track this decision further back to the place of life selection, when your soul first saw Ashley's life. Did you see the details of your carriage accident then?

S: Of course, but it wasn't an accident—it was supposed to happen.

Dr. N: Once you came to Earth, who was responsible for the fall? Was it your soul-mind or Ashley's biological mind?

S: We worked in unison. She was going to be fooling with the carriage door handle and … I capitalized on that …

Dr. N: Tell me what was going through your soul-mind in the life selection room when you saw the scene of Ashley falling and being injured?

S: I thought about how this crippled body could be put to good use. I had some other choices for body injuries, but I preferred this one because I didn't want to have the capability for much movement.

Dr. N: I want to pursue the issue of causality here. Would Ashley have fallen anyway if she had a soul other than your own?

S: (defensively) We were right for each other …

Dr. N: That doesn't answer my question.

S: (long pause) There are forces beyond my knowledge as a spirit. When I saw Ashley for the first time … I was able to see her without me … healthy … older … another life possibility …

Dr. N: Now we are getting somewhere. Are you saying if Ashley had begun her life with another soul entity that she might not have fallen at all?

S: Yes … that's a possibility … one of many … she could also have been less severely injured, with the ability to walk on crutches.

Dr. N: Well, did you see a physically healthy Ashley living happily without your soul?

S: I saw … a grown woman … normal legs … unhappiness with a man … frustration at being trapped in an unrewarding life … sorrowful parents … but easier. (voice becomes more firm) *No!* That course would not have worked well for either of us—I was the best soul for her.

Dr. N: Were you the prime mover of the fall, once you elected to become Ashley's soul?

S: It … was both of us … we were one at that moment … she was being naughty, bouncing around in the carriage, playing with the door handle when her mother said she must stop. Then … I was ready and she was ready …

Dr. N: Just how rigid was your destiny? Once you were Ashley's soul was there any way you could have backed out of this entire incident in the carriage?

S: (pause) I can tell you I had a flash just before I fell. I could have pulled back and not fallen out. A voice inside my mind said … "It's an opportunity, don't wait any longer, take the fall, this is what you wanted—it's the best course of action."

Dr. N: Was that particular moment important?

S: I didn't want Ashley to get too much older.

Dr. N: But, the pain and suffering this child went through …?

S: It was horrible. The agony of those first five weeks was beyond belief. I almost died, but I learned from enduring it all and I now see the memories of Leth's capacity for managing pain helped me.

Dr. N: Did your inner mind have any regrets during those moments when the pain was most severe?

S: As I slipped in and out of consciousness during the worst of the ordeal, my mind began gaining in power. Overriding my damaged body, I started to better control the pain … lying in bed … the doctors helpless. The skills I developed in managing pain were later used to concentrate on my studies and my counselor was helping me, too, in subtle ways.

Dr. N: So you gained a lot in this life by being unable to walk?

S: Yes, I became a listener and thinker. I corresponded with many people and learned to write with inspiration. I gained teaching ability with the young, and felt guided by an internal power.

Dr. N: Was your counselor proud of your accomplishments after you returned to the spirit world?

S: Very, although I was told I had become a little too indulged and pampered (laughs), but that's an okay trade-off.

Dr. N: How does your experience with the strong body of Leth and the weak one of Ashley help you today, or is this of no consequence?

S: I benefit every day by my appreciation of the necessity of a union between mind and body to learn lessons.

During my client's reliving of the street scene which broke her legs, I initiated desensitization measures. At the close of our session together, I then deprogrammed her generational memory of leg pain entirely. This woman later notified me she has had no further pain and regularly enjoys playing tennis.

The two past lives I have represented in this case were largely devoted to physical choices for soul actualization in two quite different environments.

Souls search for self-expression by developing different aspects of their character. Regardless of what physical or mental tools are used through the use of many bodies, the laws of karma will prevail. If the soul chooses one extreme, somewhere down the line this will be counterbalanced by an opposite choice to even-out development. The physical lives of Leth and Ashley are examples of karmic compensation. The Hindus believe a rich man sooner or later must become a beggar for his soul to develop adequately.

By surviving different challenges our soul identity is strengthened. The word strength should not be misunderstood. My subjects say the real lessons of life are learned by recognizing and coming to terms with being human. Even as victims, we are beneficiaries because it is how we stand up to failure and duress which really marks our progress in life. Sometimes one of the most important lessons is to learn to just let go of the past.

While souls carefully consider the physical attributes of an Earth body in a variety of cultural settings, they give much more attention to the psychological aspects of human life. This decision is the most vital part of the entire selection process for the soul. Before entering the place of life selection, it is to a soul's advantage to ponder the factors of heredity and environment which affect how a biological life form will function. I have heard that a soul's spiritual energy has a fluctuating influence on whether the temperament of its human host will be extroverted or introverted, rationalistic or idealistic, emotionally or analytically dominated. Because of such variables, souls need to reflect in advance on the types of bodies which will serve them best in the life to come.

From what I can gather, a soul's thoughts about certain human behavior preferences for themselves in the next life are known by guides and those masters charged with operating the life selection stations. It appears to me some souls take this responsibility more seriously than others. Yet, a soul in the prelife selection phase can reflect only so much on how they would fit into a specific body. When souls are called to the place of life selection the guesswork is over. Now they must match their spiritual identity against a mortal being. Why one soul joined, for psychological reasons, with two human beings thousands of years apart is the basis of my next case.

Case 27 is a Texas businessman who owns a large, successful clothing firm. During a vacation in California, Steve came to see me on the advice of a friend. As I took his history, I noticed he was tense and hypervigilant. While his fingers toyed with a key chain, Steve's eyes darted anxiously around my office. I asked if he was nervous or afraid of hypnosis as a procedure and he replied, "No, I'm more afraid of what you will uncover."

This client told me his employees were demanding and disloyal and the multitude of personnel complaints had become intolerable. His solution had been to increase discipline and fire people. I learned that he had two failed marriages and was a binge alcoholic. He said he had recently tried a recovery program but quit because "they were getting too critical of me."

As we talked further, Steve explained that his mother disappeared after leaving him on the steps of a church in Texas within a week of his birth. After a few lonely and unhappy years in an orphanage, an older couple adopted him. He added that these people were stern disciplinarians who seemed to disapprove of him all the time. Leaving home in his teens, Steve had many scrapes with the law and once attempted suicide.

I found this client's personality to be overly assertive and untrusting of authority. His anger was rooted in feelings of isolation and abandonment issues. Steve said he felt like he was losing control over his life and was willing to try anything "to find the real me." I agreed to short-term exploration of his unconscious mind if he would consider seeing a therapist later in his own town for sustained counseling.

As this case unfolds, we will see how Steve's soul maintains its identity while responding to physical life in a human body. The intensity of this association is increased in hypnosis when my subjects discuss their motives for body selection. One reason why I have used this case is to expose a difficult barrier to discovering our identity—that of childhood trauma. Souls who unite with people that develop early personality disorders deliberately set themselves up for a difficult life. Before taking my client into the spirit world to learn why his soul chose this life, it was necessary to relive his early childhood memories. In the short excerpt which begins this case, this subject will see his real mother again. It is one of the most poignant scenes I have ever facilitated.

✦ Case 27 ✈

Dr. N: You are now a baby in the first week of life and your mother is seeing you for the last time. It doesn't matter that you are a baby because your inner adult mind knows everything that is going on. Describe to me exactly what transpires.

S: (subject starts to shake) I ... I'm in a basket ... there is a faded blue blanket around me ... I'm being set down on some steps ... it's cold ...

Dr. N: Where are these steps?

S: ... In front of a church ... in Texas.

Dr. N: Who is setting you down on the church steps?

S: (the shaking increases) My mother ... is bending down over me ... saying goodbye ... (begins to cry)

Dr. N: What can you tell me about your mother's reason for leaving you?

S: She ... is young ... not married to my father ... he is already married. She is ... crying ... I can feel her tears falling on my face.

Dr. N: Look up at her. What else do you see?

S: (chokes) Flowing black hair ... beautiful ... I reach up and touch her mouth ... she kisses me ... soft, gentle ... she is having a terribly hard time leaving me here.

Dr. N: Does she say anything to you before leaving?

S: (subject can now hardly talk) "I must leave you for your own good. I have no money to take care of you. My parents won't help us. I love you. I will always love you and hold you in my heart forever."

Dr. N: What happens then?

S: She ... takes hold of a heavy door knocker ... it has an animal on it ... and bangs on the door ... we hear footsteps coming ... now she is gone.

Dr. N: What do your inner thoughts tell you about all you have seen?

S: (almost overcome by emotion) Oh ... she wanted me after all ... didn't want to leave me ... *she loved me!*

Dr. N: (I place my hand on the subject's forehead and begin a series of post-hypnotic suggestions which end with the following instructions) Steve, you will be able to recall this subconscious memory in your conscious mind. You will retain this picture of your mother for the rest of your life. You now know how she truly felt about you and that her energy is still with you. Is this clear?

S: Yes … it is.

Dr. N: Now, move forward in time and tell me how you feel about your foster parents.

S: Never satisfied with me … made me feel guilty about everything … controlling and judging me … (subject's face is dripping wet with tears and perspiration) don't know who I am supposed to be … I'm not real …

Dr. N: (I raise my voice) Tell me what is unreal about you.

S: Pretending … (stops)

Dr. N: *Keep going!*

S: I'm not really in control … constant anger … mistreating people to … get even … hopelessness …

Note: After additional conditioning, I will now take my subject back and forth between his subconscious and superconscious mind.

Dr. N: All right Steve, now let's go back to the time before your birth into this life. Tell me if you have ever lived in another life with the soul of your birth mother.

S: (long pause) Yes … I have.

Dr. N: Was there ever a particular life you lived with this soul on Earth which involved any sort of physical or emotional pain between the two of you?

S: (after a moment subject's hands grip the arms of his chair) *Oh, damn—that's it—of course—it's her!*

Dr. N: Try to relax and not go too fast for me. I want you to enter the life you see in your mind at the most crucial point in your relationship with this soul on the count of three. *One, two, three!*

S: (a deep sigh) Oh my … it's the same person … a different body … but she was my mother then, too …

Dr. N: Stay focused on the Earth scene. Is it day or night?

S: (pause) Broad daylight. Hot sun and sand ...

Dr. N: Describe what is happening under the hot sun in the sand.

S: (haltingly) I am standing in front of my temple ... before a large crowd of people ... my guards are in back of me.

Dr. N: What is your name?

S: Haroum.

Dr. N: What are you wearing, Haroum?

S: A long, white robe and sandals. I have a staff in my hand with gold snakes on it as a symbol of my authority.

Dr. N: What is your authority, Haroum?

S: (proudly) I am a high priest.

Note: Further inquiries revealed this man was a tribal leader who was located on the Arabian peninsula close to the Red Sea around 2000 BC. In pre-classical times, this area was known as the Kingdom of Sheba (or Saba). I also learned the temple was a large oval structure of mud bricks and stone dedicated to a moon god.

Dr. N: What are you doing in front of your temple?

S: I am on the steps judging a woman. She is my mother. She is kneeling down in front of me. There is a look of pity and fear in her eyes as she looks up at me.

Dr. N: How can her eyes show both pity and fear at once?

S: There is pity in her eyes because of the power which has consumed me ... in taking so much control over the daily lives of my people. And there is fear, too, for what I am about to do. This disturbs me, but I must not show it.

Dr. N: Why is your mother kneeling on the temple steps before you?

S: She has broken into the storage house and stolen food to give to the people. Many are hungry at this time of year, but I alone can order distribution. The food must be measured out carefully.

Dr. N: Did she act against some rule of food rationing? Was this a question of survival?

S: (abruptly) There is more to this—by disobeying me she is undermining my authority. I use the distribution of food as a means of ... control over my people. I want them all to be loyal to me.

Dr. N: What are you going to do with your mother?

S: (with conviction) My mother has violated the law. I can save her, but she must be punished as an example. I decide she will die.

Dr. N: How do you feel about killing your own mother, Haroum?

S: It must be done. She has been a constant thorn in my side—causing unrest among my people because of her position. I cannot govern freely with her here any longer. Even now, she is defiant. I order her death by banging my staff on the stone steps.

Dr. N: Later on are you sad about ordering your mother's execution?

S: (voice becomes strained) I ... must not think about such things if I am to maintain power.

At this point Steve's mind had relived two emotionally wrenching events involving voluntary actions of separation between mother and son. Although he had made the karmic connection, it was important that his abandonment as a baby not be isolated as pure historic retribution. For healing to begin we had to go further.

The next stage in our session together was designed to recover Steve's soul identity. To do this, I took him into the spirit world. In each of my cases, I try to bring the subject back to the most appropriate spiritual area to get the best results. In Case 13, I used the place of orientation. With Case 27, we will go back to relive the spiritual time just after his return from the place of life selection. In this setting, I want Steve to see the reasons for his current body choice and the role of other soul participants in his life.

Dr. N: By what name are you known in the spirit world?

S: Sumus.

Dr. N: All right, Sumus, since we are now in the spirit world again, I want us to go to the period just following your initial viewing of the man who is Steve. What are your thoughts?

S: Such a resentful man ... he is so angry about his mother dumping him on a doorstep ... and those hard-nosed people who will take over as his parents ... I don't know if I even *want* to take this body!

Dr. N: I understand, but why don't we put that decision aside for a few minutes while other things develop. Tell me what you actually do once you leave the place of life selection.

S: Sometimes I might want to be by myself for a while. Usually, I am anxious to have the opinions of my friends about the lives I look at, especially one this rough.

Dr. N: Surely, you had more than one body option?

S: (shakes head) This is one I should take ... it's a rough decision.

Dr. N: Tell me, Sumus, when you are back with your group of friends, do you discuss the possibility of yourself associating with some of them in the next life?

S: Yes, more often than not, these close friends are going to be in my life to come, just as I will be in theirs. Some of my clutch will not be in certain lives. It doesn't matter. We all discuss our next life with each other. I want to get their ideas on details. You see, we all know each other so well—our strengths and weaknesses—former successes and failures—what to watch out for ... that kind of thing.

Dr. N: Did you discuss with them any details about the kind of person you should be in your next life before actually going to the place of life selection?

S: Oh yeah, in a roundabout way. Nothing concrete. Now that I have seen Steve, and who the others might be in relation to him in this life, there are reservations. So I talk to Jor.

Dr. N: Is Jor your guide?

S: Yes, he listened a lot to what I had to say about who I thought I should be before I was sent to the place where we look at lives.

Dr. N: Okay, Sumus, you have just returned to your primary cluster group from the place of life selection. What do you do first?

S: I talk about this guy Steve who is so unhappy ... no real mother ... all that stuff ... what kinds of people will be around him ... their plans, too ... it must fit all together for us.

Dr. N: You mean which souls are going to take certain bodies?

S: Right, we need to firm that up.

Dr. N: Are soul assignments still negotiable at this point, or is everyone told which body they will be in after leaving the place of life selection?

S: No one is forced to do anything. We know what should be done. Jor ... and the others help us make adjustments ... they are sent in to round out the picture ... (subject's face becomes grave)

Dr. N: Is something bothering you at this moment, Sumus?

S: (in a cheerless manner) Uh ... my friends are moving away ... there are others coming ... oh ...

Dr. N: I gather some deliberations are about to occur with other souls. Try to relax as best you can. On my command you will clearly relate to me everything that is happening. Do you understand?

S: (nervously) Yes.

Dr. N: *Begin!* How many entities do you see?

S: There are ... four of them ... coming over to me ... Jor is one of them.

Dr. N: Who is first?

S: (subject grabs my hand) It's ... Eone ... she wants to be ... my mother again.

Dr. N: Is this the soul of the woman who is Haroum's and Steve's mother?

S: Yes, she is ... oh ... I don't want to ...

Dr. N: What's going on?

S: Eone is telling me it's time for us to ... settle things ... to be in a disordered life as mother and son again.

Dr. N: But Sumus, didn't you know this at the place of life selection when you viewed Steve's mother taking her baby to the church?

S: I saw the people ... the possibility ... it was still an ... abstract consideration ... it wasn't actually *me* yet. I guess I need more convincing because Eone is here for a reason.

Dr. N: I take it none of these newly arrived entities is from your own clutch?

S: (sighs) No, they are not.

Dr. N: Why did you and Eone wait 4000 earth years before discussing a balancing out of your treatment of her in Arabia?

S: Earth years mean nothing; it could have been yesterday. I just wasn't ready to offset the harm I did her as Haroum. She says the circumstances are right for this exercise now.

Dr. N: If your soul joins with the body of Steve in Texas, will Eone consider this karmic payment for your debt?

S: (pause) My life as Steve is not supposed to be punishment.

Dr. N: I'm glad you see that. So what is the lesson to be learned?

S: To … feel what desertion is like in a family relationship … deliberate severing …

Dr. N: The severing of the mother and son bond by deliberate action?

S: Yes … to appreciate what it is like to be cast off.

Dr. N: Allow Eone to move away and have the other entities join us, Sumus.

S: (distressed) Eone is floating back to … Jor … coming forward are … *Oh shit—it's Talu and Kalish!* (subject squirms in his chair and tries to ward off the two spirits in his mind by pushing the palms of his hands outward)

Dr. N: Who are they?

S: (in a rush of words) Talu and Kalish have volunteered to be Steve's—my foster parents. They work together a lot.

Dr. N: What's the problem, then?

S: I just don't want them again so soon!

Dr. N: Slow down for me, Sumus. You have worked with these souls before?

S: (still muttering to himself) Yes, yes—but they are so *hard* for me to be with—especially Kalish. It's too soon. They were my in-laws in the German life.

Note: We digress for a few minutes while Sumus briefly explains a past life in Europe as a high-ranking army officer who neglected his family and was the object of scorn from his wife's influential parents.

Dr. N: Are you saying that Talu and Kalish lack the capability for the assignment of being your foster parents in Texas?

S: (shakes head with resignation) No, they know what they are doing. It's just that with Kalish, it's *always* a rough ride. She chooses to be people who are critical, demanding, cold …

Dr. N: Does she always present that sort of behavior in human bodies?

S: Well, that's her style with me. Kalish is not a soul who engages easily with others. She is independent and very determined.

Dr. N: How about Talu as your adoptive father?

S: Stern … allows Kalish to lead … can be too detached … emotionally private… I'm going to really rebel against them this time.

Dr. N: Okay, but will they teach you something?

S: Yes, I know they will, but I am still arguing about it. Jor and Eone come over.

Dr. N: What do you say next at this conference?

S: I want Eone to be my foster mother. They all laugh at me. Jor won't buy my explanations. He knows I am close to Eone.

Dr. N: Do they make fun of you, Sumus?

S: Oh no, it's not that way at all. Talu and Kalish question my reluctance to tackle my faults with them.

Dr. N: Well, I was getting the impression you thought these souls were ganging up on you to force a decision to join with the Texas baby.

S: That's not how it goes here. We are discussing my misgivings about the life itself.

Dr. N: But I thought you didn't like Talu and Kalish?

S: They know about me ... I need strict people or I ride over them. Everyone here sees I have a tendency to indulge myself. They convince me an easy life without them will be like treading water. Both of them are very disciplined.

Dr. N: Well, it sounds like you have about made up your mind to go with them into the Texas life.

S: (musing) Yes... they are going to make a lot of demands on me as a child... Kalish sarcastic ... Talu a perfectionist ... losing Eone... it's going to be a rough ride.

Dr. N: What will playing the roles of your parents do for Talu and Kalish?

S: Kalish and Talu are in different ... configurations than me. I'm not supposed to get all muddled up in their business. It has something to do with their being rigid people and overcoming pride.

Dr. N: When you are on Earth, does your soul-mind always know the reason why certain people who influence you positively or negatively are significant in your life?

S: Yes, but that doesn't mean the person I am in that life understands what my spirit knows. (smiles) That's what we should be able to figure out on Earth.

Dr. N: Which is what we are doing now?

S: Yeah ... and I am cheating a little with you helping, but it's okay, I can use it.

It does seem an enigma that the knowledge of who we really are as souls is so difficult for many of us to reach through our conscious minds. By now I'm sure the reader has discerned that even in a superconscious state, we do retain the ability to observe ourselves with a portion of the critical center of our conscious mentality. Assisting clients in reaching their inner selves by linking all facets of the mind is the most important part of my work in hypnotherapy.

I want Steve to gain insight into the motives for his behavior by understanding his soul. The dialogue which follows provides us with further disclosures as to why Sumus integrated into Steve's body. The spiritual conference with Jor, Eone, Talu, and Kalish is over and I have taken Sumus to a quiet setting in the spirit world for this discussion.

Dr. N: Tell me, Sumus, how much of who you really are as a soul identity is reflected in the human beings you have occupied?

S: Quite a lot—but no two bodies are alike. (laughs) Good body and soul mergers don't always happen, you know. I remember some of my former bodies more fondly than others.

Dr. N: Would you say your soul dominates or is subordinated by the human brain?

S: That's difficult to answer because there are subtle differences with the brain of each body which affects how we … exhibit ourselves from that body. A human would be pretty vacant without us … we treat earth bodies with respect, though.

Dr. N: What do you think human beings would be like without souls?

S: Oh, dominated by senses and emotions …

Dr. N: And you believe each human brain causes you to react differently?

S: Well, that which I am … is able to utilize some bodies better than others. I don't always feel fully attached to a human being. Some physical emotions are overpowering and I … am not so effective.

Dr. N: Such as the high level of rage displayed by Steve's temperament, perhaps affected by the central nervous system of this body?

S: Yes, we inherit these things …

Dr. N: But you knew what Steve would be like before you chose his body?

S: (in disgust) That's right, and it's typical of how I can make a bad situation worse. I am able to interpret only when the storms of the human mind are quiet, and yet I want to be stormy people.

Dr. N: What do you mean by interpret?

S: Interpret ideas … make sense out of Steve's reactions to turmoil.

Dr. N: To be frank, Sumus, you sound like a stranger inside Steve's body.

S: I'm sorry to give you that impression. We don't control the human mind … we try by our presence to … elevate it to see …

meaning in the world and to be receptive to morality ... to give understanding.

Dr. N: That's all very well, but you use human bodies for your own development too, don't you?

S: Sure, it's a ... blending ... we give and take with our energy.

Dr. N: Oh, you tailor your energy to fit a host body?

S: It would be better to say I use different facets of expression, depending on the emotional drives of each body.

Dr. N: Let's get specific, Sumus. What is going on between you and Steve's brain at this time on Earth?

S: I ... have felt ... submerged ... sometimes my energy is tired and unresponsive to so much negativity.

Dr. N: Looking back to your choices of Haroum, Steve, and those other human bodies in between, do they all have traits in common which attracted you?

S: (long pause) I am a contact entity. I seek humans who involve themselves ... aggressively with others.

Dr. N: When I hear the word aggression, this means hostility to me as opposed to being assertive. Is this what you intended to say?

S: (pause) Well, I'm attracted to those who influence other people ... ah, vigorously—at full tilt.

Dr. N: Are you a soul who enjoys controlling other people?

S: I wouldn't say control, exactly. I avoid choosing to be people who have no intense involvement with those around them.

Dr. N: Sumus, aren't you being controlling when you try to direct other souls in their lives?

S: (no response)

Dr. N: What would Jor say about your human relationships?

S: Hmm ... that I like power as a means of influencing the acts of humans who are decision makers. That I crave social and political groups where I lead.

Dr. N: So, you would not enjoy being in a human body which was quiet and unassuming?

S: Definitely not.

Dr. N: (I push harder) Sumus, isn't it true you took pleasure in the way you were a part of Haroum's misuse of power in Arabia, and that you gain satisfaction as Steve from mistreating your employees in Texas?

S: (loudly) *No*, that isn't true! Things get out of hand easily when you try to lead humans. It's the conditions on Earth which screw everything up. It isn't all my fault.

Dr. N: Is it possible that both Haroum and Steve became more extreme in their conduct because your soul was with them?

S: (heavily) I haven't done well, I know that …

Dr. N: Look Sumus, I hope you know I don't think you are a bad soul. But maybe you are easily seduced by the trappings of human authority and you have now become someone who feels in conflict with society.

S: (disturbed) You are beginning to sound like Jor!

Dr. N: I don't presume to be doing that, Sumus. Perhaps Jor is helping us both to understand what is going on inside you.

S: Probably.

Steve and I have reached a productive stage of contact with his soul. I address this subject as if he were two people, while tightening the bowstring between his conscious and unconscious self. After applying additional conditioning to pull these two forces closer together, I close our session with a final series of questions. It is important his mind not be allowed to drift or his memories to become dissociated. To foster responsiveness, my questions are confrontive and spoken rapidly to increase the tempo of my subject's answers.

Dr. N: Sumus, begin by telling me why you originally accepted Steve's body.

S: To … rise above my attraction for leading others … always wanting to be in charge …

Dr. N: Is your soul identity in conflict with the direction Steve's life has taken?

S: I don't like that part of him which is fighting to be on top and, at the same time, having thoughts of escape by self-destruction.

Dr. N: If this is a contradiction for you, why does it exist?

S: … childhood … sadness … (stops)

Dr. N: Who am I listening to now? Sumus, why aren't you more active in helping yourself, as Steve, overcome the shame of abandonment by Eone and your anger from an unloving childhood with Talu and Kalish?

S: … I am grown now … and managing others … won't let people hurt me anymore.

Dr. N: Sumus, if you and Steve are now speaking to me as one intelligence, I want to know why your lifestyle is so self-destructive.

S: (long pause) Because my weakness is … using power for self-preservation on Earth.

Dr. N: Do you feel if you were less controlling of people as an adult, life would revert to the way you were treated as a child?

S: (angrily) *Yes!*

Dr. N: And when you don't get self-gratification from the body of your choice, what do you do as a soul?

S: I … tune out …

Dr. N: I see, and how is this accomplished, Sumus?

S: By not … being too active.

Dr. N: Because you are intimidated by a body in an emotional tailspin?

S: Well … I go into a shell.

Dr. N: So, you use avoidance in not actively dealing with the major lesson you came to Earth to learn?

S: Uh huh.

Dr. N: Steve, your adoptive parents were rough on you, weren't they?

S: Yes.

Dr. N: Do you now see why?

S: (pause) To know what being constantly judged is like.

Dr. N: What else?

S: To … overcome … and be whole. (bitterly) I don't know …

Dr. N: I think you do know, Steve. Tell me about the damaged self you present to people around you.

S: (after some procrastination) Pretending to be happy—covering up my feelings by drinking and mistreating people.

Dr. N: Do you want to stop this cover up and go to work?

S: Yes, I do.

Dr. N: Define who you really want to be.

S: (tearfully) I … we don't want to be hostile to people … but don't want to risk being a … non-person … without respect or recognition, either.

Dr. N: So you are on a fence?

S: (quietly) Yes, life is so painful.

Dr. N: Do you think this is an accident?

S: No, I see it isn't.

Dr. N: Steve and Sumus, repeat after me: "I'm going to give back the pain of Eone, Talu, and Kalish, which they gave to me for my own good, and get on with my life by becoming the identity I really *want* to be." (subject repeats these words three times for me)

Dr. N: Steve, what are you going to do about revealing yourself in the future, and taking responsibility for improvement?

S: (after a couple of false starts) Learn to be more honest.

Dr. N: And to trust that you are not a victim of society?

S: Yes.

This case ended with my reinforcing Steve's understanding of who he really is and his mission in life. I wanted to help liberate him as a person of value, with a contribution to make in society. We talked about his love and fear choices, as well as the necessity to get in touch with himself frequently. I felt we had laid the groundwork for his dealing with resentment and a lack of intimacy. I reminded Steve of the need for follow-up counseling. About a year later, he wrote to tell me his recovery was going well, and that he had found the lost child within himself. Steve realized his past mistakes were not failures, but the means to improvement.

Case 27 demonstrates how the hard tasks we set for ourselves often begin in childhood. This is why considerable weight is given to family selection by the soul. The idea that each of us voluntarily agreed to be the children of a given set of parents before we came into this life is a difficult concept for some people to accept. Although the average person has experienced love from his or her parents, many of us have unresolved, hurtful memories of those near to us who should have offered protection and did not. We grow up thinking of ourselves as victims of biological parents and family members whom we inherited without any choice in the matter. This assumption is wrong.

When clients tell me how much they suffered from the actions of family members, my first question to their conscious mind is, "If you had not been exposed to this person as a child, what would you now lack in understanding?" It may take a while, but the answer is in our minds. There are spiritual reasons for our being raised as children around certain kinds of people, just as other people are designated to be near us as adults.

To know ourselves spiritually means understanding why we joined in life with the souls of parents, siblings, spouses, and close friends. There is usually some karmic purpose for receiving pain or pleasure from someone close to us. Remember, along with learning our own lessons, we come to Earth to play a part in the drama of others' lessons as well.

There are people who, because they live in a terrible environment, suspect the spirit world of not being a center of divine compassion. However, it is the ultimate in compassion when beings who are spiritually linked to each other come forward by prior agreement into human lives involving love-hate relationships. Overcoming adversity in these relationships may mean we won't have to repeat certain abrasive alliances in future lives. Surviving such trials on Earth places us into a heightened state of perception with each new life and enhances our identity as souls.

People in trance may have trouble making a clear distinction between their soul identity and human ego. If the human personality has little structure beyond the five senses and basic drives for survival without ensoulment, then the soul *is* our total personality. This means, for example, that one could not have a human ego which is jealous and also possess a soul which is not jealous.

Yet my cases indicate there are subtle variations between their soul identity and all that is manifested by the human personalities of many host bodies. Case 27 showed similarities and differences in the personalities of Haroum and Steve. Our constant soul-self seems to be a governing agent of human temperament, but we may express ourselves differently with each body.

The souls of my subjects apparently select bodies which try to match their character flaws with human temperament for specific growth patterns. In one life an overly cautious, low-energy soul might be disposed to blending with a quiet, rather subdued human host. This same soul, encouraged to take greater risks in another life, could choose to work more in opposition to its natural character by melding with a temperamentally high-strung, aggressive body-type on Earth.

Souls both give and receive mental gifts in life through a symbiosis of human brain cells and intelligent energy. Deep feelings generated by an eternal consciousness are conjoined with human emotion in the expression of one personality, which is as it should be. We don't need to change who we are in relation to life's experiences, only our negative reactions to these events. Asian Buddhists say enlightenment is seeing the absolute soul ego reflected in the relative human ego and acting through it during life.

In the chapters on beginning, intermediate, and advanced soul levels, I gave case samples of soul maturity. I think souls do demonstrate their own patterns of ego in the bodies they inhabit, and they exert a powerful influence over body performance. However, making hasty judgments on a soul's maturity based solely on behavioral traits has its pitfalls. The design plan of souls could include holding parts of their energy in reserve in some lives. Sometimes a negative trait is selected by an otherwise developed soul for special attention in a certain body.

We have seen how a soul selects the person with whom it wishes to associate in a given life. This does not mean that it has absolute control over that body. In extreme cases, a fractured personality struggling with internalized conflicts may result in a dissociative reaction to reality. I feel that this is a sign the soul is not always able to regulate and unify the human mind. I have mentioned how souls may become so buried by human emotion in bodies which are unstable, that by the time of death they are contaminated spirits. If we become obsessed by our physical bodies, or carried along on an emotional roller coaster in life, the soul can be subverted by its outer self.

Many great thinkers in history believed the soul can never be fully homogeneous with the human body and that humans have two intellects. I consider human ideas and imagination as emanating from the soul, which provides a catalyst for the human brain. How much reasoning power we would have without souls is impossible to know, but I feel that the attachment of souls to humans supplies us with insight and abstract thought. I view the soul as offering humans a qualitative reality, subject to conditions of heredity and environment.

If it is true that every human brain has a host of biological characteristics, including raw intelligence and the facility for invention, which are separate from the soul, then choosing our body raises an important question. Do souls choose bodies whose intellectual capabilities match their own development? For instance, are advanced souls drawn to human brains with high intelligence? In looking at the scholastic and academic achievements of my clients, I find there is no more correlation here than with an immature soul being inclined to bodies with lower intellectual aptitudes.

The philosopher Kant wrote that the human brain is only a function of consciousness, not the source of real knowledge. Regardless of body choice, I find souls do demonstrate their individualism through the human mind. A person may be highly intelligent and yet have a closed attitude about adjusting to new situations, with little curiosity about the world. This indicates a beginner soul to me. If I see someone with an evenness of mood, whose interests and abilities are solidly in focus and directed toward helping human progress, I suspect an advanced soul at work. These are souls who seek personal truths beyond the demands of ego.

It does seem a heavy burden that in every new life a soul must search all over again to find its true self in a different body. However, some light is allowed through the blackout of amnesia by spiritual masters who are not indifferent to our plight. When it comes to finding soulmates on Earth and remembering aspects of the lives we saw in the place of life selection, there is an ingenious form of coaching which is given to souls just before the next life. We will see how this is done in the following chapter.

14

Preparation for Embarkation

AFTER souls have completed their consultations with guides and peers about the many physical and psychological ramifications of a new life and body choice, the decision to incarnate is made. It would be logical to assume that they would then go immediately to Earth. This doesn't happen before a significant element of preparation occurs.

By now I'm sure it is understood that souls returning from the place of life selection must not only sort out the best choice of who they are going to be in their next life, but coordinate this decision with other players in the coming drama. Using the analogy of life as being one big stage play, we will have the lead role as an actor or actress. Everything we do in the play affects other minor characters (minor because they are not us) in the script. Their parts can be altered by us and ours by them because script changes (the result of free will) can be made while the play is in progress. Those souls who are going to have a close association with us on the stage of life represent our supporting cast, each with prominent roles. But how will we know them?

The issue of how to find soulmates and other important people in their lives is of paramount concern with many clients who come to me seeking hypnotic regression. Eventually, most of my subjects answer their own questions in superconsciousness because finding these souls was an integral part of their preparations for leaving the spirit world. The space souls go to for this in the spirit world is commonly called the place of recognition, or recognition class. I am told the activity here is like cramming for a final exam. As a result, my subjects also use the term prep-class to describe this aspect of spiritual reinforcement that occurs just before their souls embark on the passage back to Earth. The next case represents this experience.

In order to clearly understand what is behind the spiritual activity of a recognition class, perhaps the word soulmate ought to be defined. For many of us, our nearest and dearest soulmate is our spouse. Yet, as we have seen in previous cases, souls of consequence in our lives may also be other family members or a close friend. The amount of time they are with us on Earth can be long or short. What matters is the impact they have on us while here.

At the risk of oversimplifying a complex issue, our relationships can be divided into a few general categories. First, there is the kind of relationship involving love which is so deep that both partners genuinely don't see how each could live without the other. This is a mental and physical attraction which is so strong neither partner doubts that they were meant for each other.

Second, there are relationships based upon companionship, friendship, and mutual respect. Finally, we have associations based largely upon more casual acquaintances which offer some purposeful ingredient to our life. Thus, a soulmate can take many forms, and meeting people who fall into one of these categories is no game of Russian roulette.

Soulmates are designated companions to help you and themselves accomplish mutual goals which can best be achieved by supporting each other in various situations. In terms of friends and lovers, identity recognition of kindred spirits comes from our highest consciousness. It is a wonderful and mysterious experience, both physically and mentally.

Connecting with beings we know from the spirit world, in all sorts of physical disguises, can be harmonious or frustrating. The lesson we must learn from human relationships is accepting people for who they are without expecting our happiness to be totally dependent upon anyone. I have had clients come to me with the assumption that they are probably not with a soulmate because of so much turmoil and heartbreak in their marriages and relationships. They fail to realize that karmic lessons set difficult standards for each of us and painful experiences involving the heart are deliberate tests in life. They are often of the hardest kind.

Whatever the circumstances, relationships between people are the most vital part of our lives. Is it coincidence, ESP, déjà vu, or synchronicity when the right time and place come together and you meet someone for the first time who will bring meaning into your life? Was there a fleeting forgotten memory—something familiar tugging at the back of your mind? I would ask the reader to sort through those memories involving a distinctive first encounter with someone important in the past. Was it at school? Did this individual live in your neighborhood? How about meeting him or her at work or during some recreation? Did someone introduce you, or was it a chance meeting? What did you feel at that moment?

I hate to tamper with your fond recollections of a supposedly spontaneous past meeting, but such descriptions as chance, happenstance, or impulse aren't applicable to crucial contacts. This makes them no less romantic. In cases involving soulmates, I have heard many heartfelt accounts of close spiritual beings who journeyed across time and space to find each other as physical beings at a particular geographic spot on Earth at a certain moment. It is also true our conscious amnesia can make meeting significant people difficult and we may take a wrong turn and miss the connection at some juncture. However, there can be a prearrangement here for back-up contingencies.

In the case which follows, I will begin the dialogue at a point in the session where I am asking my subject about his spirit world activity just before rebirth into his present life.

↞ Case 28 ↠

Dr. N: Is it close to the time when you will be leaving the spirit world for another life?

S: Yes … I'm about ready.

Dr. N: After you left the place of life selection, was your soulmind made up as to who you would be and the people you were to meet on Earth?

S: Yes, everything is beginning to come together for me.

Dr. N: What if you had second thoughts about your choice of a time frame or a particular human body? Could you back out?

S: (sighs) Yes, and I have done that before—we all have—at least the people I know. Most of the time it's intriguing to think about being alive on Earth again.

Dr. N: But what if you resisted coming back to Earth shortly before you were due to incarnate?

S: It's not that … rigid. I would always discuss the possibilities … my concerns for a new life with my tutor and companions before making a firm commitment. The tutors know when we are stalling, but I have made up my mind.

Dr. N: Well, I'm glad. Now tell me, once you are firmly committed to return to Earth, does anything else of importance transpire for you in the spirit world?

S: I must go to the recognition class.

Dr. N: What is this place like for you?

S: It's an observation meeting ... with my companions ... so I can recognize them later.

Dr. N: When I snap my fingers you will go immediately to this class. Are you *ready*?

S: Yes, I am.

Dr. N: (snapping my fingers) Explain to me what you are doing.

S: I ... am floating in ... with the others ... to hear the speaker.

Dr. N: I would like to accompany you, but you will have to be my eyes—is that all right?

S: Sure, but we must hurry a little.

Dr. N: How does this place appear to you?

S: Mmm ... a circular auditorium with a raised dais in the middle—that's where the speakers are.

Dr. N: Are we going to float in and sit down on seats?

S: (shakes head) Why would we need seats?

Dr. N: Just wondering. How many souls are around us?

S: Oh ... about ten or fifteen ... people who are going to be close to me in the life to come.

Dr. N: That's all the souls you see?

S: No, you asked how many were around me. There are others ... further away in groups ... to hear their speakers.

Dr. N: Are the ten or fifteen souls around you all from your cluster group?

S: Some of them.

Dr. N: Is this gathering similar to the one near the gateway where you met a few people right after your last life?

S: Oh no, that was more quiet ... with just my family.

Dr. N: Why was that homecoming meeting more quiet than where we are now?

S: I was still in a daze from losing my body. Here, there is lots of conversation and milling around ... anticipation ... our energy is really up. Listen, we have to move along faster, I have got to hear what the speakers are saying.

Dr. N: Are these speakers your tutor-guides?

S: No, they are the prompters.

Dr. N: Are they souls who specialize in this sort of thing?

S: Yes, they give us the signs by coming up with ingenious ideas.

Dr. N: Okay, let's move in close to the prompter while you continue to tell me what is happening.

S: We form a circle around the dais. The prompter is floating back and forth in the center—pointing a finger at each of us and saying we must pay close attention. I have to do it!

Dr. N: (lowering my voice) I understand and I wouldn't want you to miss a thing, but please explain what you mean by signs.

S: This prompter is assigned to us so we will know what to look for in our next life. The signs are placed in our mind now in order to jog our memories later as humans.

Dr. N: What kind of signs?

S: Flags—markers in the road of life.

Dr. N: Could you be more specific?

S: The road signs kick us into a new direction in life at certain times when something important is supposed to happen ... and then we must know the signs to recognize one another, too.

Dr. N: And this class takes place for souls before each new life?

S: Naturally. We need to remember the little things ...

Dr. N: But haven't you already previewed the details of your next life in the place of life selection?

S: That's true, but not the small details. Besides, I didn't know all the people who would be operating with me then. This class is a final review ... bringing all of us together.

Dr. N: For those of you who will have an impact on each other's lives?

S: That's right, it's mainly a prep-class because we won't recognize each other at first on Earth.

Dr. N: Do you see your primary soulmate here?

S: (flushing) ... she is here ... and there are other people that I am supposed to contact ... or they will contact me in some way ... the others need their signs, too.

Dr. N: Oh, so that's why these souls are a mixed gathering of entities from different groups. They are all going to play some significant role in each other's new life.

S: (impatiently) Yes, but I can't listen to what is going on with you talking ... Shhh!

Dr. N: (lowering my voice again) All right, on the count of three I am going to hold this class in suspension for a few minutes so you won't miss anything. (softly) *One, two, three.* The speaker is now quiet while you are going to explain a little more about the flags and the signs. Okay?

S: I ... guess so.

Dr. N: I am going to call these signs memory triggers. Are you telling me there will be special triggers for each of these people with you?

S: That's why we have been brought together. There will be times in my life when these people will appear. I must try to ... remember some ... action by them ... the way they look ... move ... talk.

Dr. N: And each will trigger a memory for you?

S: Yeah, and I'm going to miss some. The signs are supposed to click in our memory right away and tell us, "Oh, good, you are here now." Inside us ... we can say to ourselves, "It is time to work on the next phase." They may seem like insignificant little things, but the flags are turning points in our lives.

Dr. N: What if people miss these road flags or signs of recognition because, like you said, you forget what the prompter told you? Or, what if you choose to ignore your inclinations and take another path?

S: (pause) We have other choices—they may not be as good—you can be stubborn, but ... (stops)

Dr. N: But, what?

S: (with conviction) After this class we usually don't forget the important signs.

Dr. N: Why don't our guides just give us the answers we need on Earth? Why all this fooling around with signs to remember things?

S: For the same reason we go to Earth without knowing everything in advance. Our soul power grows with what we discover. Sometimes our lessons get resolved pretty fast ... usually not. The most interesting part of the road are the turns and it's best not to ignore the flags in our mind.

Dr. N: All right, I am going to count from ten down to one, and when I reach one, your class will start again and you will listen while the prompter gives out signs. I will not speak until you raise the index finger of your right hand. This will be my sign that the class is over and you can relate to me the signs you are to remember. Are you *ready?*

S: Yes.

Note: I finish my count and wait a couple of minutes before my subject raises his finger. This is a simple example of why time comparisons between Earth and spirit worlds are meaningless.

Dr. N: That didn't take long.

S: Yes, it did. The speaker had a lot to go through with all of us.

Dr. N: I assume you have the details of recognition signs now firmly in your mind?

S: I hope so.

Dr. N: Good, then tell me about the last sign you were given as the class ended.

S: (pause) A silver pendant ... I will see it when I am seven years old ... around the neck of a woman on my street ... she always wore it.

Dr. N: How will this silver object be a trigger for you?

S: (abstractly) It shines in the sun ... to catch my attention ... I must remember ...

Dr. N: (in a commanding tone) You have the capacity to bring your spiritual and earthly knowledge together. (placing my hand on the subject's forehead) Why is the soul of this woman important for you to know?

S: I meet her riding my bike on our street. She smiles ... the silver pendant is bright ... I ask about it ... we become friends.

Dr. N: Then what?

S: (wistfully) I will know her only a short time before we move, but it is enough. She will read to me and talk to me about life and teach me to ... respect people ...

Dr. N: As you grow older, can people themselves be signs or provide flags to help you make a connection?

S: Sure, they might arrange introductions at the right time.

Dr. N: Do you already know most of the souls who will be meaningful people to you on Earth?

S: Yes, and if I don't, I'll meet them in class.

Dr. N: I guess they can set up love relationship meetings, too?

S: (laughs) Oh, the matchmakers—yes they do that, but meetings can be for friendship ... getting people together to help your career ... that kind of stuff.

Dr. N: Then the souls who are in this auditorium and elsewhere can be involved with different kinds of associations in your life?

S: (enthusiastically) Yeah, I'm going to connect with the guy who is on my baseball team. Another one will be a farming partner—then there will be my life-long pal from grade school.

Dr. N: What if you connect with the wrong person in business, love, or whatever? Does that mean you missed a relationship sign or a red flag for an important event?

S: Hmm … it probably won't be wrong, exactly … it could be a jump start to get you going in a new direction.

Dr. N: Okay, now tell me what is the most important recognition sign you must remember from this prep-class.

S: Melinda's laugh.

Dr. N: Who is Melinda?

S: My wife-to-be.

Dr. N: What is there to remember about Melinda's laugh?

S: When we meet, her laugh is going to … sound like tiny bells … chimes … I really can't describe it to you. Then, the scent of her perfume when we first dance … a familiar fragrance … her eyes.

Dr. N: So, you are actually given more than one trigger sign for your soulmate?

S: Yes, I'm so dense I guess the prompters thought I needed more clues. I didn't want to make a mistake when I met the right person.

Dr. N: What is supposed to trigger her recognition of you?

S: (grins) My big ears … stepping on her toes dancing … what we feel when we first hold each other.

It is an old saying that the eyes are the windows to our soul. No physical attribute has more impact when soulmates meet on Earth. As to our other physical senses, I mentioned in an earlier chapter that souls retain such memories as sounds and smell. All five senses may be used by spiritual prompters as recognition signals in future lives.

Case 28 began to express some discomfort with my keeping him from participating in his spiritual recognition class. I reinforced his visual association of floating around a central dais in an auditorium. (other people use different names) I gave my subject time to finish taking instruction and communicating with his friends and then moved him out of the place of recognition.

It is my practice never to rush clients in and out of their spiritual settings during a session because I find this hinders the intensity of concentration and recall. When we had established ourselves away from the other souls, I talked to this man about his soulmate, Melinda. I learned these two souls were most comfortable in husband and wife roles although occasionally they chose to relate differently in their lives together. Both these souls wanted to make sure they would connect on Earth in their current lives. I thought I would follow up on what actually had transpired.

Dr. N: When you and Melinda came to Earth and were young, did you live close to each other?

S: No, I lived in Iowa and she was in California ... (musing) it was Clair that I knew in Iowa.

Dr. N: Were you interested in Clair romantically?

S: Yes, I almost married her. It was close—and that would have been a mistake. Clair and I weren't right for each other, but going together in high school had become a habit.

Dr. N: And yet you left your home town for California?

S: Yes ... Clair didn't want me to go, but my parents wanted to leave our farm and move west. I liked Iowa and was uneasy about moving and torn over leaving Clair, who was still in high school.

Dr. N: Was there a road sign—a flag of some sort—which helped you make the decision to move with your parents?

S: (sighs) It was my sister who waved a red flag at me. She convinced me I would have more opportunities in the city where my parents were planning to go.

Dr. N: Do you see your sister in the spirit world?

S: Oh yeah, she is in my circle (cluster group).

Dr. N: Is Clair one of your soulmates?

S. (pause) More a friend ... just friends ...

Dr. N: Was leaving Clair hard for you?

S: Oh, yes ... even more for her. We were sexually attracted to each other in high school. The infatuation had no real mental connection ... it's so hard on Earth to figure out what you are supposed to *do* with other people ... sex is a big trap ... we would have grown bored with one another.

Dr. N: Was the physical attraction different with Melinda than you had with Clair?

S: (pause) When Melinda and I met at the dance there was the strong physical attraction of her body … and I guess she liked the way I looked, too … but we both felt something much more …

Dr. N: I want to get this straight. Did you and Melinda choose your male and female bodies in the spirit world deliberately to attract each other once you reached Earth?

S: (nodding) To … some extent … but we were attracted to each other on Earth because inside our minds was the memory of what we were *supposed* to look like.

Dr. N: When the time of the dance rolled around, what happened in your mind?

S: I can see it all now. Our tutor was helping Melinda and me that night. My idea to go to the dance was sudden. I hate to dance because I'm clumsy. I didn't know anybody in the town yet and felt stupid, but I was guided there.

Dr. N: Had you and Melinda scripted the dance scene together during the spiritual prep-class?

S: Yes, we knew about it then and when I saw her at the dance, alarms went off. I did something very uncharacteristic of me … I cut in on the man she was dancing with. When I first held her my legs were like rubber.

Dr. N: And what else did you and Melinda feel at that moment?

S: As if we were in another world … there was this familiarity … it was so weird during that dance … a knowing without doubt that something important was unfolding … the guidance … the intent of our meeting … our hearts were racing … it was enchantment.

Dr. N: Then why was Clair in your life earlier as a complication?

S: To tempt me to stay on the farm … one of the false trails I needed to get past … another kind of life. After I left, Clair found the right person.

Dr. N: If you and Clair had taken the lesser trail together and missed your sister's flag, would that life have been a total disaster?

S: No, but it would not have been as good. There is one main course of life we choose in advance, but alternatives always exist and we learn from them, too.

Dr. N: In your lives do you ever make mistakes and take false trails and miss the flags in the road for a job change, moving to another town, or meeting someone important because the details you saw at the place of life selection or in the recognition class were not implanted firmly enough?

S: (long pause) The signs are there. But, sometimes I overrule my ... inclinations. There are times in my lives when I change directions because of too much thinking and analysis. Or, I do nothing for the same reasons.

Dr. N: Ah, so you might do something other than what was planned in the spirit world?

S: Yeah, and it may not work out as well ... but we have the right to miss the red flags.

Dr. N: Well, I have enjoyed our talk about the place of recognition and I wondered if there is anything else this spiritual class does for you later in physical life.

S: (in a far away voice) Yes, sometimes when I am confused about my life and don't know where to turn next, I just ... imagine where I might be going compared to where I've been and ... it comes to me what to do.

Helping clients recognize people who were destined to have an impact on their lives is a fascinating aspect of my practice. I believe those who come to see me about relationships are not in my office at a certain point in their lives by chance. Am I spoiling the purpose of their spiritual recognition class by assisting these subjects in recalling clues? I don't think so, for two basic reasons. What they are not supposed to know yet probably won't be revealed in hypnosis, while on the other hand, quite a few of my clients only want confirmation of what they already suspect is true.

I can speak about recognition signs from personal experience, since I was blessed by three specific clues to help me find my wife. Thumbing through *Look* magazine as a teenager, I once saw a Christmas advertisement for Hamilton watches modeled by a beautiful dark-haired woman dressed in white. The caption in the ad said, "To Peggy," because she was holding a wristwatch as a gift from an imaginary husband. An odd sensation came over me, and I never forgot the name or face. On my twenty-first birthday I received a watch of the same make from a favorite aunt.

A few years later, while attending a graduate school in Phoenix, I was washing a load of white laundry one Saturday. Suddenly, the first trigger was activated in my mind with the message, "It's time to meet the woman in white." I tried to shake it off, but the face in the ad pushed all other thoughts away. I stopped, looked at my Hamilton watch and heard the command, "Go now." I thought about who wears white. Acting as if I was obsessed, I went to the largest hospital in the city and asked at the desk for a nurse matching the name and description.

I was told there was such a person who was coming off her shift. When I saw her, I was stunned by the resemblance to the picture in my mind. Our meeting was awkward and embarrassing, but later we sat in the lobby and talked non-stop for four hours as old friends who hadn't seen each other for a while—which, of course, was true. I waited until after we were married to tell my wife about the reason I came to her hospital and the clues given to me to find her. I didn't want her to think I was crazy. It was then I learned that on the day of our first meeting she had told her astonished friends, "I just met the man I'm going to marry."

My advice to people about meaningful encounters is not to intellectualize coming events too much. Some of our best decisions come from what we call instinct. Go with your gut feelings at the time. When a special moment is meant to happen in life, it usually does.

One of the last requirements before embarkation for many souls is to go before the Council of Elders for the second time. While some of my subjects see the Council only once between lives, most see them right after death and just before rebirth. The spirit world is an environment personified by order and the Elders want to reinforce the significance of a soul's goals for the next life. Sometimes my clients tell me they return to their spirit group after this meeting to say goodbye while others say they leave immediately for reincarnation. The latter procedure was used by a subject who described this exit meeting in the following manner.

"My guide, Magra, escorts me to a soft, white space which is like being in a cloud-filled enclosure. I see my committee of three waiting for me as usual. The middle Elder seems to have the most commanding energy. They all have oval faces, high cheekbones, no hair and smallish features. They seem to me to be sexless—or rather they appear to blend from male to female and back. I feel calm. The atmosphere is formal but not unfriendly. Each in turn asks me questions in a gentle way. The Elders are all-knowing about my entire span of lives but they are not as directive as one might think. They want my input to assess my motivations and the strength of my resolve towards working in new body. I am sure they have had a hand in the body choices I was given for the life to come because I feel they are skilled strategists in life selection. The committee wants me to honor my contract. They stress the benefits of persistence and holding to my values under adversity. I often give in too easily to anger and they remind me of this while reviewing my past actions and reactions towards events and people. The Elders and Magra give me inspiration, hope and encouragement to trust myself more in bad situations and not let things get out of hand. And then, as a final act to bolster my confidence when I am about to leave, they raise their arms and send a power bolt of positive energy into my mind to take with me."

One aspect of the two council meetings which I initially found rather odd is that members of the same soul group do not necessarily go before the same panel. For a while I assumed there would always be a correlation here because all members of a single soul group have the same guide. I was wrong. In the minds of my subjects, even senior guides are thought to be a couple of steps below the developmental level of the omnipotent beings who make up their councils. They are similar to the Old Ones that Thece told us about in Chapter 11, but with more specific responsibilities toward life evaluation of souls. While a guide might, in some respects, be considered a personal confidant to a soul this same familiarity does not extend to an Elder. In time, I came to appreciate that an Elder's authority, unlike that of guides, involves a cross-section of souls from many groups.

Apparently, everyone in a soul group respects the intensely private nature of these proceedings. They all see their individual Council of Elders as godly. The Elders are bathed in bright light and the whole setting has an aura of divinity. A subject put it this way, "when we are taken into the presence of these superior beings who exist in such a high spiritual realm, it validates our feelings about the source of creation."

15

Rebirth

WE have seen how a soul's decision to come forward into the next life at a specific time and place on Earth involves an ordered progression of spiritual planning. As I bring the soul consciousness of my subjects nearer to the moment of their exit from the spirit world, most become quietly introspective, while others engage in light bantering with their friends. These reactions toward what lies ahead depend more upon the individual soul than on the length of time since a last incarnation.

Rebirth is a profound experience. Those souls getting ready for embarkation to Earth are like battle-hardened veterans girding themselves for combat. This is the last chance for souls to enjoy the omniscience of knowing just who they are before they must adapt to a new body. My last case involves the soul of a woman who offers us a well-defined description of her most recent passage to Earth.

◄◄ Case 29 ►►

Dr. N: Has the time arrived for you to be reborn into your next life?

S: Yes, it has.

Dr. N: What is uppermost in your mind about returning to Earth?

S: The opportunity to live in the twentieth century. It's an exciting time of many changes.

Dr. N: And have you seen this life, or at least parts of it, in advance?

S: Yes ... I've been through that ... (subject seems distracted)

Dr. N: Is there something else you want to talk to me about concerning your next incarnation?

S: I am having a last talk with Pomar (subject's guide) on all the alternatives to my project (life).

Dr. N: Might this be considered a final exit interview with Pomar?

S: Yes, I suppose it would.

Dr. N: Would it help you to talk to me about the contingency plans you have for the next life?

S: (voice is dry and rather thin) I … think I have them straight …

Dr. N: How did your recognition class go? I assume that phase of your preparation is complete?

S: (still distracted) Uh-huh … I've met with the rest (of the participants) for my project.

Dr. N: Are the recognition signs clear in your mind for meeting the right souls at the right time?

S: (nervous laugh) Ah … the signals … my compacts with people … yes, that's all done.

Dr. N: Without analyzing or censoring your impressions in any way, tell me what you are feeling at this moment.

S: I'm … just … gathering myself for … the big jump into a new life … there is apprehension … but I am excited, too …

Dr. N: Are you a little scared and perhaps wondering if you should go to Earth at all?

S: (pause and then more cheerfully) A little … concern … for what lies ahead of me … leaving my home here … but happy, too, at the opportunity.

Dr. N: So you have mixed emotions about leaving the spirit world?

S: Most of us do, as our time draws near. I have second thoughts before some lives … but Pomar knows when I am lagging behind my schedule—you can't hide anything here, you know.

Dr. N: Okay, let's assume it's a go situation for your next life. On the count of three, your decision to return at an appointed time is firm and you are in the final stage to leave the spirit world. *One, two, three!* Describe to me what happens to you now.

S: I say goodbye to everyone. This can be ... difficult. (tosses her head back with resolution) Anyway, they all wish me well and I move away from them ... drifting alone. There is no great rush ... Pomar allows me to collect my thoughts. When I am quite ready he comes to escort me ... to offer encouragement ... reassurance ... and he knows when I am prepared to go.

Dr. N: I sense that you are now more upbeat about the prospect of rebirth.

S: Yes, it's a period of inspiration and expectations ... a new body ... the course ahead ...

I now prepare this subject to leave the spirit world for the last time before her current life. I am as careful here as when I brought her into the spirit world for the first time following normal age-regression. Starting with a reinforcement of the protective energy shield already placed around this subject, I apply additional conditioning techniques to keep her soul in proper balance with the mind of the child she is joining on Earth.

Dr. N: All right, you and Pomar are together for your exit from the spirit world. I want you to go deep inside yourself and explain to me what you do next as if it were happening in slow motion. *Go!*

S: (pause) We ... begin to move ... at a greater speed. Then I am aware of Pomar ... detaching from me ... and I am alone.

Dr. N: What do you see and feel?

S: Oh, I ...

Dr. N: Stay with it! You are alone and moving faster. Then what?

S: (in a faint voice) ... Away ... slanting away ... through pillows of whiteness ... moving away ...

Dr. N: *Stay with it!* Keep going and report back to me.

S: Oh, I'm ... passing through ... folds of silky cloth ... smooth ... I'm on a band ... a pathway ... faster and faster ...

Dr. N: *Keep going!* Don't stop talking to me.

S: Everything is blurred ... I'm sliding down ... down into a long, dark tube … a hollow feeling … darkness … then … *warmth!*

Dr. N: Where are you now?

S: (pause) I'm aware of being inside my mother.

Dr. N: Who are you?

S: (chuckles) I'm in a baby—I'm a baby.

The hollow tube effect described by my cases is apparently not the mother's birth canal. It is similar to the tunnel souls pass through at physical death and may be the same route. The reader might wonder why I would take more care with the act of birthing when I have already brought my subjects in and out of a number of past lives during a session. There are two reasons. First, reliving a past life does not need to involve the birthing process. I help my clients go straight from the spirit world into the next life, usually as adults. Second, if I return subjects to their current body and decide to command them to relive the birthing experience, I want to remove any minor discomforts felt by some people after they wake up.

Before continuing with this case, I should offer a little more general information about souls and babies. All my subjects tell me the transition of their souls from the spirit world to the mind of a baby is relatively more rapid than the passage back. What is the reason for this difference? After physical death our souls travel through the time tunnel and move past a gateway into the spirit world in a progressive way. We have seen how the outward passage is intended to be more gradual than our return to Earth in order to allow for acclimatization of a newly freed soul. However, as souls who enter babies, we come from a state of all-knowing and thus are mentally able to adjust more quickly to our surroundings than at the end of a physical life. Then too, we are given additional time for adaptation while in our mother's womb.

Nevertheless, having this time inside our mother does not mean we are fully prepared for the jarring paroxysm of birth, with blinding hospital lights, having to suddenly breathe air, and being physically handled for the first time. My subjects say if they were to compare the moment of birth with that of death, the physical shock of being born is much greater.

At some point prior to birth, the soul will carefully touch and join more fully with the impressionable, developing brain of a baby. When a soul decides to enter a baby, apparently that child has no free choice in accepting or rejecting the soul. At the moment of first entry, chronological time begins for the soul. Depending upon the inclinations of the particular soul involved, the connection may be early or late in the mother's pregnancy. I have had cases where souls timed their arrival at the last minute during delivery, but this is unusual. My findings indicate even those souls who join the baby early seem to do a lot of traveling outside the mother's womb during her term.

Once birth has taken place, the union of spirit and flesh has been fully solidified into a partnership. The immortal soul then becomes the seat of perception for the developing human ego. The soul brings a spiritual force which is the heritage of infinite consciousness. Although I have said souls can be confined by a human in trauma, they are never trapped. Besides leaving at the moment of death, souls may also come and go when the body is sleeping, in deep meditation, or under an anesthetic in surgery. The soul's absences are much longer in cases of severe brain damage and coma.

Case 29 continues by explaining the creative beauty of a soul joining with a new human being. This coupling of an intelligent life force before birth brings us full circle from the death scene described in Case 1.

Dr. N: Well, I'm glad you arrive safe and sound in your new body. Tell me, how old is the baby?

S: Five months have passed (since conception).

Dr. N: Is this your usual arrival time as far as the maturation of a child?

S: In my lives ... I have arrived at different times ... depending on the baby, the mother, and my life-to-be.

Dr. N: As a soul, are you in distress if the baby is aborted from the mother's womb for any reason before full term?

S: We know if a baby is going to full term or not. Not being born comes as no surprise to us. We may be around to just comfort the child.

Dr. N: Well, if the child does not go to term, is your life assignment as a soul aborted as well?

S: No, there never was a full life assignment as far as that child was concerned.

Dr. N: Might some babies who are aborted never have souls?

S: That depends on how far along they are. The ones who die very early often don't need us.

Note: This issue was as hotly debated in the past as it is today. During the thirteenth century, the Christian church found it necessary to establish guidelines for the existence of souls with regard to an aborted fetus. St. Thomas Aquinas and other medieval theologians arbitrarily decided ensoulment took place forty days after conception.

Dr. N: Assuming a baby is going to full term, do you know about the convergence habits of other souls with these children?

S: (offhandedly) Oh, some float around more than others, going in and out of the baby until birth because they get bored.

Dr. N: What do you usually do?

S: I'm average, I guess. Actually, I don't spend a long time at any one stretch with babies because it can get pretty dull.

Dr. N: All right, let's take this current situation inside your mother and allow some time to pass. What do you do when you are not with the unborn baby?

S: (laughs with delight) You want the truth? I'll tell you. Me—I play! It's a fine time to leave and purely goof off ... when the baby is less active. I have fun with my friends who are doing the same thing. We bounce around Earth to visit with each other ... and go to interesting places ... where we have once lived together in former lives.

Dr. N: Don't you and these other souls feel leaving the unborn baby for long periods is shirking the responsibilities of your assignment on Earth?

S: (defensively) Oh, lighten up! Who said anything about long periods? I don't do that! Anyway, our tough exercises haven't begun yet.

Dr. N: When you leave the baby for a while, what astral plane are you on in relation to Earth?

S: We are still on the Earth plane ... and we try not to get too distracted, either. A lot of our fooling around is in the neighborhood of the baby. I don't want you to get the idea there is nothing for us to do with unborn babies.

Dr. N: Oh …?

S: (continues) I'm busy with this new mind, even though it's not fully ready.

Dr. N: Why don't we talk more about that? When your soul enters a baby to remain with this new body for a lifetime, give me the scope of this undertaking.

S: (takes a deep sigh) Once I attach to a child it is necessary to bring my mind into synchronization with the brain. We have to get used to each other as partners.

Dr. N: This is what other people tell me, but do you and the baby have an affinity for each other right away?

S: Well … I am in the mind of the child but separate, too. I go slowly at first.

Dr. N: Okay, why don't you explain what you do with the mind of the baby.

S: It's delicate and can't be hurried. I start with a gentle probe … defining connections … gaps … every mind is different.

Dr. N: Is there any conflict within the child against you?

S: (softly) Ah … there is a slight resistance in the beginning … not full acceptance while I trace the passages … that's usual … until there is familiarization (stops for a moment and laughs quietly). I keep bumping into myself!

Dr. N: As you integrate with the baby, when does it become receptive to the force of your identity as a soul?

S: I'm disturbed by your word "force." We never force ourselves when entering an unborn baby. My tracing is done carefully.

Dr. N: Did it take you many lives to learn to trace a human brain?

S: Uh … a while … new souls are assisted with their tracing.

Dr. N: Since you represent pure energy, are you tracing electrical brain connections such as neurotransmitters, nerve cells, and the like?

S: (pause) Well, something like that … I disrupt nothing, though … while I learn the brain wave patterns of the baby.

Dr. N: Are you referring to the thought-regulation circuitry of the mind?

S: How this person translates signals. Its capacity. No two children are the same.

Dr. N: Be completely frank with me. Isn't your soul taking over this mind and subjugating it to your will?

S: You don't understand. It's a melding. There is an … emptiness before my arrival which I fill to make the baby whole.

Dr. N: Do you bring intellect?

S: We expand what is there.

Dr. N: Could you be more specific about what your soul actually provides the human body?

S: We bring a … comprehension of things … a recognition of the truth of what the brain sees.

Dr. N: Are you sure this child doesn't think of you at first as an alien entity in her mind?

S: No, that's why we unify with undeveloped minds. She recognizes me as a friend … a twin … who is going to be part of her. It's as if the baby was waiting for me to come.

Dr. N: Do you think a higher power prepares the baby for you?

S: I don't know, it would seem so.

Dr. N: Is your work at unification completed before birth?

S: Not really, but at birth we have started to complement each other.

Dr. N: So, the unification process does take some time?

S: Sure, while we adjust to each other. And, like I told you, I leave the unborn baby at intervals.

Dr. N: But what about those souls who join babies at the last minute before birth?

S: Humph! That's their style, not mine. They have to start their work in the crib.

Dr. N: How far along in age is the body by the time your soul stops leaving the child altogether?

S: At about five or six years of age. Usually we get fully operational when the child starts school. Children under this age can be left to their own devices a lot.

Dr. N: Don't you have a duty to always be with your body?

S: If things get bad in a physical way—then I'm back inside like a shot.

Dr. N: How would you know this if you were off fooling around with other souls?

S: Every brain has a wave pattern—it's like a fingerprint. We know immediately if the baby assigned to us is in trouble.

Dr. N: So, you are watching the baby assigned to you all the time—both inside and out—during the early stages of growth?

S: (with pride) Oh yes, and I watch the parents. They might be having squabbles around the baby which sets up disturbing vibrations.

Dr. N: If this happens to the child, what do you do as its soul?

S: Quiet the child as best I can. Reach out to the parents through the baby to calm them.

Dr. N: Give me an example of how you can reach out to your parents?

S: Oh, make the baby laugh in front of them by poking my parents' faces with both hands. This sort of thing further endears babies to parents.

Dr. N: As a soul, you can control motor movements of the baby?

S: I'm ... me. I can push a little on that part of the brain which controls movements. I can tickle the kid's funny bone sometimes, too ... I'll do whatever it takes to bring harmony to my assigned family.

Dr. N: Tell me what it is like being inside a mother's womb.

S: I like the warm comfortable feeling of love. Most of the time there is love ... sometimes there is stress. Anyway, I use this time to think and plan what I am going to do after birth. I think about my past lives and missed opportunities with other bodies and this gives me incentive.

Dr. N: And you haven't yet had the memories of all your past lives and your life in the spirit world blocked out by amnesia?

S: That starts after birth.

Dr. N: When the baby is born, does it have any conscious thoughts of who its soul is and the reasons for the attachment?

S: (pause) The child mind is so undeveloped it does not reason out this information. It does have parts of this knowledge as a means of comfort, which then fades. By the time I speak, this information is locked deep inside me and that's the way it's supposed to be.

Dr. N: So, will you have fleeting thoughts of other lives as a child?

S: Yes … we daydream … the way we play as children … creating stories … having imaginary friends who are real …but it fades. In the first few years of life babies know more than they are given credit for.

Dr. N: All right, now it is the time right before your birth in this life. Tell me what you are doing.

S: I'm listening to music.

Dr. N: What music?

S: I'm listening to my father play records—very relaxing for him—it helps him to think—I'm a bit anxious for him …

Dr. N: Why?

S: (giggles) He thinks he wants a boy, but I'll change his mind in a hurry!

Dr. N: So, this is a productive time for you?

S: (with determination) Yes, I'm busy planning for the approaching time when I will enter the world as a human and take that first breath. This is my last chance for quiet contemplation of the next life. When I come out—I'll be running.

Conclusion

THE information contained in this book about the existence of souls after physical death represents the most meaningful explanation I have found in my life as to why we are here. All my years of searching to discover the purpose of life hardly prepared me for that moment when a subject in hypnosis finally opened the door to an eternal world.

My oldest friend is a Catholic priest today. As boys walking together in the hills and along the beaches of Los Angeles we had many philosophical discussions, but were miles apart in our spiritual beliefs. He once told me, "I think it must take courage for you to be an atheist and believe in nothing beyond this life." I didn't see it that way at the time, nor for many years afterward. Starting at age five, I had been sent by my parents to military-type boarding schools for long periods. The feelings of abandonment and loneliness were so great I believed in no higher power than myself. I now realize strength was given to me in subtle ways I was unable to see. My friend and I still have different approaches to spirituality, but we both have convictions today that order and purpose in the universe emanate from a higher consciousness.

Looking back, I suppose it was no accident in my own life that people would eventually come to me for hypnosis—a medium of truth I could believe in—to tell me about guides, heavenly gateways, spiritual study groups, and creation itself in a world of souls. Even now, I sometimes feel like an intruder in the minds of those who describe the spirit world and their place in it, but their knowledge has given me direction. Still, I wonder why I am the messenger for the spiritual knowledge contained in this book, when someone with less original cynicism and doubt would surely have been much better suited. Actually, it is the people represented in these cases who are the real messengers of hope for the future, not the reporter.

Everything I have learned about who we are and where we come from, I owe to those who were drawn to me for help. They have taught me that a major aspect of our mission on Earth as souls is to mentally survive being cut off from our real home. While in a human body, the soul is essentially alone. A soul's relative isolation on Earth during a temporary physical life is made more difficult on a conscious level by thoughts that nothing exists beyond this life. Our doubts tempt us into finding attachments solely in a physical world we can see. The scientific knowledge that Earth is only a grain of sand at the edge of a galactic shoreline within a vast sea in the universe adds to our feelings of insignificance.

Why is no other living thing on Earth concerned with life after death? Is this simply because our inflated egos hate to think of life as only temporary, or is it because our being is associated with a higher power? People argue that any thoughts of a hereafter are wishful thinking. I used to do so myself. However, there is logic to the concept we were not created by accident for mere survival, and that we do operate within a universal system which directs the physical transformation of Self for a reason. I believe it is the voice of our souls, which tell us we do have personhood that is not intended to die.

All the accounts of life after death in my case files have no scientific foundation to prove the statements of these subjects. To those readers who find the material offered in this book too unprecedented to accept, I would hope for one thing. If you carry away nothing except the idea you may have a permanent identity worth finding, I will have accomplished a great deal.

One of the most troublesome concerns of all people who want to believe in something higher than themselves is the causality of so much negativity in the world. Evil is given as the primary example. When I ask my subjects how a loving God could permit suffering, surprisingly there are few variations in their responses. My cases report our souls are born of a creator which places a totally peaceful state deliberately out of reach so we will strive harder.

We learn from wrongdoing. The absence of good traits exposes the ultimate flaws in our nature. That which is not good is testing us, otherwise we would have no motivation to better the world through ourselves, and no way to measure advancement. When I ask my subjects about the alternating merciful and wrathful qualities we perceive to be the self-expression of a teacher-oversoul, some of them say the creator only shows certain attributes to us for specific ends. For instance, if we equate evil with justice and mercy with goodness and if God allowed us only to know mercy, there would be no state of justice.

This book presents a theme of order and wisdom rising from many spiritual energy levels. In a remarkable underlying message, particularly from advanced subjects, the possibility is held out that the God-oversoul of *our* universe is on a less-than-perfect level. Thus, complete infallibility is deferred to an even higher divine source.

From my work I have come to believe that we live in an imperfect world by design. Earth is one of countless worlds with intelligent beings, each with its own set of imperfections to bring into harmony. Extending this thought further, we might exist as one single dimensional universe out of many, each having its own creator governing at a different level of proficiency in levels similar to the progression of souls seen in this book. Under this pantheon, the divine being of our particular house would be allowed to govern in His, Her, or Its own way.

If the souls who go to planets in our universe are the offspring of a parent oversoul who is made wiser by our struggle, then could we have a more divine grandparent who is *the* absolute God? The concept that our immediate God is still evolving as we are takes nothing away from an ultimate source of perfection who spawned our God. To my mind, a supreme, perfect God would not lose omnipotence or total control over all creation by allowing for the maturation of less-than-perfect superior offspring. These lesser gods could be allowed to create their own imperfect worlds as a final means of edification so they might join with the ultimate God.

The reflected aspects of divine intervention in this universe must remain as our ultimate reality. If our God is not the best there is because of the use of pain as a teaching tool, then we must accept this as the best we have and still take the reasons for our existence as a divine gift. Certainly this idea is not easy to convey to someone who is physically suffering, for example, from a terminal illness. Pain in life is especially insidious because it can block the healing power of our souls, especially if we have not accepted what is happening to us as a preordained trial. Yet, throughout life, our karma is designed so that each trial will not be too great for us to endure.

At a *wat* temple in the mountains of Northern Thailand, a Buddhist teacher once reminded me of a simple truth. "Life," he said, "is offered as a means of self-expression, only giving us what we seek when we listen to the heart." The highest forms of this expression are acts of kindness. Our soul may be traveling away from a permanent home, but we are not just tourists. We bear responsibility in the evolution of a higher consciousness for ourselves and others in life. Thus, our journey is a collective one.

We are divine but imperfect beings who exist in two worlds, material and spiritual. It is our destiny to shuttle back and forth between these universes through space and time while we learn to master ourselves and acquire knowledge. We must trust in this process with patience and determination. Our essence is not fully knowable in most physical hosts, but Self is never lost because we always remain connected to both worlds.

Perhaps the most gratifying feature of my work in uncovering the existence of a spirit world in the minds of my subjects is the effect this conscious knowledge has on them. The most significant benefit which comes from knowing we have a home of everlasting love waiting for us, is being receptive to the higher spiritual power within our minds. The awareness that we do belong somewhere is reassuring and offers us peace, not merely as a haven from conflict, but to unify ourselves with a universal mind. One day we are going to finish this long journey—all of us—and reach an ultimate state of enlightenment, where everything is possible.

Index